GAUDÍ
AND THE ROUTE OF MODERNISM IN BARCELONA

CONTENTS

GAUDÍ

Ambiguity in language 9
Architecture conceived as spontaneous ....
　　growth 9
Architecture as the delimitation
　　of space 10
Preorganic character 11
Space, a non cryptographic message 12
Space in expansion 12
Individuation of the expressive medium 13
The odyssey of a form 14
An Architecture of anticipation 14
Architecture as visible space 16
The first works 17
Palacio Güell 19
Gaudí and the Neogothic 22
La Casa de los Botines 23
The Teresian School 23
A project 23
Casa Calvet 23
Bellesguard 24
Finca Miralles 24
Parque Güell 24
The architectural restoration 44
The crypt in Santa Coloma de Cervelló 45
Casa Batlló 47
La Pedrera 49
The school of the Sagrada Familia 52
The Expiatory Temple of the
　　Sagrada Familia 53

THE ROUTE OF MODERNISM IN BARCELONA

Bullfighting ring MonumentaL 73
Bullfighting ring Las Arenas 73
The park café restaurant "Castell dels Tres ...
　　Dragons" 73
Hidroeléctrica de Cataluña 74
The Market in Born 74
Palau de la Música Catalana 75
Casa Martí 76
Café de la Opera 77
Bar Muy Buenas 77
Casa Genové 77
Hotel España 77
Hotel Peninsular 78
The old Casa Figueras/ Escribà
　　Confectioners 78
Casa Pons i Pasqual 78
Casas Antoni Rocamora 79
Casa Albert Lleó Morera 79
Casa Antoni Amatller 80
Streetlights in the Paseo de Gràcia 80
Streetlights in the Hall in Sant Joan 80
Streetlights in the Plaza Real 81
Montaner i Simón Publisher's 81
Casa Dolores Calm 82
Casa Fargas 82
Casa Evarist Juncosa 82
Casa Josep i Ramon Queraltó 83
Casa Jaume Forn 84
Casa Manuel Llopis i Bofill 84
Casa Casimir Clapés 85
Casa Josep Thomas 85
Palacio Ramon de Montaner 86
Casa Ramon Casas 86
Casa Pere Serra i Pons 86
Casa Sayrach 88
Casa Fuster 88
Casa Comalat 105
Palacio del Barón de Quadras 105
Casa Terrades "The house of Spikes" 106
Casa Romà Macaya i Giber 106
Hospital de la Santa Creu
　　i de Sant Pau 107

Vallvidrera station	108
La Rotonda, Tramvia Blau and Tibidabo	109
Casaramona factory	109
The great waterfall in Ciutadella	109
Casa Vicens "Casa de les Carolines"	110
Palacio Güell	111
Casa Andreu Calvet i Pintó	112
Casa Josep Batlló i Casanovas	113
Casa Pere Milà i Camps (La Pedrera)	115
Parque Güell	116
The Expiatory Temple of the Sagrada Familia	118
Modernism	
Modernism, an international hurricane	137
Total art, Social art	137
The plan by Cerdà and the Eixample (known as Ensanche)	139
Barcelona, the mirror of Modernism in Catalonia	140
The Catalan architects in Modernism in Barcelona	141
From Modernism to "Noucentisme"	143
Antonio Gaudí	
Biographic news	144

Written texts:
Gaudí:
Ediciones Nauta, S. A..
Gaudí and the route of Modernism in Barcelona:
Clara Garí
B. A. The History of Art.

Source of illustrations:
Pages 121, 122, 124: THEMA Equipo Editorial
The rest: from the files of Ediciones Nauta C., S.A.

EDITOR TEAM:
Editorship: J. Barnat; Production: A. Llord;
General Co-ordinator: Mª D. Mascasas

© Ediciones Nauta, S. A.,
Edited by Ediciones Nauta C., S. A..
Josep Tarradellas, 123-127, 5ª A - 08029 Barcelona
Printed by Emegé Industrias Gráficas
Londres, 98 -Interior- 08036 Barcelona
ISBN: 84-8259-135-5
Legal deposit: B- 33.137-97
Printed in Spain
9712B001
Edition: 1998

All rights reserved. It is forbidden to reproduce part or all of this work by whichever means, (whether by graphic, electronic, optical, chemical, or by photocopies etc.), or to store or transmit its contents by magnetic, sonorous or visual means, or in any other way without first having written permission from the copyright holders.

COLOUR ILLUSTRATIONS

Barcelona, The Expiatory Temple of the Sagrada Familia 2
Barcelona, The Expiatory Temple of the Sagrada Familia 3
Barcelona, Casa Vicens, the exterior 4
Barcelona, Casa Josep Batlló i Casanovas 6
Barcelona, Casa Terrades, (the house of spikes) 7
Barcelona, Casa Vicens, 1878-1880 25
Barcelona, Casa Vicens, a detail of the facade with the door 26
Barcelona, Casa Vicens, the interior 27
Barcelona, Casa Vicens, a chimney with a tile decoration 28
Barcelona, Casa Vicens, a corner of the smoking room 29
Barcelona, Palacio Güell, 1885-1889, a chimney covered with tiles 30
Barcelona, Palacio Güell, chimneys 31
Barcelona, Palacio Güell, the end of the cupola in a cusp 32
Barcelona, Palacio Güell, aspect of the hall and stairs 33
Barcelona, Palacio Güell, an angle of the hall 34
Barcelona, Finca Güell, 1883-1887, the riding school roof 35
Barcelona, Teresian College, 1889-1894 36
Barcelona, Teresian College, a detail of a corridor
  with parabolic arches 38
Barcelona, Teresian College, the iron gate at the entrance 39
Barcelona, Casa Calvet, 1998-1904 40
Barcelona, Casa Calvet, a detail of the stairs 57
Barcelona, Casa Calvet, the inside 58
Barcelona, Casa Calvet, an angle of a room: a mirror 59
Barcelona, Casa Calvet, a door with a peephole
  and a bronze door handle 60
Barcelona, Torre Bellesguard, 1900-1902 61
Barcelona, Parque Güell, 1900-1914, pavilions at the entrance 62
Barcelona, Parque Güell, a cupola of an entrance pavilion 63
Barcelona, Parque Güell, a detail of the facade of a pavilion
  at the entrance 64
Barcelona, Parque Güell, a detail of the end of a pavilion
  at the entrance 65
Barcelona, Parque Güell, entrance stairs 66
Barcelona, Parque Güell, a detail of the fountain situated
  by the entrance stairs 67
Barcelona, Parque Güell, part of the parapet of the terrace
  designed for children's games 68
Barcelona, Parque Güell, a detail of the parapet on the terrace
  designed for children's games 69
Barcelona, Casa Milà, (La Pedrera), 1905-1910 70
Barcelona, The Expiatory Temple of the Sagrada Familia,
  a detail of the facade of the Nativity 71
Barcelona, The Expiatory Temple of the Sagrada Familia,
  a fragment of the towers of the Nativity 72
Barcelona, Casa Pere Serra i Pons, 1908.
  Above: the complete facade, with the part of the new
  construction behind.
  Bottom left: the main door.
  Bottom right: balcony of the Diagonal facing facade, with the
  small roof above it. 89
Barcelona, Casa Dolores Calm, 1903. A detail of the carpentry
  of the galleries 90
Barcelona, Casa Antoni Amatller, 1900.
  Above: the upper part of the facade.
  Below: shop window of the Bagués jewellers 91
Barcelona, the Montaner i Simón publishers, 1886
The upper part of the facade and the metal
  sculpture of Tàpies 92
Barcelona, Casa Fuster, 1911. Detail of the summerhouse,
projecting galleries 93
Barcelona, Casa Terrades, (the house of spikes), 1905.
  The upper part of the towers of the facade 94

Barcelona, Palacio del Barón de Quadras, 1906.
  Above: a detail of a stone ornament.
  Below: a glass and iron door ....
Barcelona, Palacio del Barón Quadras, 1906
  Gallery windows, finished with attics ....
Barcelona, Casa Manuel Llopis i Bofill, 1903. Stone engravings
  by Jujol, a detail of the green ceramic ....
Barcelona, Palacio Ramon de Montaner, 1893.
  Above: Facade with a sculpture of an eagle.
  Bottom left: the iron work of the gate.
  Bottom right: detail of the streetlight ....
Barcelona, Casa Josep Thomas, 1898.
  Above: polychrome ceramic ornament, in the plinth of a balcony.
  Bottom: a continuous gallery from the last floor ....
Barcelona, Casa Casimir Clapés, 1908.
  The upper gallery and two balconies with columns with floral
  ornamentation 1
Barcelona, Casa Comalat, 1911. Curved balconies with plant
  adornments in Calle Còrsega 1
Barcelona, Casa Comalat, 1911. Detail of the facade
  overlooking the Diagonal 1
Barcelona, Palau de la Música Catalana, 1908.
  One of the two facades 1
Barcelona, Palau de la Música Catalana, 1908.
  A corner with a sculpted motif 1
Barcelona, Palau de la Música Catalana, 1908.
  Outside view of the roof 1
Barcelona, Palau de la Música Catalana, 1908.
  Glass and ceramic work 1
Barcelona, the market at Born, 1876. A detail of the metallic
  structure 1
Barcelona, the market at Born, 1876. The inside 1
Barcelona, The bullfighting ring, Monumental, 1915.
           The bullfighting ring, Las Arenas, 1899.
  Above: Monumental, the main entrance.
  Below: Las Arenas: the finishing of the entrance ....
Barcelona, the Vallvidrera station, 1905.
  A detail of a window with a parabolic arch 1
Barcelona, Casa Martí, 1896.
  Above: the bar "Els quatre gats".
  Below: balcony with stone ornamentation 1
Barcelona, Hidroeléctrica de Cataluña, 1897. Brick facade
  and iron frame 1
Barcelona, Casas Antoni i Rocamora, 1917.
  Above: view of the extensive facade.
  Below: cupola covered with red brick 1
Barcelona, Casa Pons i Pasqual, 1891. Conical finished
  tower crowned with pinnacles 1
Barcelona, Casa Genové, 1911. Upper part of the main
  door and large windows 1
Barcelona, La Rotonda, Tramvia Blau and Tibidabo, 1906.
  La Rotonda: detail of a pinnacle 1
Barcelona, La Rotonda, Tramvia Blau and Tibidabo, 1906.
  Above: Tibidabo: Gate of the Expiatory Temple of the
  Sagrado Corazón.
  Below: El Tramvia Azul (the Blue Tram) 1
Barcelona, Fábrica Casaramona, 1911.
  One of the "Medieval" towers 1
Barcelona, Café Restaurant of the "Castell dels Tres Dragons" park.
  Above: a general view.
  Below: a detail of the battlements 1
Barcelona, Hospital de la Santa Creu i de Sant Pau, 1902.
  The main entrance 1

Ambiguity in the language

Perhaps what makes a quick understanding difficult in Gaudí's work is its daring and fascinating ambiguity, that continuum which slips between architectural "code" and "structure", although in reality it is in the "structure" and not in formal "codes" where its spacial theme is founded.
Such ambiguity is accentuated so much more when the matrixes from which Gaudí extracts a determined stylistic "code" are not always clearly evidenced. But rather they appear, as often happens, ambiguosly confused as a consequence of a sort of intervention, prior to the adoption of the chosen "code", which by way of a distorted lens, varies the facets and the colour in it, tricking us with a free all-embracing conduct, and with an underlying energy directly emanated from an ethnic heritage which is difficult to simplify. This can only be offered by the racial and historical substrata of a land such as Catalonia in Spain, and within this Barcelona, with its mediterranean port, a centre of convergence for highly diverse cultures, " a city of merchants, conquerers and people of a good upbringing, refined, well educated and luxurious: the Athens of the Troubadours" (1).

Architecture conceived as spontaneous growth

To all of this one must add the personal character of a burning fantasy which never inhibits itself and accepts all types of stimulus, whatever their origin may be, in order to explore their possibilities until they reach breaking point, and at times without giving it further importance touching the limit of dilettantism. This same characteristic can be found in many aspects in the initial unchained expression of a Picasso, and also at times in a Miró, who are also Catalans or who have participated, as is the case of Picasso, in the cultural environment of Catalonia, and within which they have developed their activity during a period which has been, to a large extent, contemporary to Gaudí. However one can also find an explanation of this fact beginning with the ethnic substrata which is decidedly Catalan, and in as much as it refers to Gaudí and Miró, this is a substratum in which very different characteristics join up and in which the classical cultural influence is not so decisive as to condition. Though it may have an equalizing function, on the possible selections, on which it acts- and this we will see as much in Gaudí as in Picasso- as one of the various components.
In Gaudí one finds oneself facing an extremely complex expression which can be interpreted from diametrically opposed points of view, and on diverse cultural levels. This depends on the interest, and the degree of preparation and the particular desire to assimilate which all types of cultures necessarily experience facing expressions which establish contact, when these expressions offer (as in the case of Gaudí) the possibility of doing so with an inexhaustible and indiscriminate richness of fantastic inventions.
The approximation to the Gaudí's expressive world can, in effect, produce

(1) A Handbook for Travellers in Spain, London, 1847, (quoted by J. J. Sweeney and J. L. Sert in Antoni Gaudí, Stuttgart, 1960, Milan, 1961).

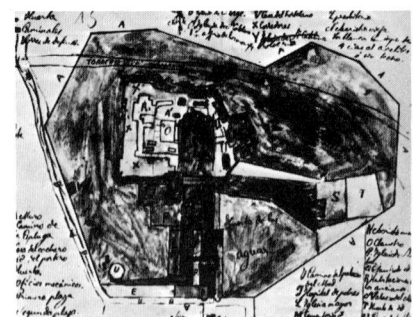

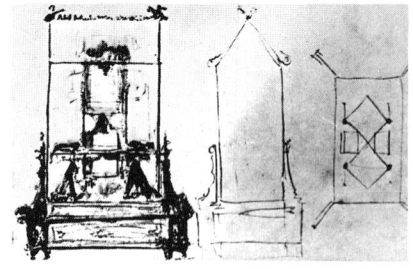

The restauration project of the Royal monastry in Poblet, carried out together with his fellow students Eduardo Toda y Güell y José Ribera Sans, 1869-1870

A project for his desk, 1878.

Project for a glass showcase for a glove factory, sent to the Universal Exhibition in Paris, 1878.

Architecture as a way of defining space

highly diverse reactions. These range from inconditional and immediate admiration to incomprehension. The first is the most frequent reaction of the general public; specially amongst Gaudí's fellow countrymen, for whom he personifies the moment of the "Renaixença", and even because, by way of a repertoire, he extracted the most outgoing elements from Catalonia. He treated succesively, or in the same context, elements from the late Gothic, from the Barroque period, from the Mudejar period, or as Casanelles (2) has observed, from the exceptional geological phenomena of Montserrat. As said, from this the reaction moves to a closed incomprehension which borders on disdain. This last point of view has tended to coincide, above all, with the prevailing of rationalist trends, and which in the name of a rigorous logic, reject *en masse* all of the statements or expressions which have a seemingly irrational content and which are apparently ridiculous. The reaction against this viewpoint (which is still alive) and the enthusiasm which the work of this great Catalan awakes today, are owed in part to the rehabilitation of "mannerism" and to the resurgence of Barroque studies, such as the discovery of the modernist or avant garde function and of the rupture brought about by the "Art Nouveau".

Consequently Gaudí has been made into an emblem of reinvindication for the Catalans, which is now expressed with that federalist feeling in which all of a new literary current is based, and which promoted the rebirth of their language, which had fallen in forced disuse in daily life in Catalonia due to the imposition of historical circumstances, The organized poetry contests in catalan, or medieval festivals incorporating poetry, music and folklore, such as the "jocs florals" (3) were a move to remedy that. Furthermore, and even because the movement for Catalan revindications was essentially a right-handed movement, after the Carlist defeat of 1876, by the Church, due to his growing mystic exhaltation, Gaudí was considered as a species of standardbearer for devout catholicism and anti reform, and who found its most tumultuous symbol in the Expiatory Temple of the "Sagrada Familia". In effective, he was an enthusiastic defender and holder of both ideals, which demonstrates, for his part, a certain lack of self criticism or lack of judgement about his own creative force, and which pushed him to accept the use of diverse expressive modes and to adhere to formulas which were imposed by fashion or by tradition. These served as "secret codes" capable of transmitting a type of cryptographic message (which sometimes had a symbolic sense, and other times an analogical or mystic meaning). The structural motivation then is what in reality raises the true problem of his conception of architectural space.

This last question, is in spite of everything, what most deeply interested him, and what represents in him, on the other hand, his only true direct message in the field of architecture, and what for us is the most interesting aspect of him, because it is founded on an experimental methodology, which is based on investigation. His method is, in the final analysis, experimental but it is also empirical. His "structural" theme is essentially explainable through the application of the most recent discoveries of the constructive technique, and in terms of functionalism. Although this can be seen in respect of materials of traditional use (stone, forged iron, brick, and wood) and with handcrafted methods which he employed in an effort to transform the same structure into an expressive object, making it appear to be the result of a "natural" growth. Thus this places itself, as seen from solipsistic viewpoint, in an attitude which emulates its creation. This is perhaps due to a wish to integrate itself to the "divine" function, by means of reconstitution of its own means. Should we also see romantic aftertastes in this behaviour as expressions of the collective soul? Expressions which are within a wagnerian or nietzschean framework and are on a provincial level, or expressions which stood out so much, in the environment of the cultural eclecticism so typical of that epoch, that all of the expressions had echo and gained immediate popularity.

I have referred now to a direct architectural message (rather than a cryptographic one), in order to consider its value as a "denotation of space". I have done this as it seems to me that - even sharing the conclusions to which the present semiolo-

---

(2) E. Casanelles, Nueva Visión de Gaudí, Barcelona, 1965
(3) The ancient festivalof the "Jocs Florals" was reestablished in 1867

gical search is directed, particularly through the observations of Dorfles (4), Brandi (5) and Eco (6)- and according to whom "architecture presents a challenge to semiology..., given that the objects in architecture do not "communicate"...but rather "function" (Eco), and that all architecture fulfills a placement in itself, that is, an actual/real presence (Brandi), without "communicating" its function so far as " being" is its own function (7) - they recognize in the character of the "denotation" of space (a way of calling the whole spacial idea) that belongs to architecture and not to the indifferenciated, "techtonic" idea which is its most direct communicable and communicative content, its most exact deciphering key.

The fact that in his work the premises of movements and successive formal facts/events which belong to the contemporary artistic world have coincided is owed to the incredible phagocytosic force of the gaudian method. This is due to his capacity to transform completely unrelated elements. These emerge from an exasperated cultural background, thus allowing the recovery of a substratum of an ancestral prohistoric nature (perhaps on a freudian level), together with elements which appear to belong to an artificial paradise of the Orient. A paradise conceived in the style of Huysmans, without of course, any of the cloudy and sensual implications with which Huysmans would conceive it.

Without question this background has been looked at when critics have wished to see Gaudí as one of the initiators of Surrealism, and it is perhaps for this reason that Salvador Dalí, in 1933, commented in an article published in "Le Minotaure", under the title "La beauté terrifiante et comestible de l'architecture Modern Style) about the sensation of pleasure which Gaudí's art gave him on entering in his "grottos through tender doors made from cow's liver".

It could be said, if it were necessary, that the zoomorphic alusions in Gaudí are always of a prehuman type and that they arise from diffunct species: enormous antediluvian monsters, whose flesh has been reduced to a thick (coreaceic) mummified mass covered with wrinkled skin, without having any appearance of being tender. We sense scaley crests and excretions of a hornlike material, shiny and pearly, mountains transformed into dragons and doted with latent life, the bony structures of lethargic dinosaurs, in whose fossilized veins a black and dense blood is found staunching, as often lead, and on whose awakening everything will burn and explode, as though waking inside a volcano. W. Boech underlines, while puntualizing this, the preorganic character of that which the Spanish representitivity is capable, and the dominant role that is played in it; " not only aspects of the animal world, but also the step from inorganic forms to living ones" (8). But in spite of all of this it doesn't seem at all possible to bring up, in respect of this, the *Cadavre Exquis* of the surrealists, with its nauseous smell of flowers in a withering and rotting trance. Gaudí resorts , on the other hand, to his allusions to primigeniuos elements because of a need (characteristic, for another part, of someone who, like he, was a solitary person and closed inside of himself), to abandon himself, as children do, to dreaming, and thus to the fabulous and the magical, and to close himself inside a world of fantasy and visions, and to unite himself, in a certain sense, to the object of his creation, in an attitude which seems closer to that of "pop" than "surrealist". This is because his disposition in relation to the object is not one of involvement or sensuality. He does not surrender himself to the forms of the unconscience or to the oneiric and neither does he evoke the disturbingly subtle ambiguities of the subliminal world, according to the procedures of the surrealist poetics. It still remains to be seen, what is his relationship to the "magical realism" in which Alberto Sartoris insisted in 1952 (9). But it may also be the case that this interpretaton results as being rather forced.

Preorganic character

Drawing of a neogothic chapel in Alella (Barcelona), 1883.

(4) G. Dorfles, Il devenire delle arti, Turin, 1959.
(5) C. Brandi, Elianti o dell'Architettura, 1956; Segno e immagine, Milan, 1960:Strutture e architettura, Turin, 1967
(6) U.Eco, Appunti per una semiologia delle comunicazioni visive, Milan, 1967, y Proposte per una semiologia dell'Architettura (en Marcatré, nºs 34-36), Milan 1967. See also S. Bettini, Critica semantica e continuità storicica dell'Architettura (en Zodiac, nº 2), Milan, 1958; S. Langer, Sentimento e forma, Milan 1965; G. C.Koenig, Analisi del linguaggio architettonico, Florence, 1964; R. De Fusco, L'idea di Architettura come mass-Medium, Bari, 1967.
(7) L.V.Masini, La Cattedrale gotica come denotazione e individuazione di spazio (in Le grandi cattedrali gotiche), Florence, 1968.
(8) W. Boeck, Meisterwerke von Antoni Gaudí, in the catalogue of the exhibition of Gaudí's works, in the Gesellschaft der Freunde junger Kunst of Baden Baden, 1961.
(9) A. Sartoris, Gaudí poliforme, in "Número", year IV, nº3, 1952, y Polimorfismo de Gaudí (in Papeles de Son Armadans, volume XV, nºXLV bis), December 1959.

A design for streetlights to illuminate the disappeared sea wall in Barcelona, 1880

The ambiguous character of these aspects which are found in Gaudí's art is probably more deeply rooted: an unconscious ambiguity, as a phenomenon which develops on an interior level. It belongs to a giantism which is more nietzschean and wagnerian, that is more *ochocentista* in so far as its capacity for anticipation and prevision, which is seen in Bosco, Brueghel or to Dalí. It is something which we can see as conditioned at the moment of "nationalities" in the development of European civilization in which it is not permitted to foresee, with full consciousness, those ferments which the avant garde novecentistas would make evident. For example; the sociological and political approaches or the struggle for democratic liberty during this century, something which the revolutions and the wars of independence of the XIX century, within a a framework of patriotic ideals did not know how to specify or resolve. These ferments do exist latently in Gaudí's work without flowering into the conscious level, and from time to time these have allowed us to recognize an anticipation of the avant garde movements in him. This is seen from the Art Nouveau to expressionism, and from Cubism to Dadaism, or to informal Abstractism and to Art Brut through the mudejar orientalism of his first works. It can also be seen through the organic forms which are found integrated in blocks in the walls of the Casa Milà and in the bewitched warriors of its chimneys, as well as in the roof and in the undulated walls of the Sagrada Familia School. Again we find these in the prestigious collages of tiles in the serpentine bank which surround the suspended terrace (destined for children's recreation) in Parque Güell and also in the blurred and delicate colour of the façade of the Casa Batlló, with its cornice formed by a shiny greenblue crest.

All of these hypothesis which have been formulated around Gaudí's work are convincing, and true in themselves, but we are dealing with a posteriori verifications which are not always justified from the viewpoint of the author's artistic consciousness and intentionality. That said, in Gaudí the imaginative strength was such that whichever formular assumed by him remained inexorably transfigured, and doted with vibracity and liveliness, to such a point as to become something new and consequently to convert the author in an anticipator of forms.

Space, a non cryptographic message

The way in which Gaudí developed the combination of elements which he employed in each case can be better explained beginning with the structural entity. This seems to me to be more unequivocal, although it is not always obvious and is evidenced, -in respect of other more visible aspects in its process which refer to the control of its forms-, by its nature of overcoming a determined "code" and so produces its true message (no secret) which is the message of its spatial nature of his architecture.

Space in expansion

When talking of the type of space which Gaudí intentionally proposed, I would say that above all we are dealing with a space that was conceived in expansion, thus giving this term the value of the result of the compressed force which tends to become apparent as an outward explosion.

In expansion gothic space was conceived based on elastic tension. Here howevever, we are dealing with a univocal expansion which follows fixed vectors and and is strictly directed in only one direction until it constitutes (specially on the inside of a building) a mesh which progressively tightens and closes in spite of its dilated scale. This, due to being formulated outside of the human scale, contributes to the accentuating of the sensation of feeling oneself to be smaller. A move against closed space was also conceived in expansion as well as classical or Renaissance blocking, or Baroque space. At least this can be seen in the appearance of the prototypes. In this case we are looking at a dynamic space, which was tense but constructed and designed, and connected to what the possible explosion really was, a curve in expansion previously programmed and pre-established.

The hyperbolic curve, which typifies Gaudí's spatial search, is in reality a curve in expansion, which from the plane tends to project itself plastically. It is not a sinuous curve (rich in vitality but not organic) which is linear and non spatial as in the Art Nouveau. That said, one cannot exclude a connection between Gaudí and Catalan "modernism", given that one shouldn't forget that he lived in the full eclosion of modernism and that parallel to his work Catalonia witnessed that of Domènech i Montaner, Martorell, Vilaseca, Berenguer, Puig i Cadafalch, Granell y Rubió i Bellver, all of whom Oriol Bohigas takes note (10). His is a curve which changes direction continually, forced by natural expansion and by its organic birth. It is charged internally by a type of dynamite which is always on the point of exploding in any directon and of destroying itself as an entity. The curve in Borromini's work is dynamic but once designed it opens and confines itself in a surrounding movement and never breaks the rules of elastic force. It is highly resistant and this permits it to slide and gives it an impetus without abandoning its confinement. The curve in Gaudí's work grows, struggling and contorting itself, as a natural element; it contains straight sections which finish and then begin their curse a new, and every so often, his work seems to conquer and dominate space, arousing as it develops, then contracts and syncopates... Then there comes a moment in which Gaudí's fantasy becomes an "evocation of monsters". It is dragged by a subconscious urgency to identify itself with the object that it is creating. This is a phase where it is feasible to perceive some freudian elements in its performance. It throws shapeless material against its structure and makes this explode and fall on itself in order to lie, as an enormous beast, in a burning bed of heaped lava. It is blinded by the pyrotechical games which surge from its ashes. But at the bottom of this violence, and in spite of it, we can detect the seriousness and the severity of Gaudí the constructor and designer.

In reality this architect begins his fight testing his own talent and his own culture to the point of wanting to correct the styles which he tries to recreate *ex nova*, beginning with the world's underlying force of invention.

Take a special look at the Sagrada Familia, and its link with the gothic which is its clearest touch stone. With this he achieved the opposite of what had occurred in the revival phenomenas in the English Eighteen hundreds. These were originated in an evasive manner, or under its stimulus, in formulas which had no connection with a true need to express themselves and justified special politico-social conditions. He recreated in virtue of a lucid delirium of religious fervour which contains the value of passionate energy nourished in the humus of his land. It is that same uncontrollable psychic and spiritual energy which had made the development of gothic space possible during the middle ages in the form of a collective effort.

Gaudí's case is not however a simple case of revival in the sense that this term holds at the moment. In reality Gaudí can be situated in competition with the same spirit of the Gothic style, in the middle of its vital and constituent elements which on re-examining the structural context he proposes diverse solutions. He breaks the rational rigor of his tripartite structure (ogive, arch buttress and buttress) in which he balances the thrusting forces. He then sets it out on the basis of the hyperbolic curve which transforms into a spatial element of a full incurvature and hyperbolic paraboloid. He does this to the point of cancelling any other mediating element which divides or balances the forces and so delays its thrust and its rising projection. This is obtained by means of columns "which follow the inclination of the resultant dynamics, suppressing buttresses and rampant arches and absorbing the forces in a new static structure, without the heaviness of supplementary weights" (11).

Project for a fountain in Plaza de Cataluña in Barcelona, 1870.

Project for a gate of a cemetery, 1870.

Project for a cooperative society in Mataró (Barcelona), 1878-1882.

Individuation of an expressive means

The force, which has been made to recover what constitutes the basic structures of his architectural formulations from the cultural tradition or perhaps from a cultural eclecticism (something specially visible in the chapel crypt of the Colonia Güell, in Santa Coloma de Cervelló, and in the covering project of the Sagrada Familia) surpasses itself in the discovery of the infinite series of formal possibilities contained in the individuation of this structural central nucleos which is found in the hyperbolic curve. This, if indeed in use in the traditional Catalan vault (and whose presence we can easily identify on a level of spontaneous architecture), on acquiring individuality is newly created, transferred to its original value and transformed from an element of artesanal elemental language, and still popular, into an outstanding fact/acheivement which is giving character specially on being magnified in all of its possibilities for application and transformation until it creates a means of expression within it.

(10) O. Bohigas, L'architettura modernista. Gaudí e il movimento catalano. Turin, 1969.
(11) J. Perucho y L. Pomés, Una arquitectura de anticipación, Barcelona 1967.

The odisea of a form

Without any doubt one of the most valid guiding threads to help interpret the gaudian development correctly can be no other than that of following one basic element: the hyperbolic curve. We can see it transform from a linear element into an element of dynamic and spatial form, that is, the hyperboloid, until this in turn transforms, on a level of complex plastic structure, from paraboloid to hyperboloid and to helicoid. We could begin, in this examination, with the parabolic curve which appears with cupola wings, from the parabolic section of the fountain project for Plaza Cataluña in Barcelona (1870). R. Pane however, also refers in his examination of Gaudí's first works to the "acroteras" "linked in curvature" and which "begin from two opposite cones, that is, with the generational form of the hyperboloid" (12). These were built in the balustrade of the monument to Arribau in the Parque Ciudadella in Barcelona (1876-1877) and in which the majority of biographies on Gaudí observe his collaboration with the engineer Fontserè, at a time when our architect was still a student. However recent studies, particularly that of Martinell (13) negate the value of this contribution, as well as negating Gaudí's supposed collaboration in the lady chapel of the Virgin of Montserrat of F. De P del Villar.

The theme of the hyperbolic curve deepens in the project of an industrial pavillion roof for the "La Obrera Mataronense" ("The Mataró worker") co-operative in (1878-82), which has clear references to Viollet-le-Duc as one of the gaudian gospels. This connecting thread continues across the great brick and ceramic facade in the Finca Güell (1883-1885) in its main door and in its riding ring as well as in the sketched doors and in the ogives of the stained glass windows in the Palacio Güell (1885-1889) and also in the radiant doorway of the Astorga episcopal palace (1887-1893).

One of the clearest examples of the application made use by Gaudí of the hyperbolic arch is in the Convento de las Teresianas (1889-94), where that arch becomes a subtle element of spatial partition to such an extent that it enters a project for a Franciscan Mission residence in Tanger (1892-1899), and where the path followed by this gaudian element reaches its goal. It is transformed into a spatial synthesis which unites the metaphysical-abstract motifs of gothic space to the arabian fantasy of an Orient transported to fabulous ends. The steeples in the Tangiers plan still have a cone profile rather than a parabolic one, but they herald the towers of the Sagrada Familia in their disposition and reciprocal links. In the following works all the odisea of a form may be considered completed and explained in all its expressiveness: especially in the inclined columns of the chapel in Santa Coloma de Cervelló, in the arches and arboreal columns of the Parque Güell viaducts, and even in the masks of the roof openings in the form of a crest in the Casa Batlló. It is found in the curved wall and in the complex conformation of the roof of a small school built next to the Sagrada Familia, and in the facade of the Casa Milà with its complex plastic applications and in the chimney that rises from its roof and finally in the tapering parabole in the bell-tower of the Sagrada Familia.

Project for a patio for the provincial council building, 1870.

Project for the centre for the Franciscan Mission in Tangiers, 1892-1893.

An architecture of anticipation

The perseverance, constancy and obstination with which gaudí continued expanding, perfecting and modifying a form all through the course of his life constitutes a highly noteworthy testimony to the seriousness of his search. Such an effort appears, on the other hand, more coherent and conscious in light of his fantastic inventions and from the illusions and fantasmagorical ideas to which he abandoned himself and even through his extravagances and contemporizations with the " fashion of being of his time". All this constitutes the other side (the less evident and in many ways the most fascinating) of Gaudí's architecture as it unites the continuous and stimulating revision of the past styles with those which he tries to arouse, verifying the experiments of his new building techniques with those of his technological discoveries, in the attempt to save, from alienation and progressive barreness, that cultural environment which was subject to a mechanical technology which had alredy taken hold of the world. This was a world which Ruskin and Morris had previously tried to direct and

(12) R. Pane, Antoni Gaudí, Milan, 1964.
(13) C. Martinell, Antoni Gaudí, Barcelona, 1967.

A six light streetlight in Plaza Real, Barcelona, 1878.

steer (even at the risk of guiding it along regressive paths, something which Van de Velde would do later).

The Art Nouveau would also try to resolve this problem beginning with art as a guide, as a creator of models for industrial-technological production. With this, however it did no more than create the "luxury object", of which the neo-capitalist society, against which all of these forces were aimed, would take it and boast it as theirs. We could say that we are talking of the same danger, that of being embraced by a system, which has observed in our epoch all the movements with a revolutionary intention, such is the destructive force that is contained in the system. Look at the fortune that the Rational architecture found in Italy, chosen as the official architecture by the fascist regime. To some extent this also happened to Expressionism, destroyed in Hitler's Germany. Observe also a great part of the attempts of "response" of the present young generation, from the "beats" to the "marcusists" and the university movements which run the risk of becoming over academic in themselves.

In Gaudí this struggle is ideologically evident almost as a reactionary proposal. We should not forget that, apart from having shown some interest in socialist forms in his youth, where he joined the "Societat Obrera Maratonina" and being involved in projects for workers' houses, factories and social centres, he always worked for the upper bourgoise, as well as for sponsors who proved to be rather well educated. The fate of an artist is always connected to that of the person who contracts him, and it is probable that without Eusebio Güell we wouldn't find such an important collection as is offered to us in the totality of Gaudí's works, at least in a society such as ours still is, or in a society such as the Spanish one was (or rather the Catalan one). This connotation, on the other hand, is proof of the capacity to overcome obstacles which our architect had. It is proof of the very poetry and of the extraordinary power of his creative inventivness which allowed him to openly and effectively show his work, his architecture as Perucho defines it as of "anticipation" (14). The substantial difference between Gaudí and Modernism has been well observed by Zevi: "Gaudí... rejects the use of a style based on the yuxtaposition (not even furious) of the separated symbols of his own context..., he directs his gaze toward an open but organic architectural product, a polyhedronic mass which although dilated and torn in order to vitalize all its fibre and to make all its dynamic potential rise from it, conserves in spite of this its unity and fluidity as though it were an emptied terra-cotta".. Domènech i Montaner rape and blaspheme the past without managing to loosen themselves from the nets of stylistic eclecticism... Gaudí respects the old because he discovers it through his own intimate adventure. He does this through a leap of fantasy which ignores vileness and committments and is as a brushstroke which shows the outrage inferred in classicism" (15).

Architecture as visible space

In short, Gaudí's attempt to conquer an expressive form in space (an idea already cheapened and inadequate) and aimed at contemporary man, for an already shapeless and dehumanized space of the present day city, can be compared to all the later attempts at the reconquest of visible space. It is the same temptation found in Wright and also in certain present day architecture which tries to develop within the plane of human experience. One could point to the work of Louis Kahn, or that of Kinsler or even to that of Michelucci. This can not be put on the same side as that which Le Corbusier has tried to found in the chapel in Ronchamp, in which an "irrationalizing" inflection can be seen in the organistic sense of his experiments (Pevsner) (16). For this reason it has been wrongly compared with certain of Gaudí's attempts. The line applied by Le Corbusier in his work in Ronchamp has the significance of a precise and highly rational indication of architectural methodolgy and of a re-thought out project within the framework of verifiable constituent variables. It is an act of intelligence and sensibility on the part of somebody who, on considering reality, is able to avoid the weight of whichever slogan (even of those which he has formulated, as he feels free to interpret that reality within his own specific demands). (17).

(14) J. Perucho y L. Pomés, ibid
(15) B. Zevi, introducción a la Op. Cit de O. Bohigas.
(16) N. Pevsner, Pioneers of Modern Architecture, New York, 1949.
(17) E. Rogers, il metodo di Le Corbusier e la forma della Cappella di Ronchamp, en "casabella-continuità", nº 207, Milan 1955, and in Esperienza dell'Architettura, Turin, 1958.

Neither does it make sense to put Gaudí's efforts next to those of successive historical avant guard works which do not try to reconquer man's freedom by means of returning to the world's origin or to its inorganic nature which is loaded with uncontrolled and underlying ferments and impulses, but rather which claim it from the cultural and historical contingencies in an act of intellectual public mindedness and overcoming. (Malevic's white canvas is the absolute zero, the blank page, *a lu tous les livres,* and in white discovered the sum of all the colours).
Gaudí feels himself immersed in the colour; he is blinded by colour in all his culturalist, symbolic, analogical and physical works. An unsatisfied spirit always hidden in itself and without a communicative relationship; unadapted. At the bottom of this, or in reality, he was frightened of living without the support of compensating superstructures. So he hid in colour which dazzles as though he were a child. In colour he would base his "functionalism"and his "decorativism" as well as his continual desire for dynamism. In the colour of his refuge, which was increasingly deep we find his religiosity. Colour would be the symbol with which he would recharge his representations, already overloaded in the Nativity doorway in the Sagrada Familia.

Barcelona, Casa Vicens, 1878-1880. The exterior in its original form.

Barcelona, Casa Vicens, the veranda in its original form.

The first works

The first of Gaudí's works show him to adopt a rather mundane attitude, and in a certain way, a self advertising one. This was an attitude that didn't exlude recurring to the use of bright and colourful forms, in order to encourage intellectual snobbery in Barcelona in its sectors which were inclined to look paternalistically at certain initiatives which were vaguely socialistic. The aim of this was to absorb them in the more general movement of ardent nationalism which had decided that the young Gaudí should adhere to the *Centre Català d'Excursions Científiques* which organized youth group excursions to places which were sacred for the Catalan racial claims (Montserrat, Mallorca, el pic de la Maladeta, Toulouse and Carcasonne). It is interesting to recall an episode which must have heightened his enthusiasm; that of his visit to the city of Carcasonne. This coincided with the moment in which Viollet-le Duc was going to begin his reconstruction works. Some of the inhabitants in Carcasonne mistook him for Viollet-le-Duc on seeing him lost in deep contemplation of the ancient city walls. This fact indicates to some extent how clearly defined and precise his inclinations were at this stage (one should remember that at that time he studied and took escrupulous notes on Viollet-le-Duc's texts. There is a copy of the *Dictionnaire* which Gaudí had borrowed from a fellow student and which has numerous handwritten comments in the margins and penned by his very own hand).

Whilst still a student, Gaudí had built a close relationship with the organizers of the Catalan cooperative movement in the *Societat Obrera Mataronina* for whom he carried out, amongst other things in 1978 having recently graduated in architecture, a series of urbanistic projects. For example, factories, and an urban complex which would be the social centre for the workers' society. In fact he only completed a small kiosk in Mataró and a machine store room, where he employed a series of wooden parabolic arches to support the rooves following a method which had been used in the old catalan building tradition as well as following examples of old French models. These were known at this time not only through the Viollet-le-Duc's (18) *Dictionnaire* but also through distinct publications carried out by Rondel and others (19).

So far we have observed various of his early works, from the project of an entrance gate for a monumental cemetery, to the streetlights in the Plaza Real in Barcelona, or the later planned but not completed projects (1880) for the illumination of the Seawall or the Paseo Nacional in Barceloneta, both in Barcelona. These indicate his persistence in his constant search for an "expressive" form. In his first important completed works, those of, Casa Vicens (1878.1880), the Finca Güell, in the then suburban area of Las Corts (1883-1885) both in Barcelona and the "El Capricho" villa in Comillas (Santander), we can see the clear desire to define himself in a precise cultural position without separating himself from his aspirations toward an *éclatant* personalism with the aim of professional success.

But this doesn't mean to say that we can reasonably talk of him, as has been

(18) Le Dictionnaire raissé de l'architecture du XIéme siecle, Paris, 1854-69.
(19) R. Pane, ibid.

done, (20) as the "forerunner" of "modernism" fourteen years before Horta. Horta consciously created a modern style according to a revolutionary social and cultural programme. This can be seen in the *Maison du Peuple* in Brussels while Gaudí's intention in the Casa Vicens, the Finca Güell and in El Capricho (21) doesn't mean other than "the affirmation of a new tendency in taste", in respect of the premisses of the rich chromatism in mudejar art, which until that moment had been transmitted in Catalonia.

The "visible" use of stone and brick, the abundant use of tiles, the frequent recourse to elements which like forged iron (according to an artesanal tradition then on the increase and rooted in Catalonia from the Middle ages) shows a clearly "revivalist" attitude on Gaudí's part. Let us not forget certain episodes however (that whilst noteworthy and personal) allow us to place such traits as forming part of a wholly autonomous performance, which from a formal viewpoint, show what was his temperament at that time. Such episodic aspects are the beautiful brick waterfall in the Casa Vicens, which was destroyed soon after the house, which was originally to be lived in, was built. We can also see angular elements and a palm sheet motif developed in hyperboloid which were used in wrought iron gateways and in end areas in the El Capricho villa. This would later be one of the precedents of Art Nouveau in a "religadura" planned by Mackmurdo and with time would become one of the characteristic models in Gaudí's "naturalist" inspiration. In the Finca Güell we can see the free distribution of interior spaces, the lighting factor, that is to say the individuation of the function of light in the architecture. In short, these characteristic indications would be the fantasy inventions and the disposition of the elements in function with the plastic structure. It shouldn't be forgotten however that at this time the Chicago school was developing its experiments and that the Brooklyn suspension bridge designed by John Roebling in New York was another example of structural innovation dating to 1875.

The Casa Vicens (1878-80), has a curious history, Gaudí built it for a brick maker who almost went bankrupt due to its construction, but who later would make great profit from the expanding fashion of ceramic flooring which precisely had been initiated in his house. The house was extended and modified in 1925 by the architect J. B. Serra Martínez, (with Gaudí's consent, who at that time was immersed in the complex task of solving structural problems in the Sagrada Familia and consequently showed little interest in the fortune that would befall his first work). It is for this reason that today it is difficult to have a true picture of what was its original configuration. The interior shows a preponderance of decorative motifs chosen from an eclectic repertoire and which at times is oppressive, however this was in keeping with tradition. The moorish roof offers a point of noteworthy interest, it is stalactitic and of the *fumoir* style (and elaborated with originality), it surrounds the lamp thus creating a lighting which combines both elements of natural light with those of artificial light.

The villa or the hotel El Capricho (1883-1885) in Comillas shows more original characteristics. These are visible in the free disposition of its interior spaces as well as the evident luministic intention in the sliding emphatic forms in the exterior, which because of the rhythmic motif of the sunflower in deep relief, and because of the small ceramic pilasters which are found throughout the building, offer an infinity of possibilities for the light to reflect on. We see then the new interpretation of the light possibilities in the open relatioship between the interior and the exterior as well as in the original function of the decoration (luminous itself, and obssessed with compositional rhythms), and which is well cared for in all its details. Gaudí never went to Comillas on the Cantabrean sea and the buildings' construction was directed by him at a distance, something which seems contradictory to Gaudí's normal habit, as he always liked to direct the progression of his works personally. It is probable that he sent a large scale and highly detailled plaster model of the finished building. All of the floors of this building are developed with great freedom and at various levels, around a large glasshouse. This allows openings and passages which give this construction (which is not free of "culturalisms" and of a certain exhibitionist stamp), the value of being a noteworthy plastic creation, which culminates in the round tower (or viewpoint) that finishes with polygonal dome, appearing to be suspended in space above the aerial ornament, which is an iron balaustrade of a phytomorphic nature.

Barcelona, Casa Vicens. The garden's monumental fountain with a parabolic arch, which is no longer there.

Comillas, the villa El Capricho, 1883-1885. The garden wall made of brick and white tiles.

---

(20) Pevsner ibid; E Cirlot, El arte de Gaudí, Barcelona, 1950
(21) Whose erection is owed to the family connection of Eusebio Güell to Claudio López, Marquis de Comillas.

Robert Pana was the first to publish a reproduction of a brick and white ceramic "exedra" of this villas garden, while J. F. Ràfols who was the only witness to so many of Gaudí's lost works, who not only doesn't refer to this discovery but neither to the very existence of the building. This enclosing construction, "exedra", made of brick and white tiles which serves as a containing wall for a garden embankment, is resolved by means of two pilasters which finish off projecting with scaled elements an effect obtained by overlayering and crosslayering bricks. This is in reality a first idea or attempt at rustic vases which appear in the highest parts of some of the "grutescos" pilasters in one the viaducts in Parque Güell. Consequently one cannot help but mentally establish a striking affinity (which is not the only one as we shall see in the "mushroom form" colomns in the same Parque Güell and also in Santa Coloma de Cervelló) with some of the projecting motifs which were characteristic of Wright's first period. The two pavillions in Parque Güell, in Las Corts (already mentioned), and now in the Avenida de Pedralbes, are also indebted to mudejar inspiration. This is the first work which Gaudí completed for Eusebio Güell (1883-1887), which was meant to form a part of the terminal of that suburban property.

Las Corts de Sarriá. Barcelona, Finca Güell. The pilaster of the iron gateway.

These two pavillions, show great imaginary powers with their lively and bright colours euphuistic luminosity and whose forms are seen to be plastically evolved from the great elements which emerge from the chimney of the doorway and from the lantern placed above the figure of the enormous winged dragon (of wrought iron) of which the inner door is composed. And while the arabian insinuation is shown in the decoration of the wall, composed of semicircular terricotta elements, it presents certain other characteristics which would become part of the gaudian world. We can observe for example, the free arrangement of tiles, (which in reality were ceramic fragments used in function with their luminous vibration and their chromatic effect, according to the incidence of light, in a decoration which was neither figurative nor naturalistic, as was that of the flooring in Casa Vicens or in El Capricho). We can also note the free explanation in the plastic sense of the elements: that species of architectural trajectory which seen in the roofings developed in a series of episodes between that which establish ties with flat terraces, small vaults, domes and lanterns united together by daring brick stairwells. This motif is also found in the cornices in Parque Güell, and in the aggressive end part in Casa Batlló and above all in the splendid and impressive architectural adventure in the roof in Casa Milà with its massive intonations. We also see that in these pavillions that the arrangement of interior space is already presented in an organically defined way. The square is developed on the sequence of parallel parabolic arches, seated on corbels and separated by small heavy vaults, while the *manège*, placed at the end of the square, is closed at its highest point by a lowered dome from which arises a cylindrical lantern above which the last set cone shell opens its radiant petals.

Add to this the fantastic use of wrought iron above the jewelled pilaster summit of the inner door and above all the invention of the fantasmagorical figure of the wrought iron dragon which seems to be leaving due to the art of magic or bewitchment, from a mannered medieval composition and which lends an unquietening fantasy with a surrealistic ending. Even the allusive character of the non descriptive image where the only naturalistic element is seen in its head induces one to think of the late gothic period. It reminds us of the countless figures of Saint George and the dragon which in the XV century were a popular theme of the xylographs.

The other elements which formed a part of the Finca Güell were a stone stairway which is now destroyed, with a brick and ceramic door, actually remade via a rather oppressive restoration which has given it an almost pharaonic appearance. This can be seen in its original state in an illustration in Ràfols book (22). It was developed above a parabolic arch in its totality and exhibited its material in earthenware and is found connected to the wall of the grounds. Today it is isolated and has lost a great part of its character.

Palacio Güell

The construction of this palace (1885-1889) is located within the height of Gaudí's activity.
In respect of this building the Italian commentators have often pointed to

(22) J. F. Ràfols, ibid.

Las corts de Sarriá, Barcelona, Finca Güell. Entrance gateway with zoomorphic representation.

Barcelona, Palacio Güell, 1885-1889. Iron wrought crest between two parabolic gateways.

the Venetian Gothic style as a source of influence, although here he freely adopted a stylistic diversity with a fully conscious and intentioned selective value.

In this work we do not find elements of the English "revivalism", everything in it shows a diligence to produce forms of a culture which was wearily conquered through books and which shows a certain affinity of spatial modulation with the ornate moorish architecture (or perhaps the Venetian Gothic). The picturesque flexibility belongs to the Spanish school, open to the patio and it makes one appreciate the motifs of filtered light in the relationship between the interior and the exterior, showing itself to be jealous in the secret on its intimacy, but wanton to reflect it in some exterior way.

The Palacio Güell facade clearly shows the relationship of the configuration between the building and the street. It achieves by means of the parabolic arches in its two great doorways and which for the first time do not use wooden panels, but use wrought iron inner doors (an innovation which would later be very popular in Barcelona, but that at this time was frowned upon). We can see the large corbel held gallery which crosses the full width of the first floor and fulfills a mission of filtering light between the interior and the exterior, as do the window slits at the ends of each. These serve in the illumination of the large central hall and whose height is that of the three upper floors of the building. All of this establishes direct contact between the prior and posterior facade, (with the free filtration of light), which opens out to a patio which is also designed with a gallery and guarded by two iron cones.

The hallway descends, on the one hand (through a beautiful helicoidal stairway), to the stables- and from where arises the wise articulation of the terracotta pilasters which support the building-, and on the other side it rises passing by the main staircase to the three upper floors, and developed around the already quoted central hall which was destined to serve as the concert and celebration hall. This hall finishes in a brickworked parabolic vault which alights in parabolic arches and is found surmounted by another vault which ends in a high summit which surges into the terrace which covers the roof and of which it is the central and dominant element.

In reality, this ending rises finishing with a succession of four conical vaults and through which the forementioned hall receives direct light. As well as the light that penetrates through the openings in the same vault of the dome. Apart from this principal detail, the conical chimneys create a fabulous landscape in the roof of this building. This is due to the richness of the colours (monochromes or polychromes, enamelled or in stone or brick or obtained with fragments of coloured tiles). This last procedure is used, without beating about the bush, in a cornice similar to that of the Palacio Güell and that was designed to give authority and above all to leave a mark in the culural and aesthetic education of the citizens of the epoch. In effect, this palace would be a characteristic sign of the gaudian presence within the Barcelona topography. It is located on the extreme of an ideal axis whose other extreme is constituted by the "summa" of the intentions of the entirety of Gaudí's work. The steeples of the Sagrada Familia, which are surrounded scenographically by some of the maestros' other works, represent the aspiration of an entire city to recognize itself in a highly meaningful symbol of one of the most bubbling epochs.

In Palacio Güell the parabolic arches of the facade doorways repeat themselves, with some variation, in the arches of the interior galleries, whose columns connect with them by means of geometric motifs, which are generally based on the hyperbole and are already part of the Gaudí's mature language or they constitute one of the first examples of his concept of architecture which was originated as if by germination (or almost by spontaneous generation), as though it were an element of nature.

Gaudí meticulously studied all the details of this palace, from the great heraldic Catalan coat of arms, in wrought iron, which explodes with expanding vitality between both doorways of the facade which it adorns, until the bars, the rooves, the balustrades and some of the pieces of furniture, thus trying to create a "syntheseis of the arts" which W. Morris had invoked and which H. Van der Velde was beginning to claim. In this case Gaudí's is an exceptional attiude, one which in our technological civilization, and at that time, only exceptionally gifted people are and were capable of. The epoch corresponds fully to the culture of the "specializations" in which there practically isn't any

Axonometric perspective of the doorway and the exercise ring for horses in the Finca Güell in Las Corts de Sarriá, Barcelona.

Finca Güell. Brick and ceramic glairway, no longer existent.

Finca Güell. Brick and ceramic door, today highly modified.

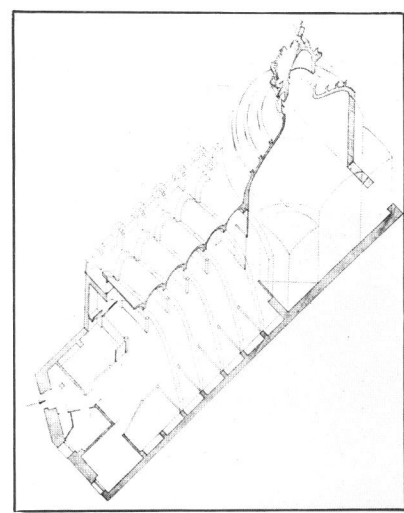

The exterior of Palacio Güell, Barcelona.

room for the figure of the "total" artist, according to the renaissance sense of the word.

As we were saying, we only find cases of artistic "synthesis" in the modern framework in the presence of special artistic personalities (Le Corbusier for example), or it is found within an area of inter-artistic collaboration. Though Gaudí's personality pushed him to adopt a leading role he also valued the collaboration with diverse artists such as the painter Clapés, in whom he entrusted the work of the interior of Palacio Güell itself. The painter produced some *decorationa al fresco* and the now lost decoration of an outside wall. He also decorated the Casa Milà. Later on, Gaudí found in Jujol a refined collaborator, who showed himself to possess great artistic sensibility in his fantastic decorations made from tile mosaics and to be seen in Palacio Güell and in the iron railings in the Casa Milà.

Gaudí had met Clapés, an industrialist who worked in the textil trade, in Eusebio Güell's house (his protector-client). He was a fervent Catalan nationalist and a man without prejudice and of an open mind and who had widespread international interests. In his house he often reunited artists, musicians and literary figures. It was probably in the rich library of that Maecenas where Gaudí met Ruskin and Morris, and in dealing with the later gained a fervour for the music of Wagner.

Gaudí and the Neogothic

Plan for the hunting pavillion which should have been built in Garraf, Barcelona for Eusebio Güell, 1882.

It is a typical phenomenum in Gaudí's tireless fantasy and worry along with the psychological anxiety which he felt for completing his possible projects, the fact that, at the same time he changed the use of diverse linguistic codes trying out various styles and elaborating new forms. He was pushed by a desire to define himself and to recognize what was his own force, as though in a temporal delay which surpasses the limits of his own moment in history, perhaps with the intention of discovering a constant in past styles in which it were possible to find a point of contact for the desired discovery of new possibilities of solutions and means of expression by means of updated techiques, even if responding to traditional formulas.

So that while he was building Palacio Güell, Gaudí planned and completed the restoration of the Episcopal palace in Astorga (1889-1893), in an inspired work of gothic fantasy. This had been completely destroyed by fire shortly before. Further he designed the plans for a pavillion for the Transatlantic company (in a moorish style which was even reminiscent of the Alhambra). This he did to celebrate the Universal Exhibition in Barcelona of 1888. He later built a house known as Botines (1891-1894) in León. This was neogothic in style. Finally he built the Teresian College in Barcelona (1889-1894) (El Colegio de las Teresianas) in which the ancient formulas would be transformed into the "live word". But apart from all of this he began the work that would increasingly absorb his thoughts and all of his aspirations as a builder, artist and believer. This was the continuation of the Expiatory Temple in the Sagrada Familia, whose long meditated and polymorphic execution would coincide with a progressive "cloistering" of Gaudí's character in that which refers to his social relationships, and of the definitive religious devotional orientation, which it would give to his life.

The Episcopal Palace in Astorga (whose reconstruction was entrusted to Gaudí in 1887 by the bishop of that diocese J. B. Grau i Vallespinós, a fellow countryman of his), was finished when the architect was still occupied in the works at Palacio Güell. (He had already assumed the responsibility for the Sagrada Familia). In that work he tried to approximate the severe gothic style belonging to certain nordic mansions. He developed his work according to spatial and volume capacity which was more complex than that which the real scale of the building allowed. He achieved a result which diminished the elements of genuine invention and which are found in the great sketched arches of the hyperbolic opening- below which are the doorways, conceived in agreement with the effects of the "prospectic" deformation caused by the shadow of these very same arches- in the distribution of the internal spaces, in the falsifying of the plans and in the interior lighting plan from the highest point, which was not applied as the bishop died in 1895 and Gaudí had to abandon Astorga. The reason for this was that he had generated great hostility as, instead of using local labour to carry out the task, he had brought Catalan workers with him who were used to his way of working.

Astorga, The episcopal palace, 1889-1895.

This house in León, which today is the main base for the local building society, was built in white granite, as was the Episcopal palace in Astorga, but not in the neogothic style. It was developed in the form of a compact block inside a quadrangle with an irregular perimeter and was determined by the character of the internal spatial distribution.

One of the characteristics in Gaudí's neogothic style is his spatial use, which is always real and precise. His work is also different in this respect from all of the revivalistic contemporary forms. One of the elements in the revival is conceptive unidimensionality, that is the diverse parts are found distributed as thpugh they were theatre wings. The internal and external façades are often yuxtaposed without offering any real cohesion. In Gaudí's work, on the other hand space is always defined. The "façade" is also something that involves and hides, and that has its "epidermis" and its "mucus" related by specific and solid thickeners. The definition of "spatial thickener" given in respect of Borromini by Cesare Brandi (23) and from which this problem has arisen, and which for Borrromini has a particular meaning, can also be applied to the intelligence of some elements of Gaudí's work.

In the Casa de los Botines we can observe, the greater width in the lower part of the window openings which in the first floor adopt a "triforium" form. Another notable element in this building is the use of iron in the inner door of the doorway and in the railings which surround the house and the series of half windows in the semibasememt.

La Casa de los Botines

León, Casa de los Botines, 1892-1894.

Easily the most interesting work of this period and with a difference, is the Colegio de las Teresianas-(Teresian School) (1889-1894), in Barcelona. In this, the same limitations of means which did not allow the elaboration of a decorative superstrucure, as was normal in Gaudí, made possible the development of a precise and extremely clear architectural deployment, in which the use of gothic motifs as seen in the limpid transcriptions, and in the white cloister corridors (and with parbolic arches) of the purest type of certain interios of that style, is the cause of an intimate expressiveness and of a sensation of calm which is rarely found in Gaudí's works which are usually full of tense energy. This work shows frenzied rhythm from its austere exterior -harmonically shared by the distribution of the two materials of which it is composed, brick and masonry, (treated with that special sensitivity which Gaudí showed in all his wall reconstructions). It is defined by the central projecting body (overvalued for its incredibly beautiful iron railings at the entrance), and by the crenalated ending of the flat roof and also by the lively angular culminations. The interior is totally coherent with the rest of the building and simple in its distribution of spaces. It is in perfect correspondence with its external definition, it impresses, even in its urbanistic appearance, and because of its severe intimacy and inusitated expressive force, which is seen in its unusual lack of ornamentation.

Colegio de las Teresianas

The assigment of building the Misión Franciscana in Tangiers gave Gaudí the opportunity of visiting Andalucía and to go as far as Tangiers. It should be noted that he was not a travel lover, and as we have seen El Capricho was built without him going once to Comillas. He went to Tangiers accompanied by the Marquis of Comillas (Eusebio Güell's nephew) who had requested the project. It was not carricd out, but it is intcresting that thc cxpcricncc of that journey gave Gaudí a starting point for the elaboration of the idea of some towers (conical yet in the African plan), which would evolve into the hyperboloid towers in the Sagrada Familia.

A plan

With the construction of Casa Calvet (1898-1904) in Calle Caspe, in Barcelona, Gaudí focused his interest toward solutions which unite Barroque memories with certain "modernist" anticipations (as in the end motif, in a double curve in the facade which finishes with the flat roof with two small balconies *ajourés* and in the rich iron decoration of the *trilobados* balconies and the gallery located above the doorway). The internal installation of the lift using an incredible

Casa Calvet

(23) C. Brandi, Struttura e Architettura, Turin, 1967.

richness of folding and wrought iron shows great inventiveness as do the details of the exterior iron railings and the insides of the doors. However, the most noteworthy element and that which has the most meaningful anticipatory value is perhaps the "functionalist" solution to the posterior facade. This was developed in the form of a succession of continuous verticle "sashes" in the windowed galleries which alternated with balconies.

Bellesguard

If the fantasy component of the minaret-city is the dominant motif in the plan for the missionary centre in Tangiers then the gothic component, here transfigured into a vision of a legend, becomes again what the Bellesguard tower informs us of (1900-1902), in n⁰ 46 of the present day street of this name. It is located at the feet of Tibidabo, and continues all along the Vilana stream. This tower was built in the memory of King Martín I of Aragon who had maintained one of his suburban residencies in that very place. Gaudí had a street deviated over the a stream, Vilana, with the object of taking the scarce remains of the old residence into the adjacent land of the new construction in the form of a garden. This gave him the first chance to construct the first vaults with inclined columns, instead of using escarpment, with the aim of containing the force exercised by the embankment. This was a solution which he would apply with great frequency in the successive systematization of Parque Güell.

The modern Bellesguard building which has a high angulum crowned steeple finished by a four armed cross (an almost floral motif which can be considered as a typical gaudian sign). This is found completely refloored in its exterior with pieces of gravel whose fragments create a highly delicate chromatic contrast. Windows of various forms, in a happy distorted arrangement mark rhythms in the external surface and correspond to a spatial definition which can be considered as one of Gaudí's most interesting attempts. The interior is refloored in stucco with chamfered angles in both the stairs and large rooms. It is organized in sharing columns, pilasters and arches which are above corbels in a fantastic game of rational but daring structures. For example in the attic, pilasters of the width of two bricks rise until it creates a plane of rest formed by two threads twenty-two bricks wide and two in thickness. Above this plane rise lobed arches which sustain the roof. There are other characteristic elements in this: the presence of a visible and external discharge pipe, which is covered in gravel stones and surrounded by rings. The interconnected ironwork of the beautiful innerdoor, finished in *ou de fouet* denoting a heightening of the modernist spirit (remember that Obrist's folding screen is dated 1895 and that the decoration of Atelier Elvira de Endell, in Munich, was dated 1897-1898 and that in Barcelona itself the furniture designer Gaspar Homar had used this ondulated trait in some forms of his furniture by 1891). Another notable detail is the star in relief that crows the stairway window slit, which is made of colourful glass and has an appearance which is at once *mandala* buddhist and kaleidoscopic image.

Las Corts de Sarriá, Barcelona, the gate to the Finca Miralles

Finca Miralles

At this moment in Gaudí's career (1901), he built the wall and the gate to the Finca Miralles, close to Parque Güell in Las Corts in Sarriá. In this task he collaborated with the architect Sugrañes who was both his friend and compatriot and who worked at his orders. The wall presents a base stone element, with curvature development in both horizontal and vertical directions. It has an iron cornice which repeats alternately with itself. In the gate whose roof is by Sugrañes, it is worth noting the plastic sinuosity of the arches, and the lateral inner door, where Gaudí developed the motif of the linear overacceptance of two series of opposing curved lines which follow parallel courses.

Parque Güell

Following this came one of Gaudí's most prestigious and unbridled works, and one which continually demanded the applied and attentive control of rational concepts on his part. Parque Güell (1900-1904) was opened due to a plan for "green space". It was yet again Eusebio Güell, who having constituted an association for the garden cities in London the previous year, encharged Gaudí with this task. The park occupies the space called *Muntanya Pelada* at the bottom of Tibidabo and looks directly toward the city and to the sea. There had been plans

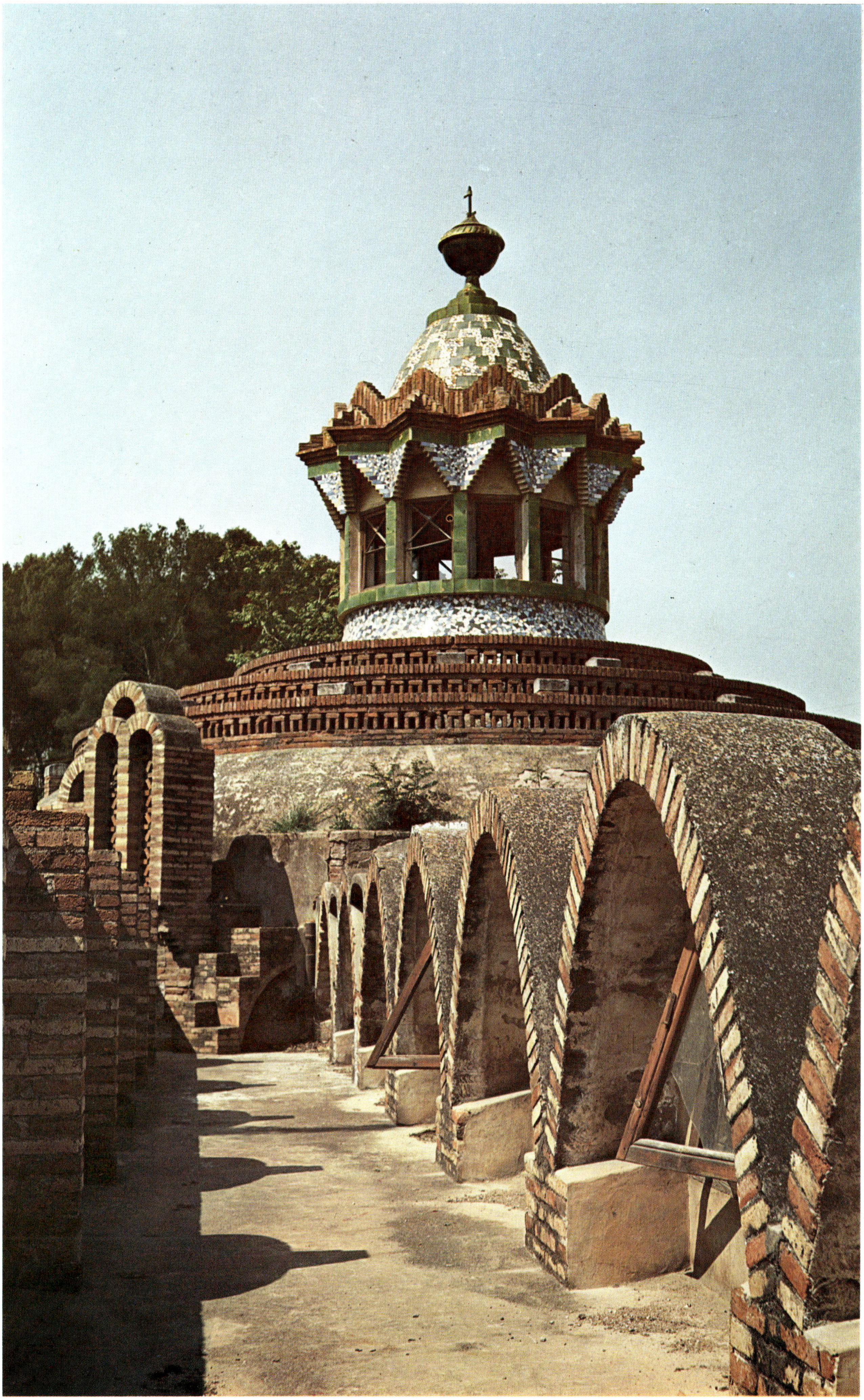

36

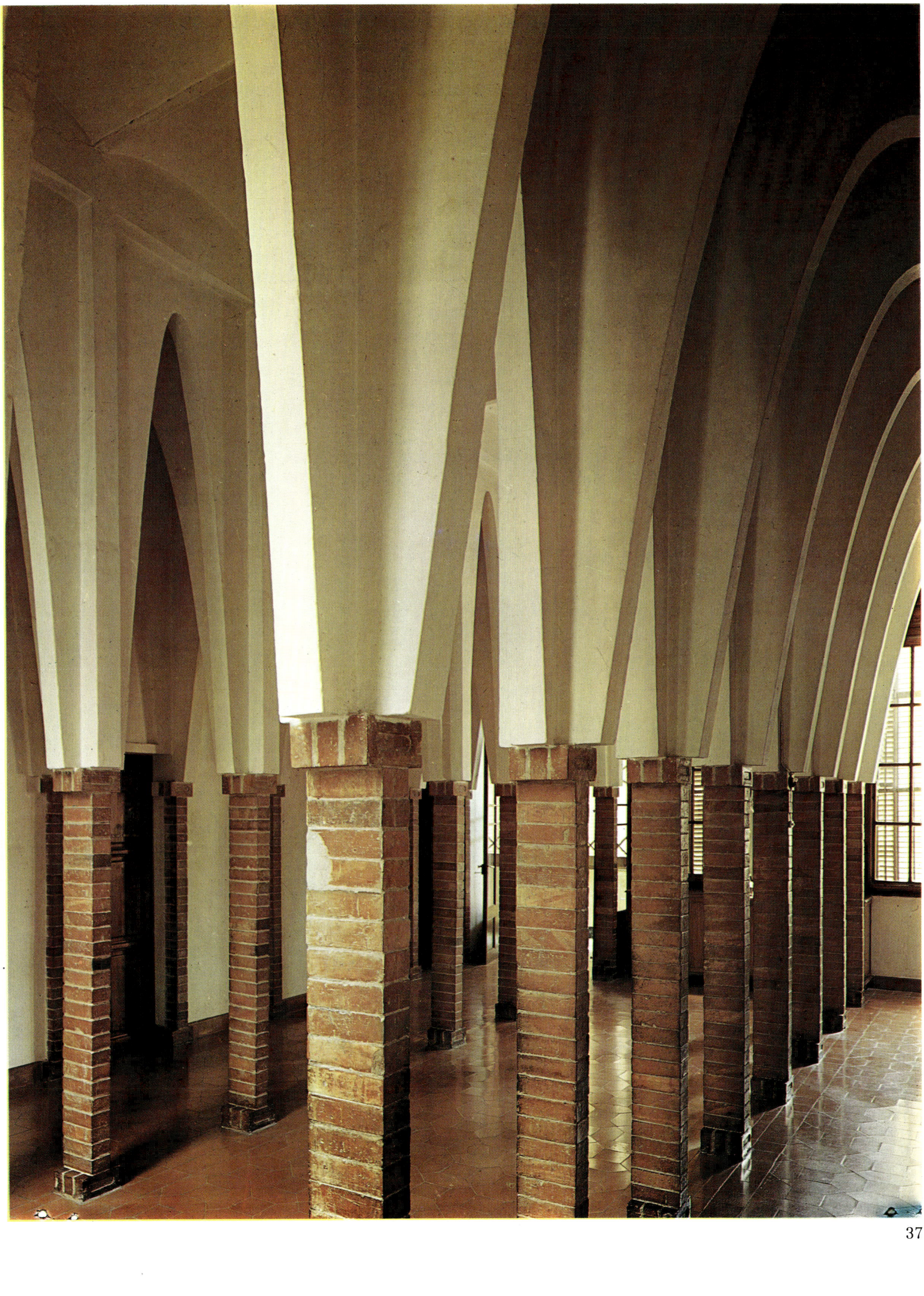

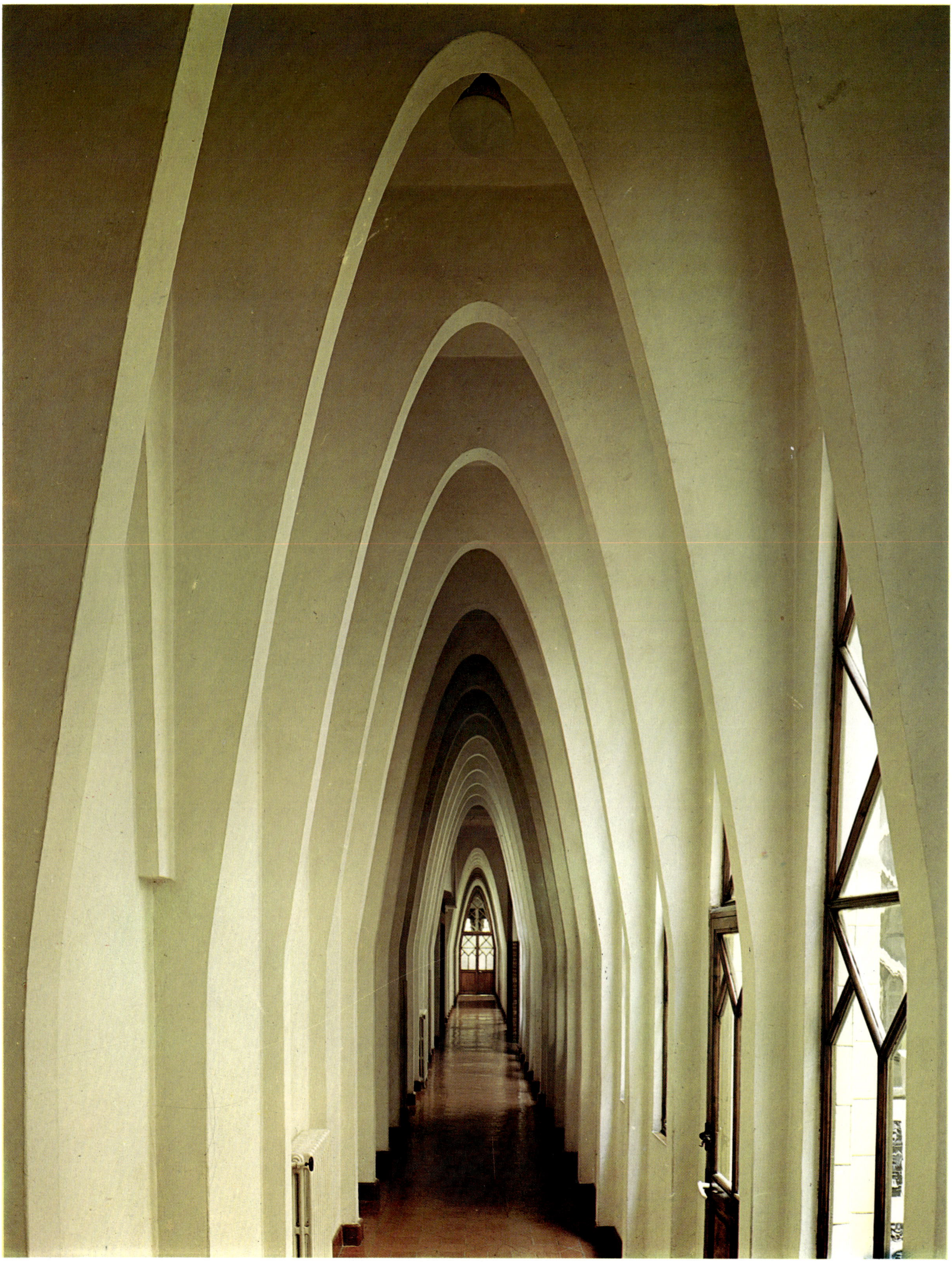

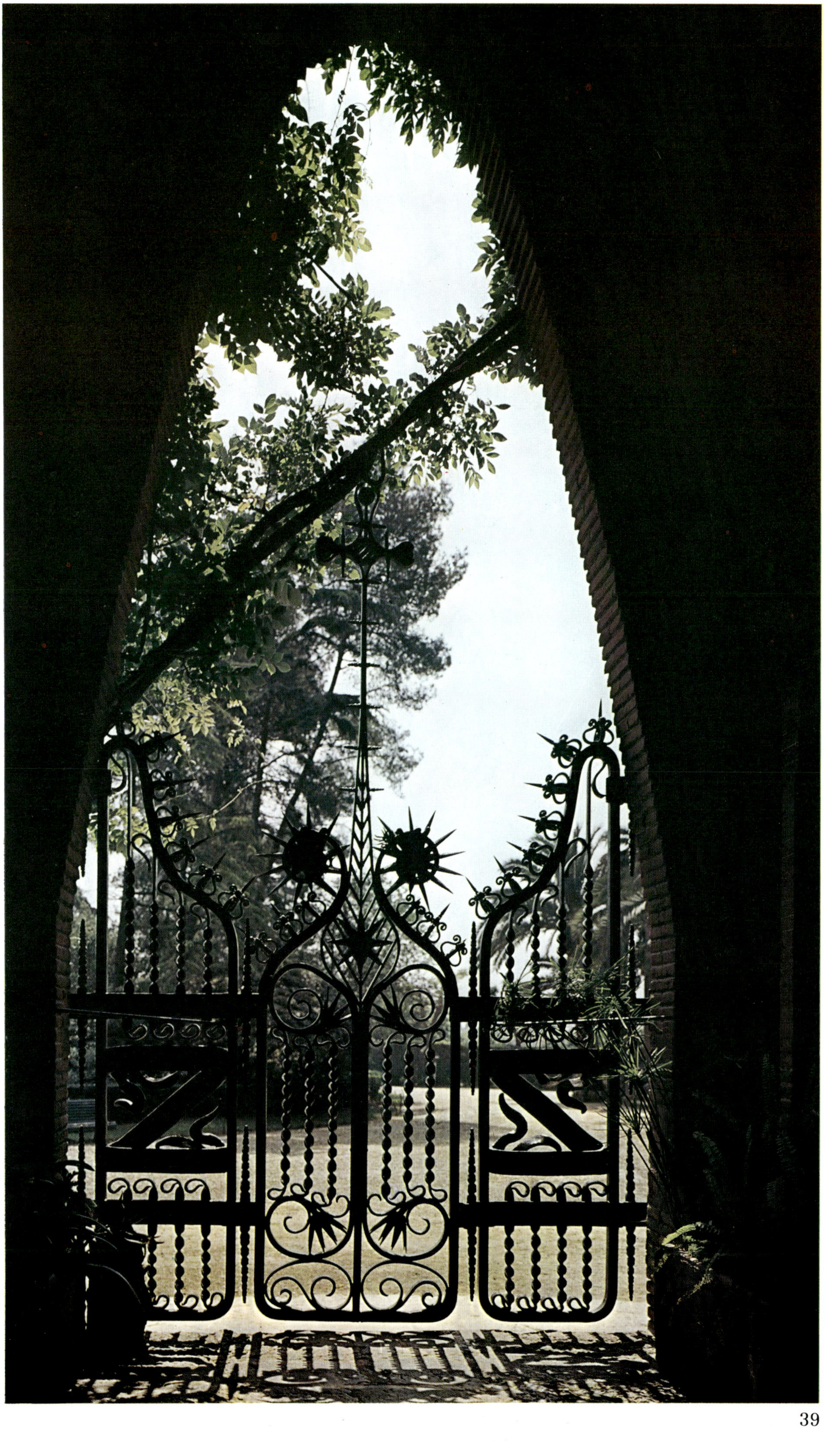

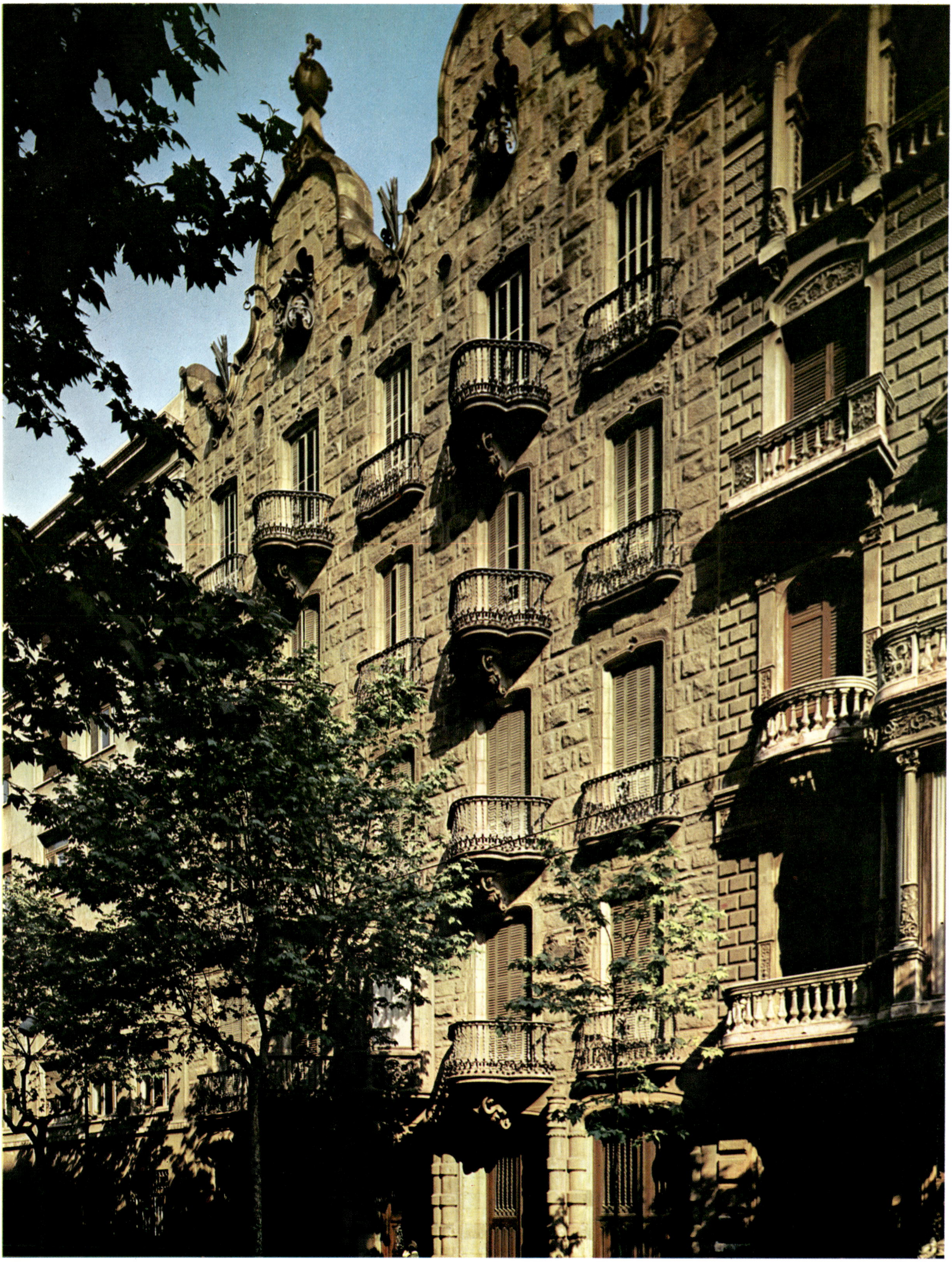

Barcelona, Torre Bellesguard (Tower), 1900-1902. The attic.

Barcelona, Parque Güell, 1900-1914. Arboreal columns.

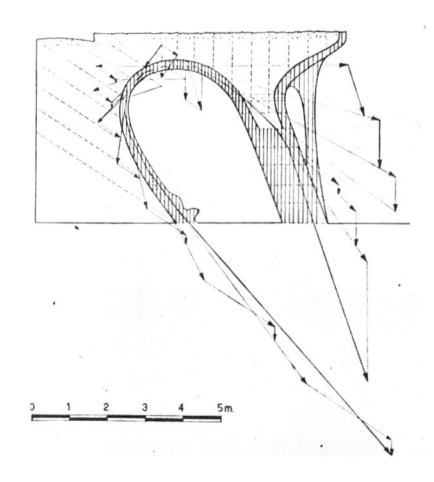

A drawing of a section of a curved passage of Parque Güell, (Barcelona), with a diagram of the weights and forces.

to construct an urbanization of sixty buildings surrounded by gardens; but the plan of using it as a "green city" did not gain approval. For this reason the park was given to the city as a public place. Although Gaudí's sensibility toward the natural element is clearly evident, as is his desire to recover the creative process of nature, in all its elements, do not adopt the opinion that it was his mimetic instinct which led him to begin such a fantastic adventure. Nothing in this vast work (with its infinite variations and inventions) was left to chance, or to the risk of uncontrolled discovery. Quite the opposite, all of this apparent freedom in this vast plan in which stone continually disguises in tree, ramification, or even an incisive blackberry tree as "organic" or natural data, is in fact the result of a precise calculation which begins with the laws of elasticity and the relationships between forces and counterforces, and those between weights and forces.

There is no element of the fantasy that has not been constructed on a reasoned basis (and this is seen in each of the parks' details). So that, it doesn't seem that the unbridled "productivity so characteristic of Gaudí is continually orientated, above all in a rational and technical sense, until this technological rationalism becomes an aim in itself. On the other hand, we do find daring technological solutions which border on the virtuoso for the type of rational gaudian "mania" and this desire he has to get to the bottom of things at "whatever cost". We see a meaning in a type of fear to feel himself sufficiently up to date with the new tecnological discoveries. Gaudí's solutions seem out of date and elementary in comparison to Dutert's famous machine gallery, with its arches with three 115m opening hinges for the Universal Exhibition in Paris in 1889. However, in reality this apparent insecurity contrasts with the more genuine intention in gaudian investigation whose innovative character is exlusively expressive.

The study of certain constants in Gaudí's vision, in the sense of his behaviour, will probably lead us to discern sign of an "untireable productive mind" in our investigation. (This is specially so if we start with his tendency to use surrounding, radiant and parabolic and "agglutinative" forms, in order to take advantage of a foreign psychiatric language which belongs to the study of certain manifestations which have a pathological root.)

I would like to make clear, that with all that has been said, that I do not wish to raise the question of Gaudí on a psychoanalitical level and thus convert it into a "case study". That said, certain searches along these lines, if carried out scientifically, could prove to be revealing.

To affirm however that certain investigations may result as deviant to the aims of achieving a critical judgement is nothing more than to underline the need to use them as in the same way we use all types of documents or background study sources. This only seems possible through part time studies which may offer solid evidence to a judgement.

Parque Güell takes in more than 56 hectares of land which is made up of roads, viaducts and diverse types of paths, exploiting the natural landscape characteristics of the mountain to the full extent. This continued respect for nature and this desire to investigate and continually recreate his forms in the same constitutive character has contributed in the evaluation of Parque Güell as the definitive result of garden architecture of the XVII and XVIII centuries, specially in that which refers to English gardens. Certain references which have been made in respect of this should not in my opinion be excluded. I would incline, as does Ragghianti (24), in seeing a connection with the Italian and French architecture of the fifteen hundreds, with more allusions to names like Buontalento than to Ammanati. Roberto Pane directs his references to "ancient and complex structures which exploit the available stones in the area of the work, modelling transitions between walls and vaults, so approximate and naive as they are ingenious" (25), in reference to Catalonia and the Balearic islands.

One loose thread which remains to be considered is that of the connection between Gaudí and nature which seems to be too direct and too deeply felt to justify just any indirect cultural reference. It is more, there exists a moment in which all connection of cultural dependence in Gaudí is descarted. I would say that this moment can be placed in Parque Güell itself, if we omit the naive or perhaps ironic presence of the support of the large end terrace with its thick

(24) C. L. Ragghianti, Antoni Gaudí (in "Sele Arte" nº 35), 1958
(25) R. Pane, idem.

A plan for the iron baldaquin in the Palma de Mallorca Cathedral, 1904-1914.

doric columns, something unusual in Gaudí, though later he would give the name "griego" to the Portal de la Natividad (Nativity Doorway) of the Sagrada Familia.

Next to the entrance and between the two fantastic splendid coloured pavillions, thanks to its ceramic decorations (which reflect light at all hours of the day, depending on the angle of incidence), and which culminate in the highly elaborate white-blue steeple, one enters a a type of enchanted garden in which an enormous lizard-dragon greets us. This dragon is covered in majolica which descends between the double balustrade of the stairwell. Above this a fountain opens below a great arch which forms its protection. At the bottom the great doric column which contributes to accentuating the sensation of "disorder" provoked by its irrational presence with the anormal inclination of its columns (at least in the classical sense). If we see in this an anticipation, a "macroscopization", "a la pop", but presented on a Kitcsch level in the style of Disneyland, it would be in such a case not a verification but rather an indication of analogy which would serve to help us in the comprehension of vast cultural phenomema. (We should note that the ceramic mosaics in the terrace which extend over the columns have been considered a posteriori in Gaudí as Cubist and Dadaist premises.)

On the other hand, it would be fair to insist in the playful character of this landscape architecture. Look at the accentuation of the acute verticality of the inclined columnal stones and in the vaults of the viaducts for example. Note also the sensation of intentionally provoked vertigo in the curved passages, as though that to which the section design refers, together with the diagram of weights and forces in which the vault continues sustained by the treelike columns at a steep angle, is violently bent against the embankment whose wall accentuates the curve of the opposing columns. This would be a possible reference to the ""Scherzi" in the Italian gardens of the XVII century, (as labyrinths, or visions in *trompe l'oeil*, streams of secret water which suddenly reveal themselves), if it were not for the fact that here we are dealing with a more intense game: one which is a complete mind game.

The problem of the "playful" element in Gaudí could be focused in respect of the admirable derivation of the serpentine parapet mosaic which borders the terrace and which was planned for childrens' games. In Jujol, Gaudí had a brilliant collaborator in this part of the work. Jujol was the author, amongst other things, of the beautiful ceramic decorations of the roof in the so called "doric hall". That terrace is one of the most free and happy expressions of Gaudí's inventiveness, and where here he doesn't seem to be overly worried about cultural order.

Some have insisted in their views on the gaudian anticipations in respect of Cubism and Dadaism amd Informal Art while referring to such decoration. This is specially because numbers also appear in some of the mosaics. These are nothing other than "manufacturers numbers" of the destroyed tiles or incrustations of strange elements and complete examples. This view is also held because the compositions denote a refined non-figurative vision. It is in such works where Gaudí appears to have reached the most perfect balance between invention and reason and strangely that distention that self realization that seems to have been his ungraspable dream: a *joie de vivre* in which many of his fantasy and colourful inventions would seem to wish to impose themselves by force, thus provoking with their violence a certain sensation of "distancing" or of "alienating" us which leaves us at times rather perplexed.

Architectural restoration

Let's turn now to Gaudí's intervention in the work which occupied him in Mallorca Cathedral from 1904-1914 (this is seen as a "reform" in the definitions of the majority of Spanish texts, or the architectectural-liturgical restoration according to Ràfols term) (26). The problem which arises here is that of to what extent it is licit to talk of a direct intervention which is not limited to works of consolidation and conservation, given that we are dealing with ancient architectural monuments. The problem is complex, and in no moment can it be resolved starting with a general point of view which is universally valid. If it is true, as Brandi writes, that direct intervention on an ancient work is not possible in a modern epoch (there is a century and a half of difference in this example), because the formation of the "historical consciousness of the monument" dates to that epoch and in consequence of the "necessary recognition of an irreversible status of the present historical consciousness" which impedes us from intervening in past monuments, then it is no less true that clean breaks do not exist in history and that its course is certainly irreversible and that not even artistic heritage can be considered as "mummified". Churches and other monuments have a history that continues and in whichever case they are not museums! On the other hand everything is relative and situations never repeat themselves in an identical way. It is a question which should not be treated as question of principle but rather one of making it an object of continual annotation on a scientific level and that each time that the case demands then we move to a critical evaution.

In the specific question of Gaudí's architectural-liturgical restoration, which raised so much dust and generated so much argument, we are dealing with, in my opinion, a personal intervention which is neither irrespectful nor wrongful. At the bottom it was limited to the insertion of iron diafragms in stained glass windows of the large windows of the apse, which were restored according to a procedure in which Gaudí used the superimposition of three diverse stained glass panes, in order to obtain blurred tones, in the creation of the beautiful aerial baldaquins and in the systematization of light in the basilica. We should add that this isn't the sort of task that you give to just anyone. This is shown in the same cathedral a few years after the distancing of Gaudí, when other anonimously created stained glass windows were installed which were totally unacceptable. According to Bergós (28), Gaudí had commented in respect of his intervention in the Mallorcan Seo: "Let's practise architecture without doing archeology: in the first place there are the relationships between things, in a predisposed situation; for this reason we shouldn't copy the forms but rather be in condition to produce them within a determined character which possesses their spirit." These words seem to be a precise criticism of all the tiring problem of the eighteenth century restorations based on "repristining" archeology which was always arbitrary in Viollet-le-Duc's style.

(26) J. F. Ràfols, Antoni Gaudí, Barcelona, 1960.
(27) C. Brandi, L'inserzione del nuovo nel vecchio, idem.
(28) Bergós, idem.

Another of Gaudí's uses of the concept of "playfulness" can be found in the crypt of the chapel in Colonia Güell (1898-1915), a workers colony in Cervelló, Barcelona. The project had been encharged to Gaudí by the great industrialist and maecenas Güell along with a project for houses and social service centres for workers. The concept is understood as an overcoming of structural laws and static equilibrium in order to obtain a freer fantasy game to such a point that all the problems seem to be voluntarirly provoked by the happines of being able to overcome it immediately. The chapel, even thugh we are talking of an unfinished work, represents one of the greateast achievements in gaudian investigation. It is in this work where Gaudí freely applied his new structural laws with which he understood how to subvert those other fundamental laws in the tripartition of the gothic forces, coming closer once again and with profound adhesion, to the natural laws of growth consequently he discovered, if not through the cultural path but rather through the natural one, a connection with archaic and barbarous forms which possessed an intense dramatic expressiveness.

The chromatic rapport provoked by the contrast of the diverse materials, (different coloured stones, bricks, cement, iron, enamel, and stained glass), achie-

The crypt in Santa Coloma de Cervelló

Santa Coloma de Cervelló, Barcelona, the crypt of the church in Colonia Güell, 1898-1915.

Crypt of Colonia Güell: a detail of the exterior.

Crypt of Colonia Güell: aspects of the interior.

ves a force of fantastic application which adequate lighting (which Gaudí had foreseen), would have duly heightened and prized. An absolute independance from whichever form of "revivalist" worries or even formal ones makes this crypt an insuperable model of emotive expressiveness (given that here form is born from the fact of total experience independent of its individual relationships), and above all free of whichever decorativist link which could be considered as a unifying element.

Heads have turned to look at this totally pure example of faith in the possibilities of the fantasy of man's creator, when the premisses of a new mystic-religious symbolism have tried to be recreated, and it was through these premisses that Gaudí managed to make us relive the most genuine gothic spiritual condition. But if we look at the most elaborate preparatory studies and the splendid "funicular" models which served Gaudí in the experimental calculation of the forces and weights and to determine the inclination of the columns and the pilasters (for which he hung a series of wires from the roof of his studio in parallel directions to both extremes, and from which he hung small weights in proportion to the foreseen weights for the vaults and then after photographing the model worked on it looking at it from an inverted perspective); then one would have of the clarity of vision with which he focussed on the technical problems and of the transformation it experienced in the course of its elaboration, until it formed a consitutive part of his fantastic invention. We could say of his models, they constituted a precedent of what later have been *mobiles*. That Gaudí had not invented the test for the static curve of the arch and the vault with the overhead power cable, doesn't seem to me to add or to detract anything from either the originality or validity of his method.

Barcelona, Casa Batlló, 1905-1907. A partial detail of the façade.

In a quick analysis of the gaudian works as is this it is impossible to offer a brief commentary on the Casa Batlló, which Gaudí built in the Paseo de Gracia, almost on the corner of the Calle Aragón, in Barcelona (1905-1907). Such is the complexity of the themes which this building presents with its difficultly describable concatenation in respect of the interior and exterior, that it is one of the most perfect examples of plastic "organism". In order to realize this, it is sufficient to think of the modelled facade full of sensibility, whose delicate effect of chromatic and clear

Casa Batlló

A roof detail of Casa Batlló, Barcelona.

A room from the Casa Batlló, Barcelona.

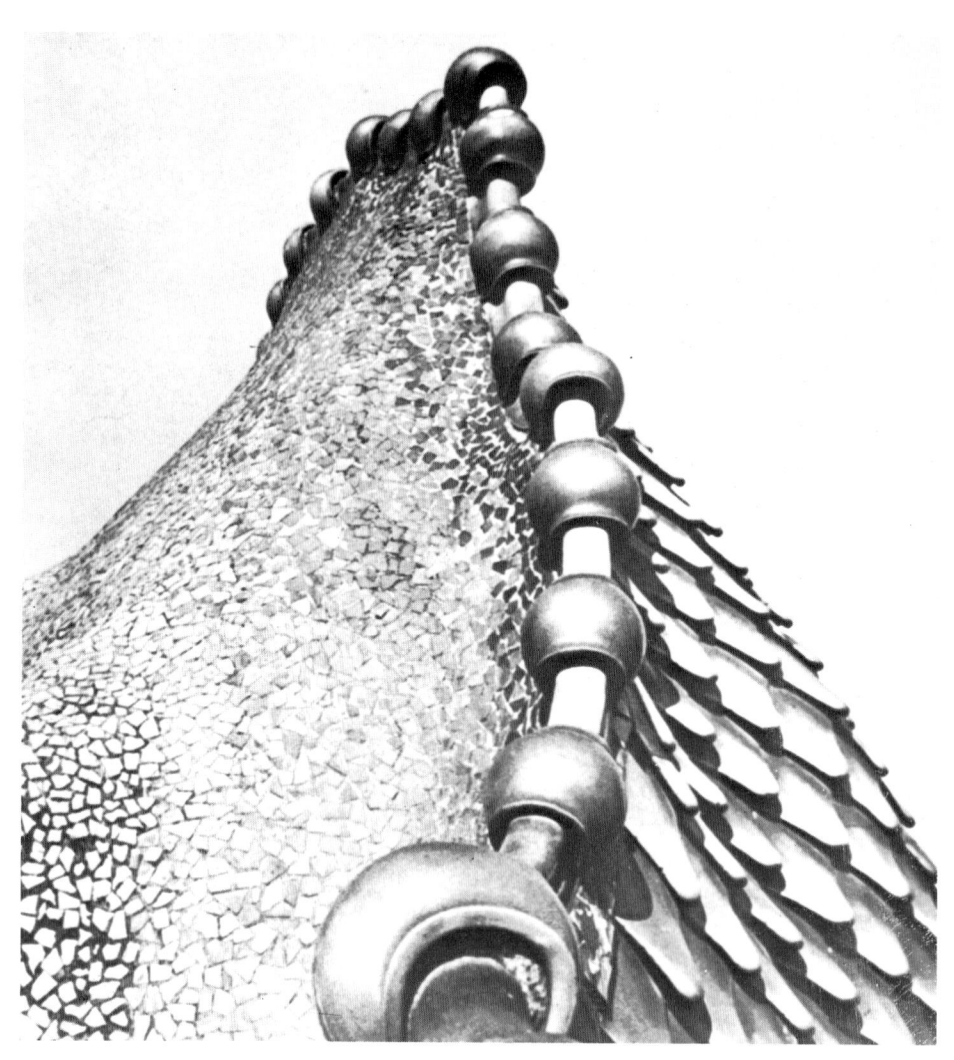

and dark contrast which is seen to become lighter as it moves toward the bottom of the house. This is accentuated, on the other hand, as it ascends toward the green imperious and bright scaley crest which forms part of the roof in relief and projects forward in the central balconies. This forms a viewpoint on the first floor in a structural area which continues in the two lateral galleries of the second floor, with delicate modelled ornaments which form floral motifs in the centre of the thin columns which support Casa Batlló. It was named the "Casa de las Tibias Descarnadas" (The house of the emaciated tibia), due to a journalistic expression. But in this building all organistic reference is overcome by the refinement of a game (almost seventeen century) which contributes in the accentuation of the silent iron balconies in the form of masks. These are capricious forms which play with the mixed background and are elements which evoke a Venetian carnaval with gondolas and crinoline.

In reality, this lightness and this type of *insouciance* happiness are apparent and not real, given that rational control is exercised so continuously in the structure of the house that it gains the function of a complex organism in which all the exterior elements are found connected in tight continuity with the flexible, slow and uninterrupted internal development. From the stately stairs all of which expressed "by hand" (in that which it is possible to show for the first time precise formal analogies with the linguistic modalities of a certain Surrealist magic in the style of Arp or Miró), even the splendid and luminous interior rooms control a unique and continuous modelling "gesture" which never leaves us. We observe this in the morbid development of the light-dark walls, up to the wide staircases of the roof (which are full of sensibility), and even the chamferred angles on whose surfaces light is obscured.

Roberto Pane reproduces a phrase which was attributed to Gaudí, and which here appears to have a symbolic use: "The corners will disapear and matter will manifest itself abundantly in its astral emphaticness; the sun will enter here from all sides and it will produce an image as though in paradise, we will have to make the most of the contrasts, and so my palace will be more luminous than light itself (29)."

(29) R. Pane, ibid.

Another thing that is worth noting, in respect of the house's beautiful facade, is the way in which it avoids looking out of place with "la Casa Amatller" by Puig i Cadafalch, the beautiful neogothic small palace which is next door. We couldn't say the same of the of the house on the other side in which the relationship of the good neighbourhood with Gaudí's work has not been respected, to such an extent that a nine floor building was constructed on the site without showing the due respect to Gaudí's monument.

Another important characteristic is the facade's cornice, and the way in which the ceramic pinacle arises from it, whic supports the habitual four armed cross and the sharpened end section with its shiny crest which forms the end of the roof (perhaps an allusion to Montserrat), and adorned with a series of large green ceramic pearls. The same is true of the cornice formed by two cavities covered with floor tiles through which natural light penetrates into the interior of the house. These are found in the upper skylights held up by parabolic supports. The posterior facade reminds us of Casa Calvet, due to its glass elements which are arranged vertically and the chimneys covered with ceramic mosaic which are visible on that side (which is not the case of the anterior façade), and which in a compact group preannounce the disturbing presence of fantastic and watchful forms which people the end forms of the roof of Casa Milà.

Casa Milà (1905-1910) gained a popular nickname during the time of its construction: La Pedrera (La Cantera)(Quarry) which is still the name by which it is known in Barcelona.

La Pedrera

In this house Gaudí made the maximum use of his concept of architectural work as a compact and uninterupted plastic organism. This was a concept already used in Palacio Güell which had led him to leave out the direct elements of the columns and the arches, with the result that the capital and the vault were born directly from the column. In Parque Güell he had conceived the columns to be twisted which when magnified created a vault.

Seen from this angle, Casa Milà is an immense block of fusion, which conserves its imperfections and the dents and swellings. This architectural creation offers a compact block character. It is like a work hand modelled in plaster which is later melted in lava. In the eyes of present day viewers it appears similar to forms which are characteristic of this century, for example the large lying statues of Henry Moore. But the way in which Gaudí treats this compact form immediately places all his searches in the height of expressionism ten or fifteen years before the "explosion" of the architecture of the German expressionism with the Einstein tower, by Mendelsohn in Potsdam which dates to 1920, or the works of Finsterlin in Poelzig or Bruno Taut which date to 1919 and 1920 respectively.

We should not forget however that Gaudí conceived La Pedrera as a public monument in praise of the "Virgin of the Rosary" (La Virgen del Rosario) and whose image had thus to dominate the architectural mass in order to transform it into a natural base and into a rocky, craggy mass on which the figure would rise toward the sky.

For this reason Gaudí never considered this to be a finished work. In fact he abandoned it (leaving its direction in the hands of Jujol and Clapés), when his client; who was worried because of public disorder which had broken out in Barcelona in July 1909, at the time of the so called "tragic week", asked him to give up the idea of placing an enormous image above the house in the project. He was worried that the building on being confused with a convent would provoke the iconoclastic wrath of the revolutionaries.

For all of these problems, this immense construction, developed according to an undulating conception of form in its horizontal areas remains a unique example. It is admirable for its representative force and for the visionary capacity which its author demonstrated in it, who anticipated in certain formal inventions that which more recent techniques have made possible.

Here Gaudí developed his plan using traditional means as always in his customry attempt to to want to show the possibility of applying new methods to instruments which were already in current use.This brought out of him, as usual, the necessary precision to overcome the resistance of the material and the difficulty of continually inventing new methods for the use of the materials.

Barcelona, The façade of Casa Batlló (next page).

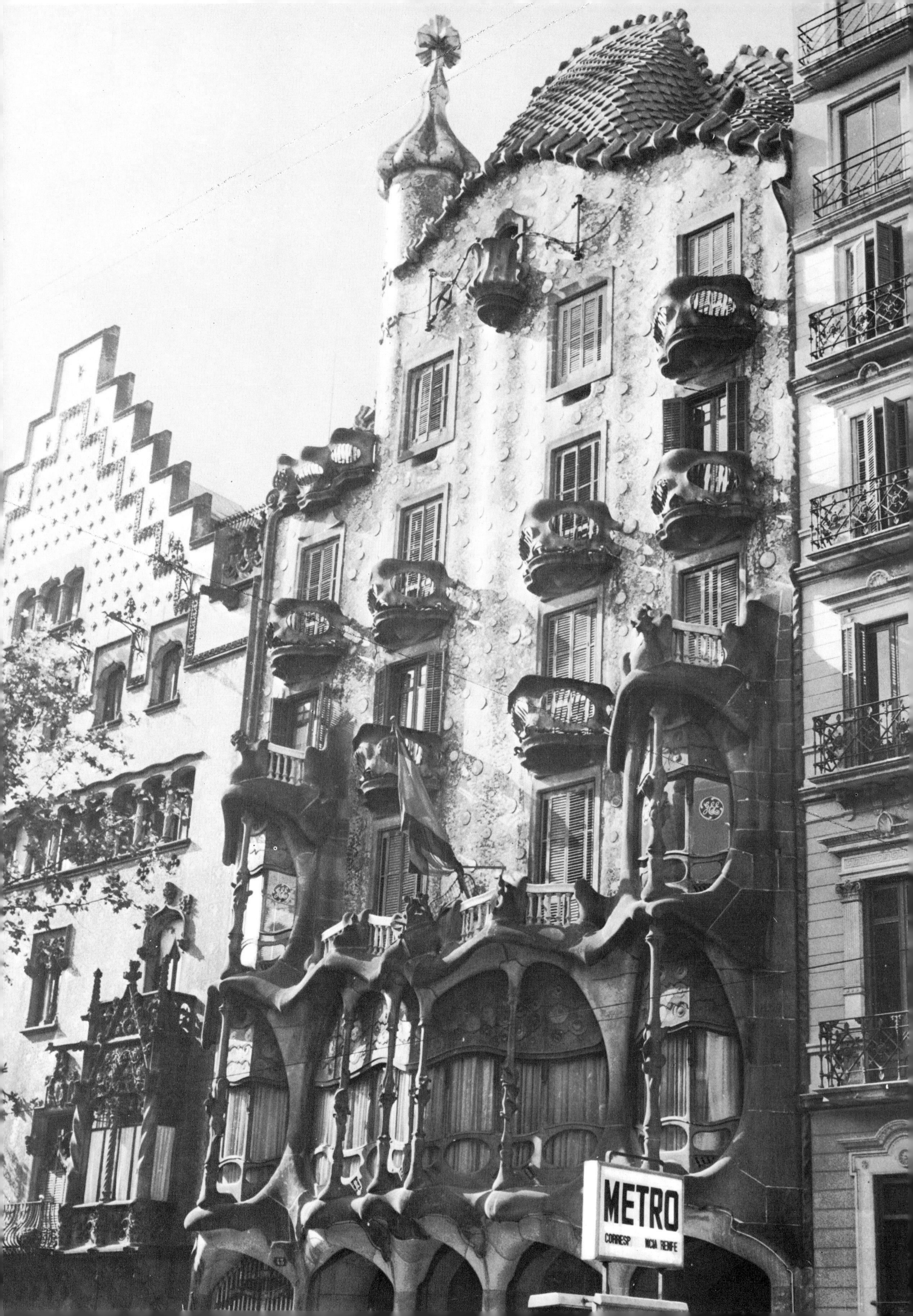
METRO
CORRESP NCIA RENFE

The plan of Casa Milà, in Barcelona.

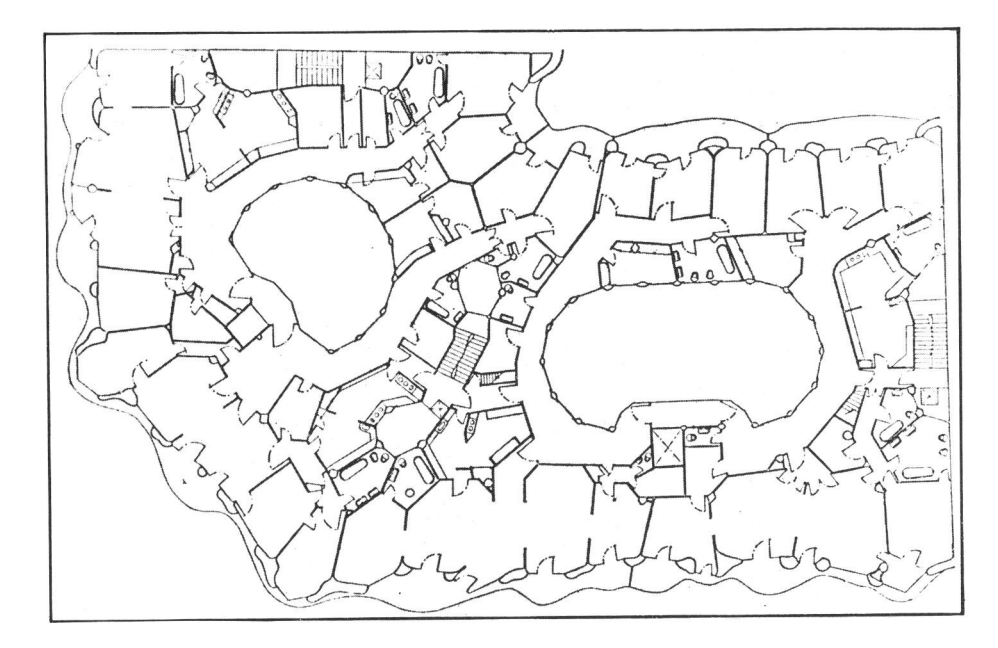

Barcelona, Casa Milà, 1905-1910.

Think only of the multiplicity of resources he must have used in order to carry out a plastic development so free and complex, using great stone blocks, and not cement, and the acuteness with which he saw, as in Parque Güell, the need to use a sort of "tailored brick" with the aim of transforming a structure which is so complex and dynamic as is Casa Milà into a static entity. This is something worthy of remembering as a demonstration of the way Gaudí always managed to translate the results of geometric laws into free expression. All of this is organized in the movement of the parabolic and hyperbolic arch which he interprets with his own free fantasy. This is a most interesting solution in the use of the parabolic and hyperbolic arch with horizontal lines and a crested pfrofile appeared in Casa Milà (a meeting of inverse parabolic vaults developed in a vertical direction). In these the totality of the plan is analytically refringed thus provoking the almost physical diffraction on the undulated horizontal line, which is the same as tailoring the floor high and synthezising it in the meeting point of the levels. It is like the reverse experiment which Borromini carried out in the facade in San Carlino. There Borromini discovered the continuous line as the last limit of Baroque. Gaudí rediscovered it through the complete destruction of the compact baroque structure with the aim of giving the architecural mass a formal component which would be readible (as was rediscovered in the tense curve in the crest oin the balcony of the riased area in Parque Güell).

A drawing by Le Corbusier (1928) in which the roof of the School of the Temple of the Sagrada Familia is studied.

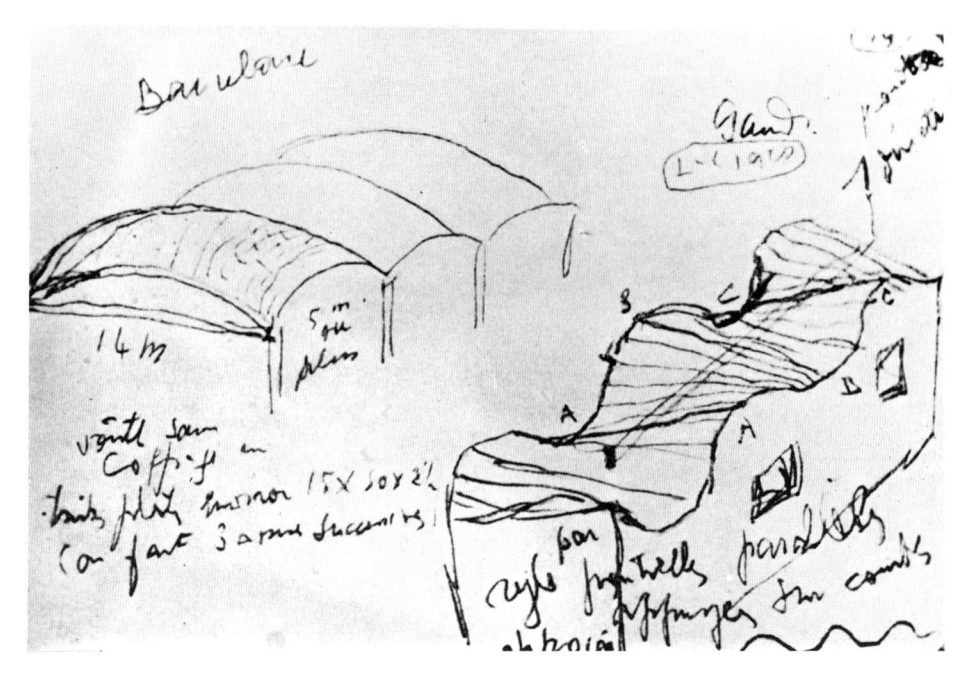

Barcelona, the School of the Temple of the Sagrada Familia, 1909.

Held above enormous pilasters which liberate the lower floor (underneath which a garage has been made), Casa Milà develops above the large continuous projecting terraces. Interrupted by interwoven phytomorphic wrought iron which forms the rails which continue on a horizontal level of the terraces. This permits light to filter into the lower flats.

The terrace is found lower than the level of the rooms, and this is in order to allow an open view onto the street. This is an intuitive and interesting vision of the communicative and extrovert spirit of the citizens environment. Such intuition may seem strange in a person such as Gaudí who was introverted and possessed a rather non communicative temperament.

The Casa Milà, which is an interesting monument due to the free development of internal space which it has, shows its greatest moment of originality in the rich and unsuspected complexity of the roof cover. It is really populated with ghosts: for example, the chimney pots in luxurious colours, or the bodies of the attics and the small rooves of the access stairways. These are independent formal elements which make up a disturbing landscape, and which at times, is dramatically intense in its expressiveness. There is where Gaudí demonstrated his power as an evoker of monsters to such an extent that it is impossible to escape miraculously from such evident presentments. These "facts" which are not only artistic, would be exploited a few years later. This can be seen in the anxious motifs in German architectural expressionism as the presentment of future wars, through the obsessive presence of monstuous warriors (with the incorrect appearance of Sarracens or Teutonic knights or of robots which chase as though they are terrible deadly weapons). This is seen in certain forms of Mendelssohn's style. Let us not forget the spikey and twisted forms which arise from tragic screaming masks, a style evoked in Munch's famous painting. To this we must add the effect caused by the iron bars and railings which further complicate this nightmare vision. All of this happens without Gaudí having proposed, not even once, to mimic the naturalistic representation with human figures, given that these immense totem forms are based exclusively on the development of geometric forms. That is to say, in the continual variation of parboloids, helicoids, hyperboloids which are transformed into fundamental and structural cores and in generators of living forms.

The School of the Sagrada Familia

Before examining the Sagrada Familia (Holy Family), the colossal work in which Gaudí saw the culmination of his mission as a builder, as a believer, and as an inventor of forms, a form in which Alighieri thought that he was capable of emulating God in creating microcosms in the likeness of macrocosms, I would first like to refer to one of his last works and one of the most perfect. The building in question is the small school of the Sagrada Familia, built in 1909.

Drawings of the plan for the Temple of the Sagrada Familia, Barcelona, 1891-1926.

This small and humble building totally unfolds in the use of the hyperbole in the *mouvementeé* wall in which small windows open and which follow the alternate inclinations of the roof of the building and the undulated vaults beginning with the dynamic development of the hyperbole above the sliding of parallel straight sections so that they each one moves according to a vertical axis although the cntre stays firm, so that it determines intersecting levels within itself. It does this in such a way that the convexity of one side corresponds to the concavity of the other. (Think for a moment in the results to which later dynamic research conducted about linear elements, in a Gabo, or a Pevsner, or a Moholy Nagy.) The result of this original concept is a small unitary organism which is dynamic, complex and at the same time full of vivacity and sensibility. This last detail is due to the fact that Gaudí conceived geometry not as an abstract exercise but as a study in which he newly discovered the laws of the natural and organic structures.

The roof of the school, which has light sheet bricks, seems to owe its line to a natural "gesture" which is only directed and guided by one law, the most exact law of nature. It is easy to understand that an organism of such character has caught the attention of Le Corbusier who keeps a rough draft in a small studio of this extraordinary solution which is owed to Gaudí.

Barcelona, Expiatory Temple of the Sagrada Familia. The interior of the crypt.

The Expiatory Temple of the Sagrada Familia

To talk about the Sagrada Familia implies dealing with a series of problems which almost have no possible resolution. Above all the difficult pursuit of this gigantic work in which Gaudí left his mark so deeply that after him the intervention of anyone else seems to have been impossible. It isn't any less difficult to pursue the work following Gaudí's ideas, in a company and situation in which he was used to make his effort day after day, with the enrichment of always renovated inventions. Today the continuation of the Sagrada Familia can easily seem to us to be the progressive mummification of an idea that was once original and full of fantasy.

We would try to set up the question in a new critical light based on the greater or lesser reasonableness in an operation of this magnitude but it seems to me that the problem also subsists on the religious level. The gothic spirit manifests itself in a collective way, so much so that Gaudí's energy was capable of assuming the force of that spirit on a personal level. It is moving to see the people's reaction after Gaudí's death, especially their wish to continue his work and with such a collective spirit. We cannot hide from the fact that the unanimity of forces which this requires can hardly be autocratic, or lasting, having already given its first great effort. However, here is no shortage of a large number of prepared studies which Gaudí completed, and which have been conserved with the sketches. Many of these were destroyed in 1936 and have been reconstructed. All of this is an indication of an incessant inventive effort in pursuit of an

A detail from the interior of the reconstructed model of the Expiatory Temple of the Sagrada Familia.

expressiveness which was increasingly evident in that which refers to his interpretation of the Gothic spirit.

Gaudí dedicated many years of work to the Sagrada Familia. Beginning around 1914, and continuing until the end of his life, his concern was no other than that of the construction of this temple (it is possible that this was a personal impulse and maybe motivated by the events in Europe and the world). His concern for this project was such that at one point he even lived inside the work during its construction with the aim of not ever separating himself from the object which had become his dominant thought. Perhaps he thought that this was his only path of salvation and one which would save him from his own death... It is in this way that we can explain the complex religious symbolism to which all of this project, even in its smallest details, seems to be subordinated. The architect Francisco de Paula del Villar had started the crypt of that temple in 1882 contracted by José María Bocabella, a bookseller from Barcelona who bought the land and sponsored the construction of a church to be dedicated to San José (his patron saint), and to the Sagrada Familia with the aim that it would be an emblem of the growth which the city had experienced.

Del Villar began the temple. Shortly after building the crypt in neogothic style, he had an argument with Bernardo Martorell who was Bocabella's advisory architect. The result of this was that Del Villar left the company. As Martorell did not want to assume the charge of the project he put forward the name of an architect who at that time was thirty years old: Gaudí, who took on the responsibility of continuing the church works on November 3. 1883.

Gaudí used all the structural solutions already studied and previously tried out. He carried out tests in function with the completely transfigured use which he had in mind and would make use of in this masterwork. Such new solutions had been elaborated with the intention of "correcting" the "errors" of the gothic style. It is for this reason that the famous internal rampant arches appear. The "crosses" or "crutches" as he called them which would transfer the balancing forces of the construction to the inside of the church. For the same reason we see the appearance of the columns which follow the inclination of the dynamic resultant forces and which have become trees in the interior of the church, with their ramifications and flowerings, exploding with decorative structural order. Even in the plans these seem to possess a type of "macroscopization".

The Sagrada Familia was thus conceived as a great mystic poem. A poem full of allusions and containing a coherent and detailed symbolism, which was closely tied to liturgy. At the end of his life Gaudí not only saw the crypt but had also built the Portal de la Natividad (Nativity Doorway) as well as the four incredibly high bell towers in the facade, which rise in the middle of Barcelona as brilliant polychromatic symbols beneath the sun. Through its irrealism and fantasy it opposes the delirium of the natural forms which nervously move and mix in the unexpected flowerings of the mentioned doorway. "This contrast is the object of great appreciation by those who prefer extravagant elements and who are here faced with large figures which possess a disturbing naturalism. It is also a little macabre, or at least cold and lifeless. Gaudí obtained these sculptures of the reality through models which he got *ad vivum*, and with this gained the result that the contrast between reality and dream was more disturbing, and within which we can see that which is definitively dead and that which is alive. This is a tendency based on a misunderstanding because in effect it is in the imaginary where we find life, and on the other hand, what has been traced faithfully and directly from life is where, in our eyes, we see death. (30)".

These words of Perucho seem in the last analysis to be perfectly applicable to the programme of continuation, based on "replicas" of a work which precisely because it had been thought out in this way, doesn't leave any possibility of later vital expansion. It is something which seems implicit in the hallucinatory involvement of that "mental productivity" and to which we have referred and which pushed Gaudí to the most daring structuralistic virtuosity.

Bohigas, in his last work (31) refers to the " obsessive lexical which frequently found an absurd end with Gaudí". He adds: "It is then when he distances himself from the European avant-garde cultural line, together with formal speculation that he forgets basic architectural problems. Around the "twenties", the most opportune idea was to correct and criticize the temple's anachronic and naive symbolism, or to attack the absurdity of pursuing a church with five naves and an impenetrable forest of columns, or to criticize the spatial disposition which is so badly resolved. He wouldn't have stopped offering solutions if it weren't for the fact that he was in full creative flight immersed in the works of La Pedrera and the Colonia Güell."

I do not share the substance of these observations. We should't forget that the Sagrada Familia represents a kind of synthesis for Gaudí of all his work and in this synthesis he aimed at reaching the summit of his architecture in the sense of its expressiveness. To say as Bohigas does that "in those years Gropius and Meyer had built the Fábrica Fagus (1911), J.J.P. Oud the first popular houses in Rotterdam (1920), Le Corbusier the pavillion of *Esprit Nouveau* (1925), and Gropius had inaugurated Dessau's *Bauhaus*" is to make a comparison. This however can deviate our reasoning toward seeing a low intelligence in the most complete of Gaudí's works, for whom architecture was always a means of the expression of emotional fantasy in spite of (or perhaps because) of structuralist virtuosity.

The active and vital lesson in Gaudí resides in this inextinguishable and anxious search for expression. It lies in this wish of his to resolve the representative function of art in the daily experience of architecture, and to have recovered for man the meaning of an artistic practice, which is, *in situ*, the will and the possibility of surpassing oneself on the level of one's own existence.

---

(30) J. Perucho y L. Pomés, ibid.
(31) O. Bohigas, ibid

57

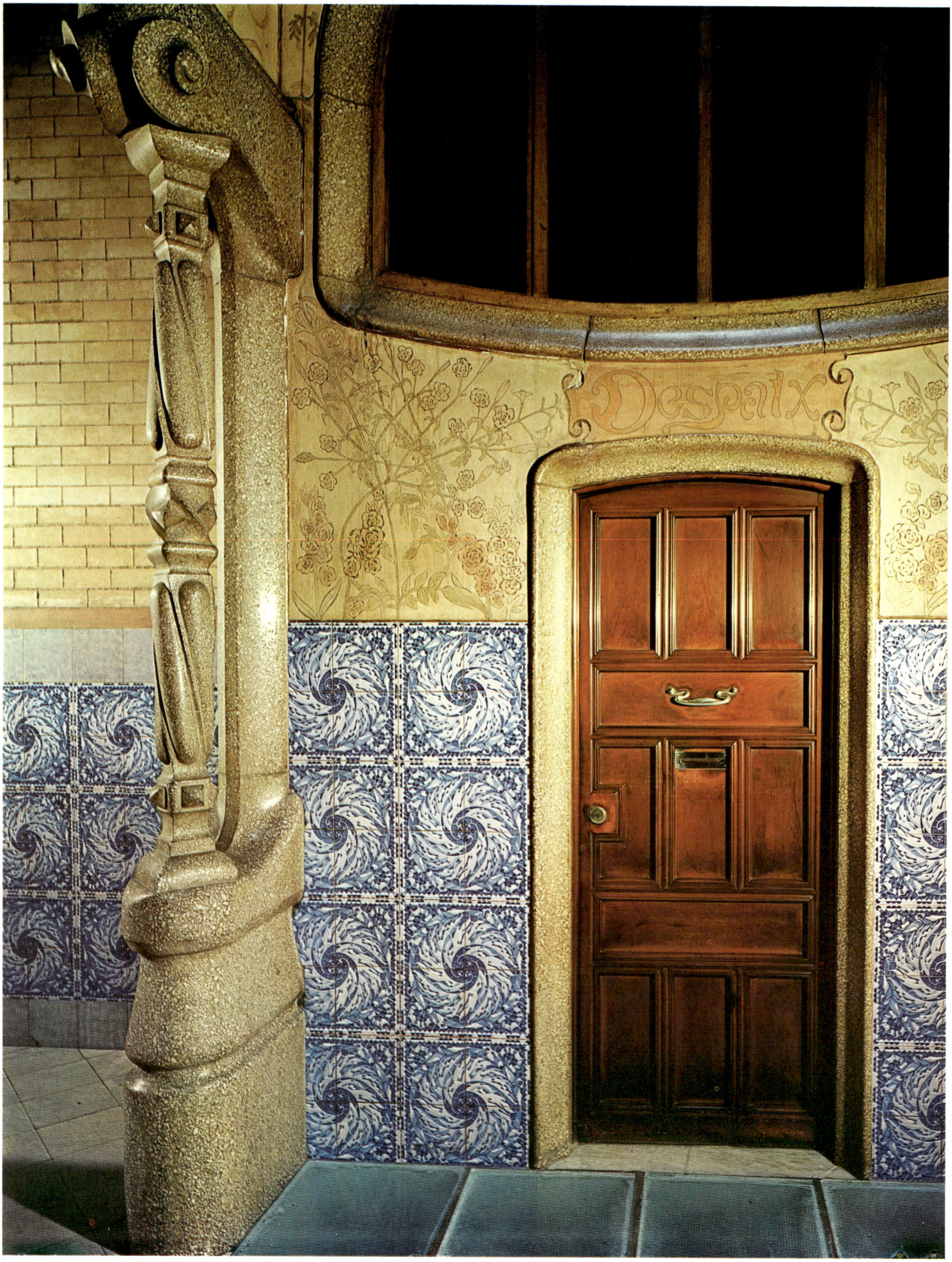
Despalx

59

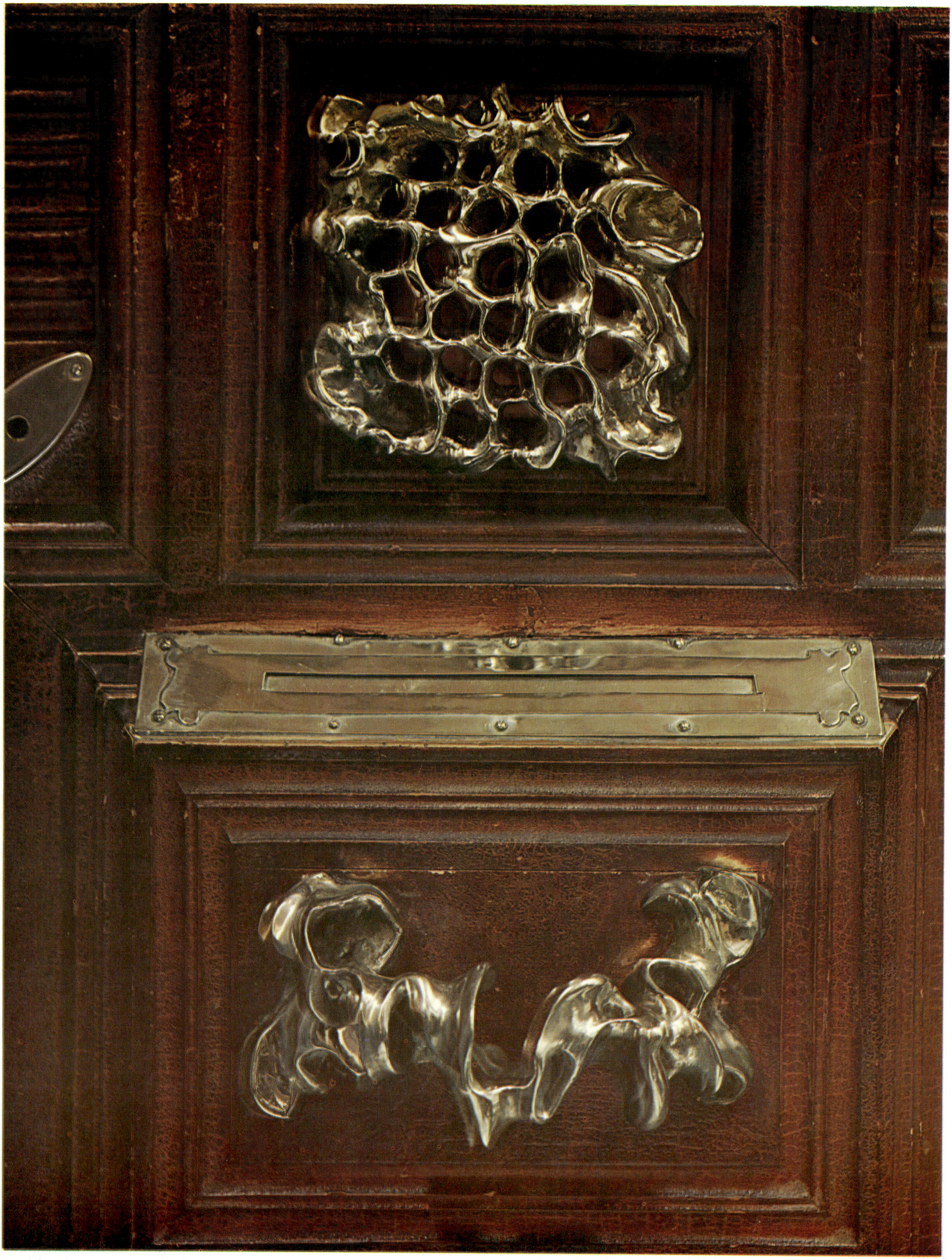

61

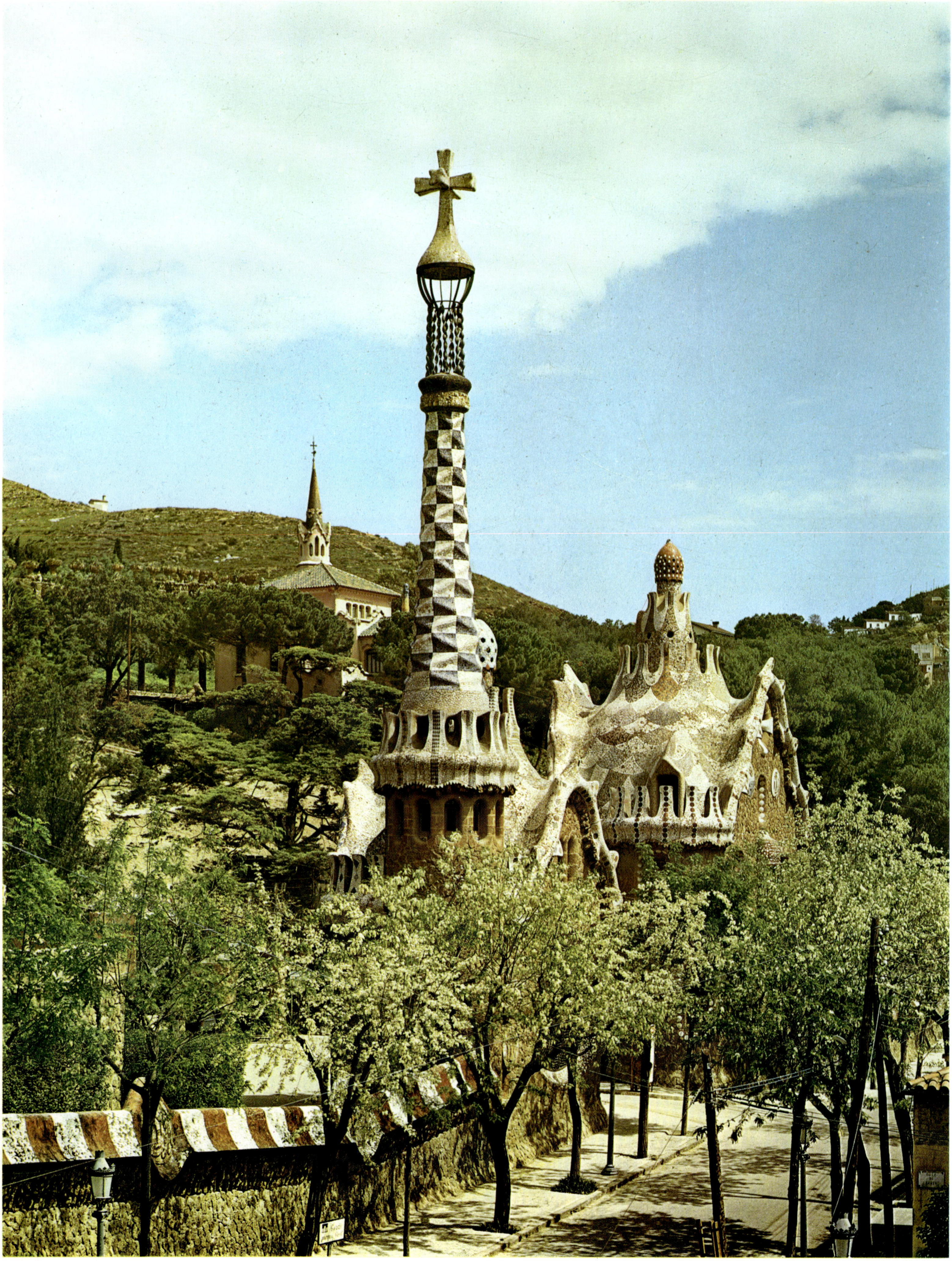

63

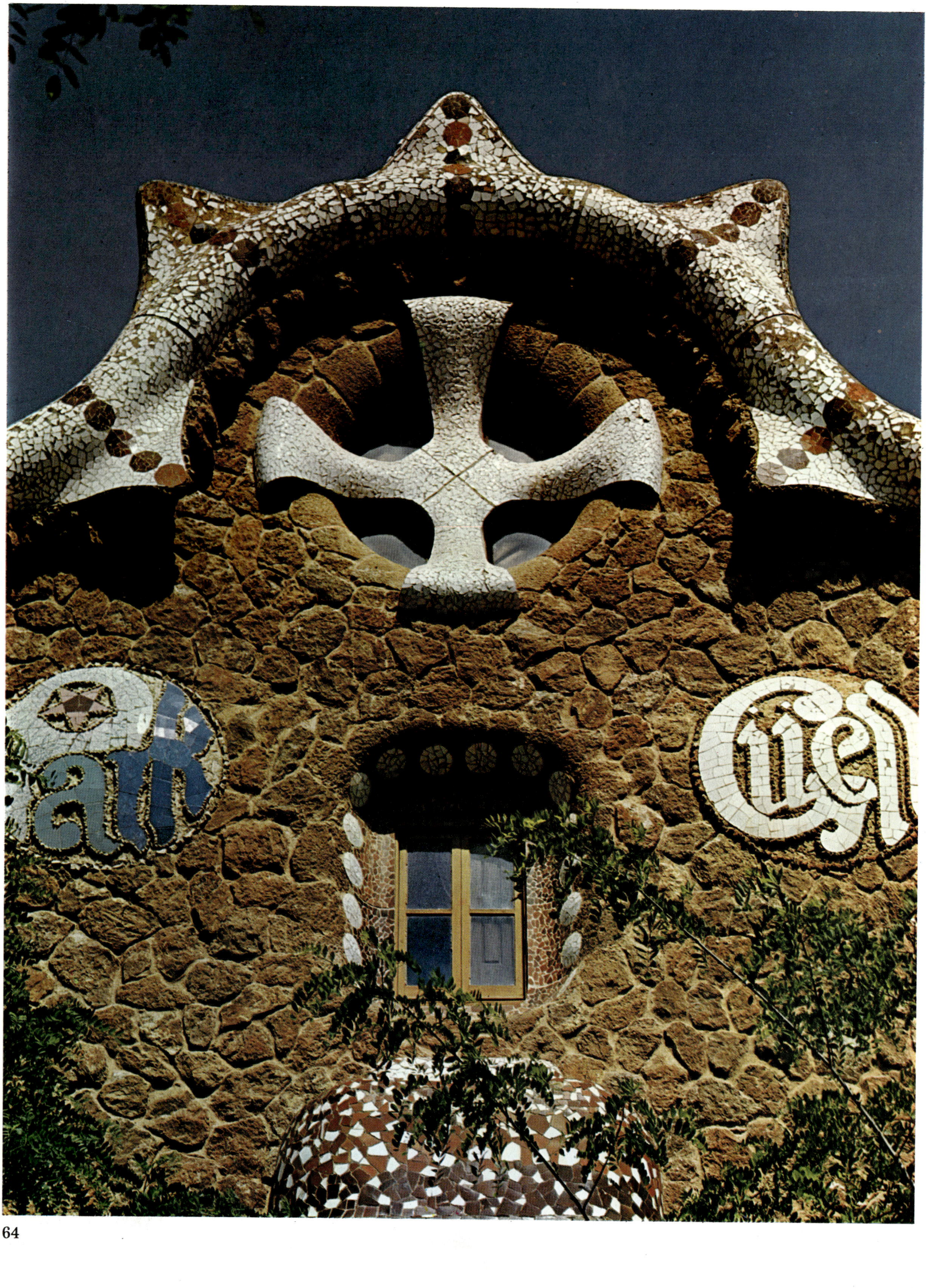

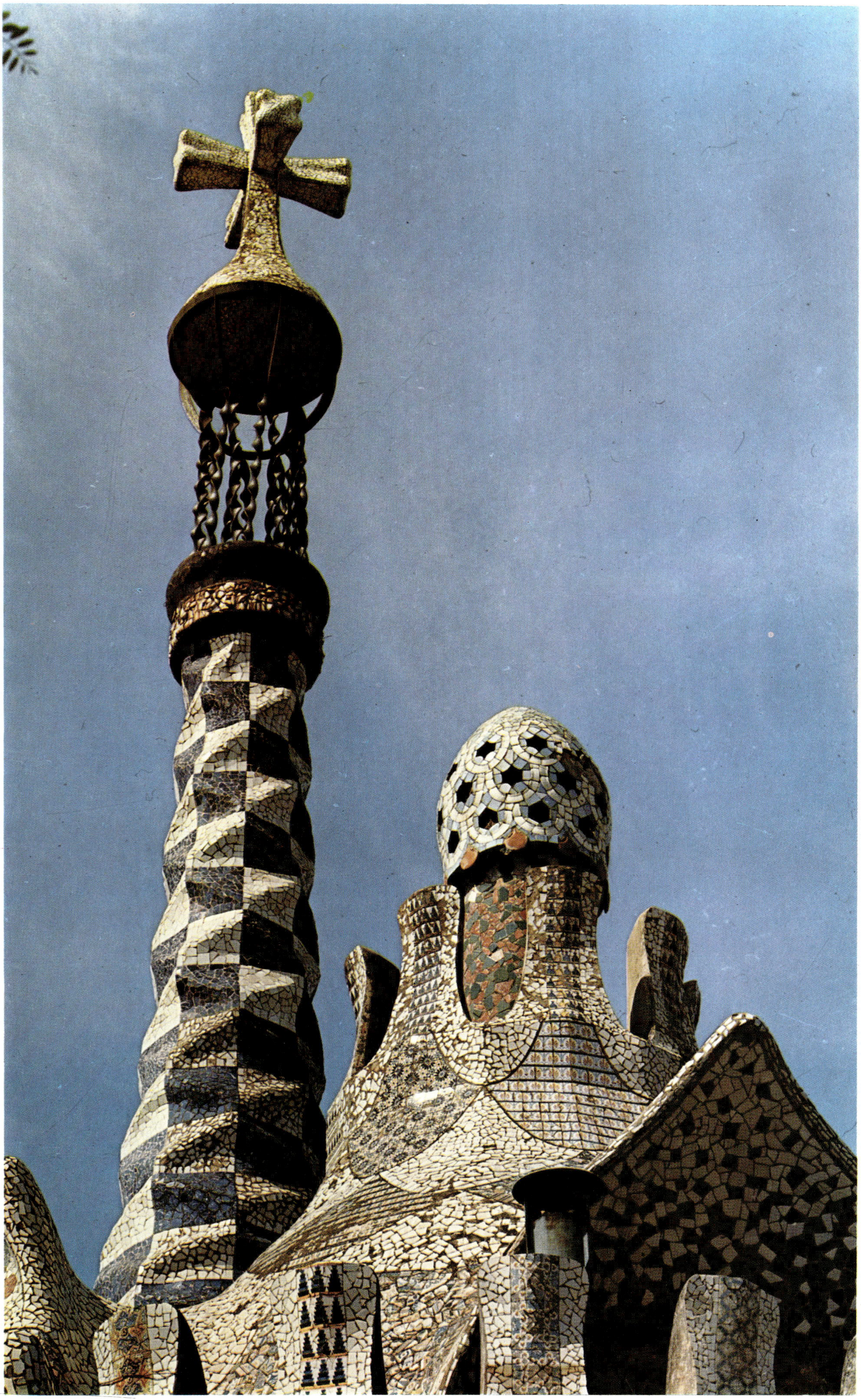

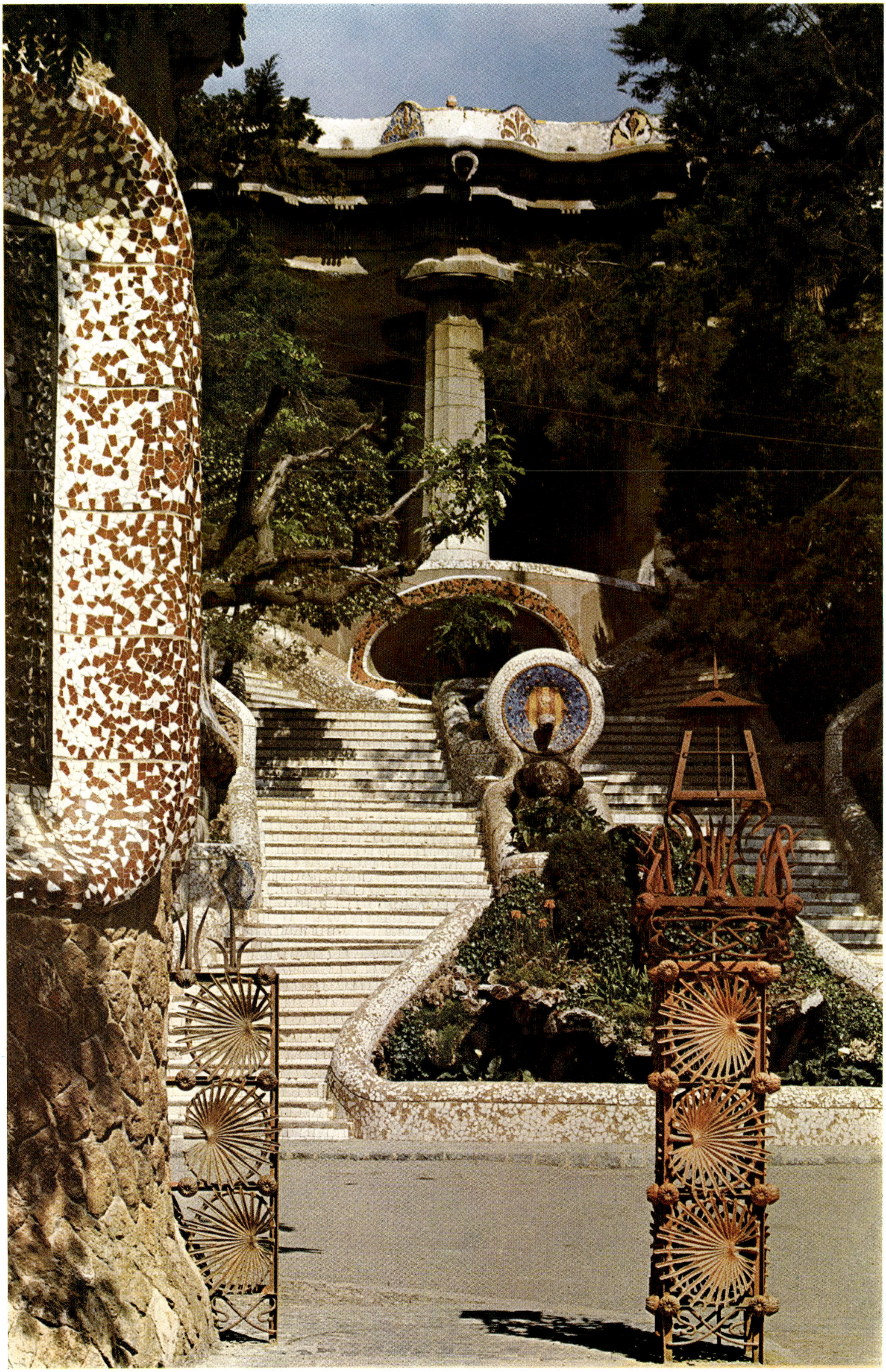

67

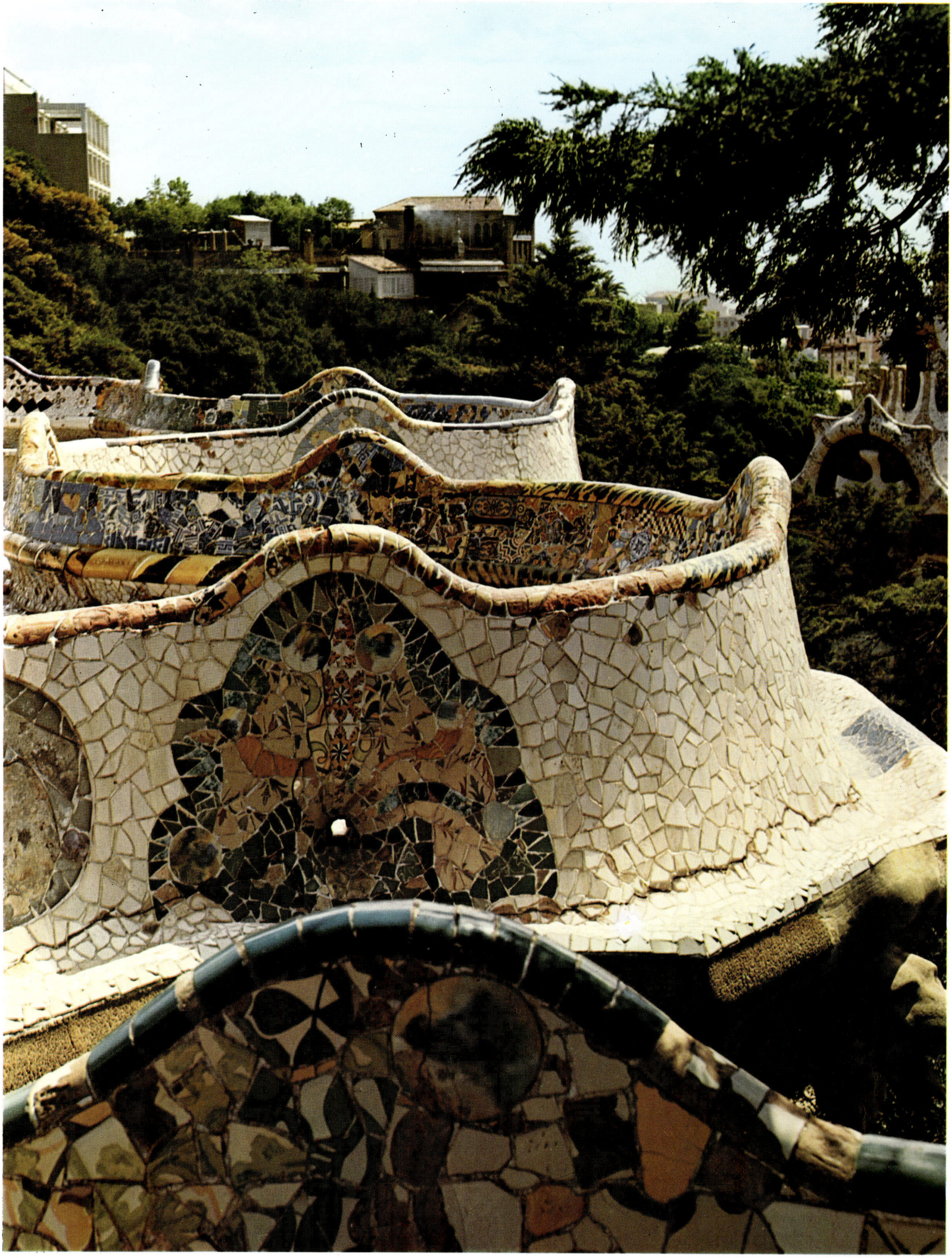

69

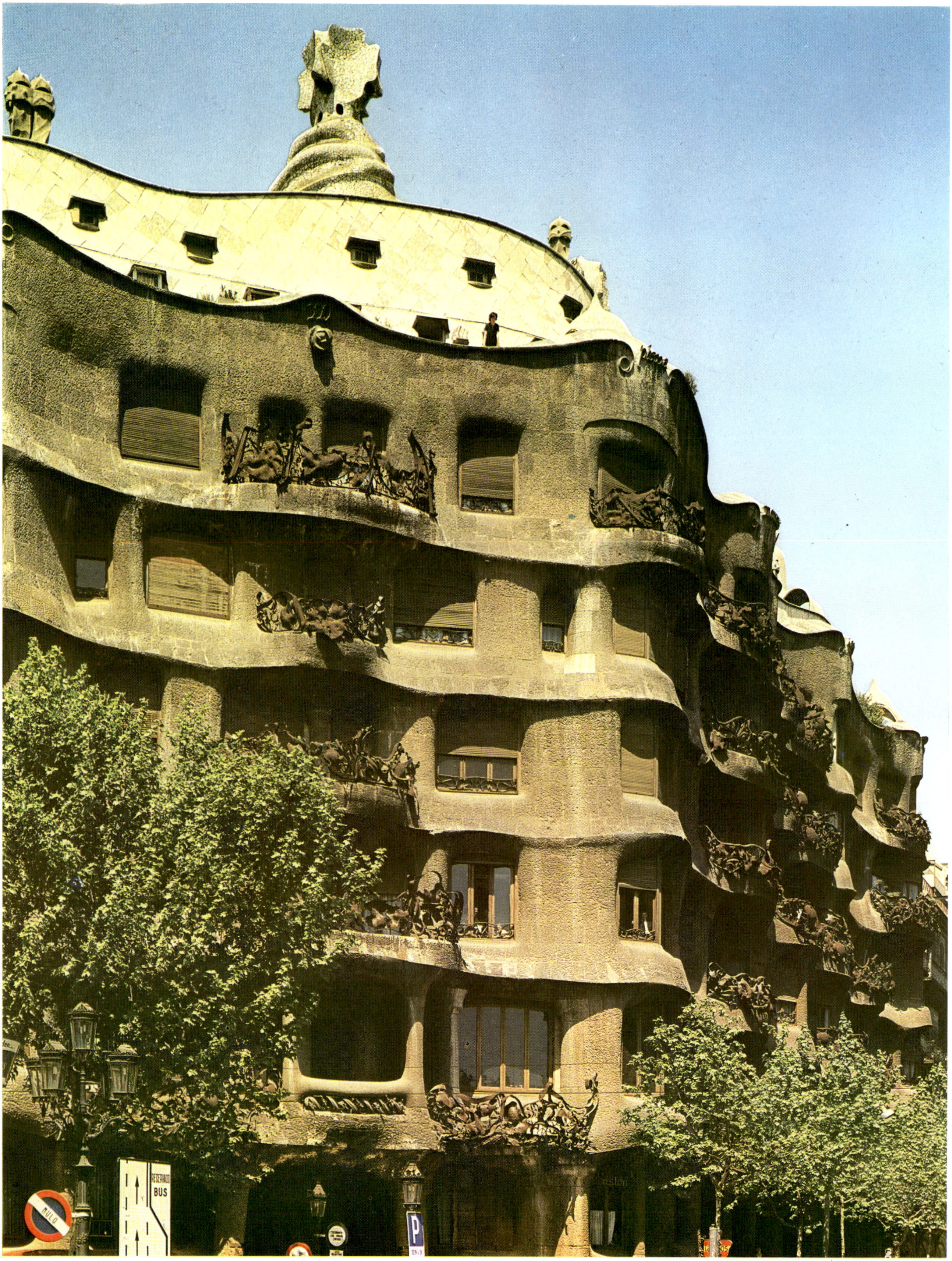
RESERVADO
BUS
P

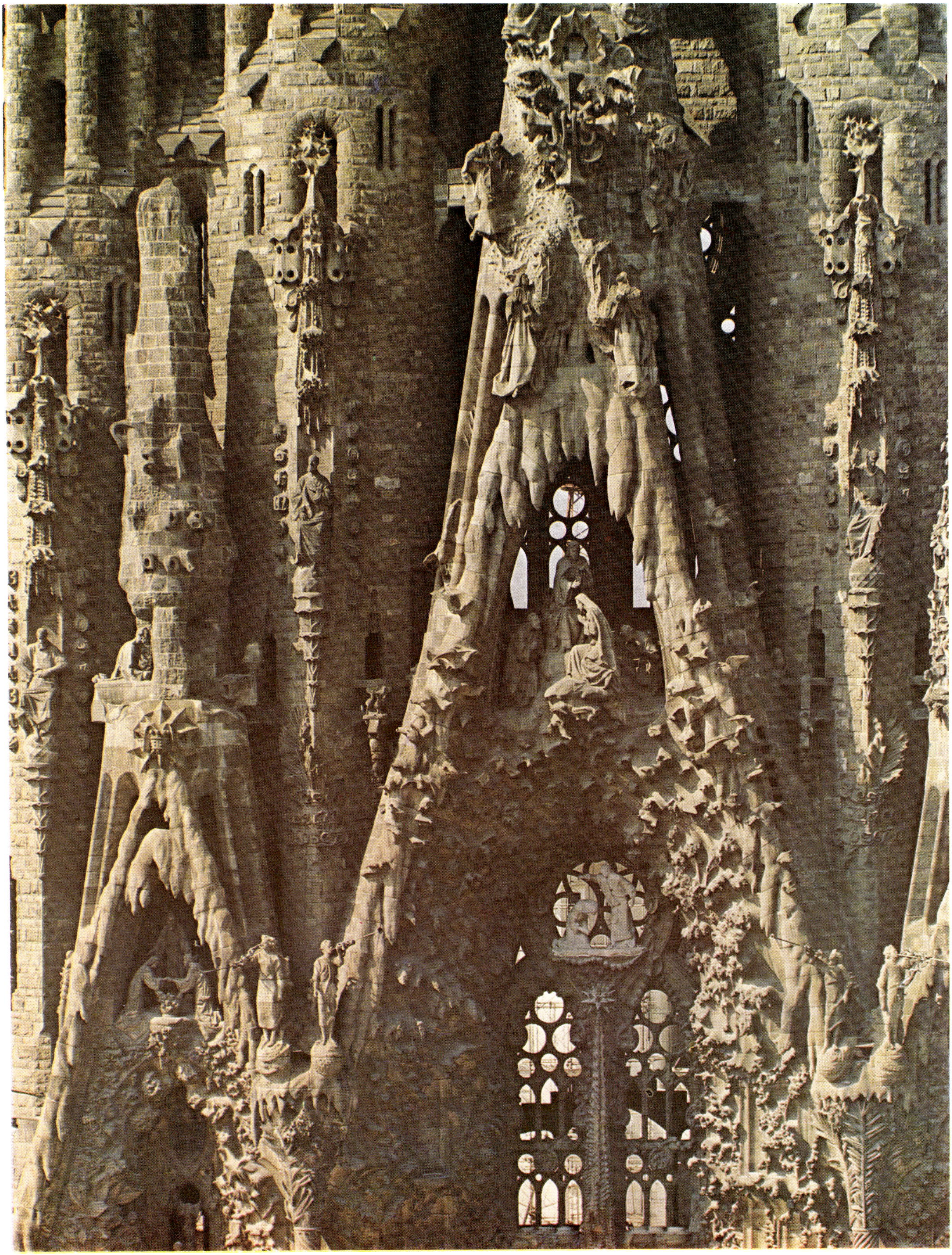

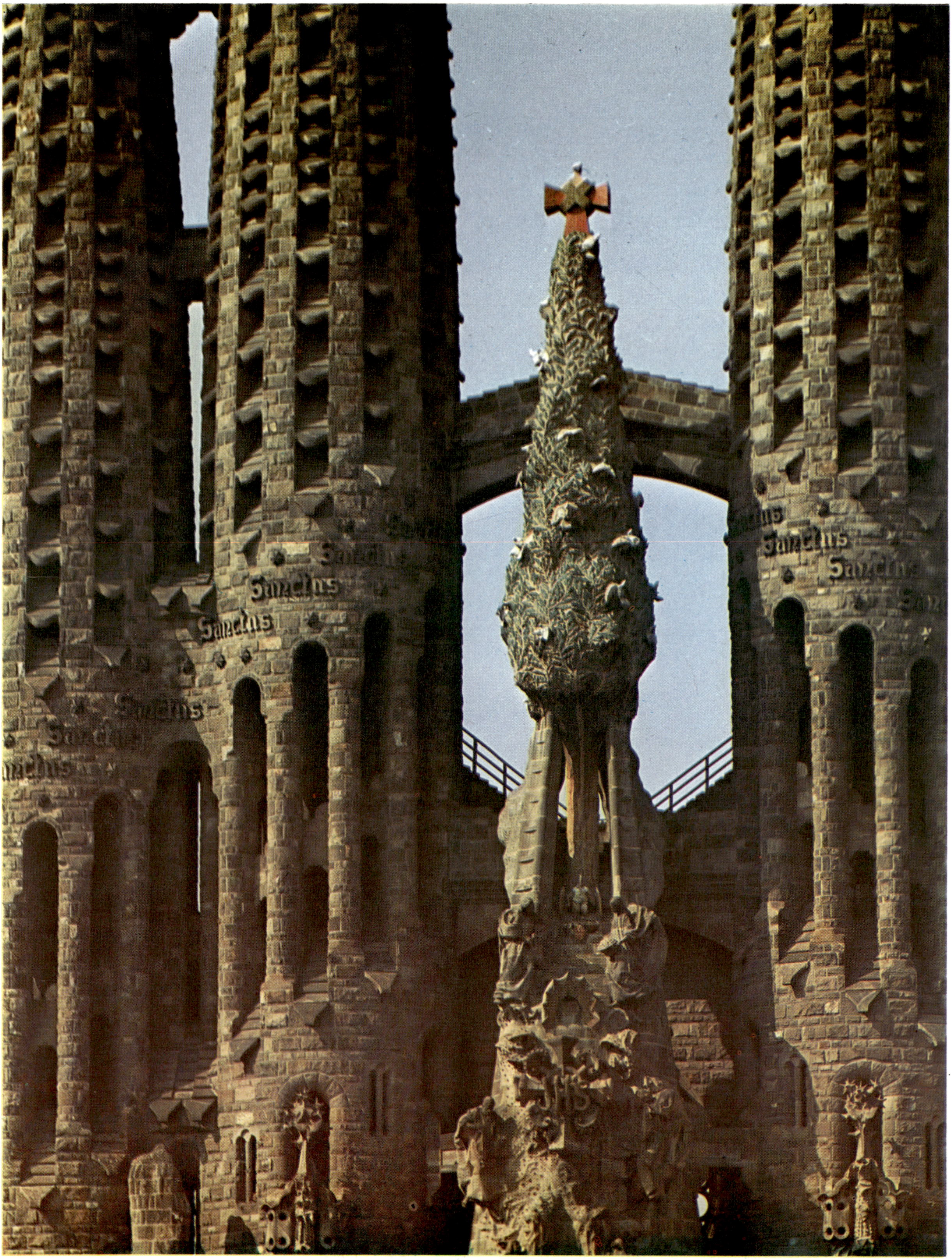
Sanctus
Sanctus
Sanctus
Sanctus
Sanctus
Sanctus

THE ROUTE OF MODERNISM IN BARCELONA

The Monumental is a late modernist work, of lesser importance but of considerable charm. We can appreciate in this building distinct functions to those which we can find in houses or in industrial production. It was conceived as the square of the sands within the Islamic spirit, it was projected with much greater freedom and fantasy. The work is composed of brick alternating with mosaic in geometrical forms which have a distant Arabian inspiration. The circle is surrounded by pillars which mark thin arches. In the finishing there are small pediments with brick and mosaic. There are towers at regular intervals with stepped arches, finished by rooves "a cuatro aguas" or by great eggs of colourful mosaic which is the most modernist element in the construction.

Plaza de Toros Monumental
Address: Gran Via de les Corts Catalanes 749
Architect: Ignasi Mas i Morell
Date of Construction: 1915
Remarks: Headquarters of the Museo Taurino

This bull fighting ring was built before the urbanisation of the Plaza de España, which took place in 1929 due to the Second Universal Exhibition. It is 52 metres in diameter and holds 15.000 spectators. The architecture is of Islamic inspiration and quite orthodox it was conceived in three registers of horse shoe arches progressively smaller. This brick work is adorned here and there with regular motifs and contrasts with the two colour stone of the arches and doors. In the finishing there are small triangular battlements.
The ticket offices are small towers which also have horse shoe arches and flank a monumental staircase. The style of the whole work is austere and fits perfectly with the purpose of the building. It is not strange to see the exotic element nor the oriental propitiated by the turn of the century literature, as well as the romantic image of the bullfighting and Andalusian world.

Plaza de Toros de Las Arenas
Address: Gran Via de les Corts Catalanes 387
Architect: August Font i Carreras
Date of construction: 1899

One of the motors of Modernism in the architecture in Barcelona was the Universal Exhibition of 1888, put forward by the mayor Rius i Taulet. The land occupied by the old military fortress was converted into a park of large dimensions. Many of the buildings in the Exhibition were demolished after this one, but fortunately many reained standing as a testimony to that important event which launched the city of Barcelona on to the European and international scene.
Domènech i Montaner's building was destined to be the park's restaurant, although finally it was not finished until after the exhibition. It is a splendid Neogothic construction in natural brick and crowned with battlements. In it one can surmise the influence of the French architect Viollet-Le-Duc. The building's popular nickname "The castle of three dragons" comes from a comedy by Serafi Pitarra.
The new possibilities of industrial materials (iron and brick) were used with

Café Restaurant del Parque "Castell dels Tres Dragons"
Address: Paseo Pujades/Parque de la Ciutadella
Architect: Lluís Domènech i Montaner
Date of construction: 1887
Remarks: It is currently the headquarters of the Zoological museum

great talent by Domènech i Montaner in the construction of the restaurant, as can be seen in the size of the rooms and the enormous openings which allow great lighting effects. The cleanliness and sobriety of the interior show an exquisite elegance.

It is interesting to note that this building is the forerunner of the famous Stock Exchange in Amsterdam by the architect Hendrick Petrus Berlague (1897-1903) in respect of the utilitarian forms, the use of natural brick and the open use of iron structures.

Later this building would house the workshop for industrial artists, a first rate centre dedicated to research and circulating of the old crafts of ceramics and wrought iron work, with the consequent recovery of the Decorative Arts in Catalonia.

Hidroeléctrica de Catalunya
Address: Avenida Vilanova 12
Architect: Pere Falqués
Date of construction: 1897

Hidroeléctrica de Cataluña: Projecting window next to the main door.

After the Universal Exhibition of 1888, the Catalan electric company at that time called "Central Catalana d'Electricitat" entrusted Pere Falqués with the construction of a new central headquarters. The project was begun in 1896 and was finished the following year. It is made up of two great parallel blocks which are connected and which house the machines and the steam generators. We find the control room in the basement a floor was built above the machine room in order to house the storage batteries.

In a display of architectural engineering worthy of the epoch, Pere Falqués made the most of the metal structure in order to absorb the steam engine's vibrations and to use brick in such a way that it could hold the weight of the machinery without any danger. The Hidroeléctrica is one of the first examples of industrial architecture which doesn't hide but rather highlights the function of its machines, not only using them practically but also finding in them a great expressive beauty. The exterior facades show us a great machine-building made of brick and iron with many ornamental variations.

In the original project a facade adorned with bronze in relief had been foreseen. Both buildings had to be finished by a pyramid which was never built. However, our present observation shows us that this ornamentation was not necessary and that the building is splendid just as it is. The brick is used in different forms and relieves forming an interesting game of lights and shadows which are strengthened by the iron.

There were some reforms in 1910 directed by Telm Fernández, and in 1980 there was a correct restoration by the architects Sanz, Torra y Fochs in order to house the central offices of the Catalan Hidroelectric Company. The machines are left open to view and the original work is respected, procuring to make as few compartments of the space as possible and not to alter the structure of the stream room.

Mercado del Born
Address: Plaza Comercial 12
Architect: Josep Fonseré i Mestres, Josep Maria Cornet i Mas
Date of Construction: 1876

Towards the middle of the XIX century, Barcelona needed new installations for its markets, which until then had been organised in the open air. As the population grew and with it the quantity of jobs in the market, a number of important health problems began to present themselves. On the other hand, the open air markets on being held daily were totally open to the inclemencies of the weather, something which was extremely uncomfortable for the shoppers and sellers.

In 1870, the Sant Josep market was finally covered, (Rambla 91). The initial project of 1836 foresaw only one uncovered ionic column but at the beginning of the works popular protest provoked a change of stance on the part of Barcelona's city council. The glasswork roof of 1914 is one aspect which stands out in this building.

In 1882 the Sant Antoni market in Calle Urgell was finished, the only one which strictly follows urban norm agreed in the Eixample project (Ensanche) and sketched out by Idelfons Cerdà (the Cerdà plan).

The works in the Born market were begun in 1873 and it was opened in 1876. Although we can not talk in all propriety of a modernist building, the born market marks the beginning in Barcelona and Spain of metallic architecture, one of the great elements of progress in contemporary architecture. The introduction of iron as a building element and the use of its potential to create higher and lighter buildings, was a bet which not everyone was prepared to make at the beginning. The meccano constructions which today seem to be archaeological appeared to many people to be anti aesthetic and the iron, open to view, a poor and graceless solution. However the modernist architects knew, later, how to use humble materials such as iron and brick in order to create an ornamental vocabulary which was not only seen in the most expensive houses but also in those of the more humble.

The market roof is subdivided into two large plants of unequal length and which meet in the centre beneath an octagonal cupola. Small secondary plants complete the market. The use of two colour brick which is applied to the walls and the roof is a clear hint to the future.

Palau de la Música Catalana
Address: Calle Sant Pere Més Alt 11
Architect: Lluís Domènech i Montaner
Date of Construction: 1908

In 1904, the Orfeó Català, a choir founded by Lluis Millet and Amadeu Vives, had grown sufficiently as to aspire as to having a decent base. The choral movement was in its peak in Catalonia, specially in the city of Barcelona and the surrounding towns of (Gràcia, Sants).

The Orfeó entrusted the work to Domènech i Montaner who converted the Palau into possibly the most important work in his life. The plot which was

Palau de la Música: A ticket office.

chosen had an irregular form and is located between two narrow streets in the old part of the city next to Via Laietana. In his place the architect managed to produce two wonderful facades covered with rich sculpted ornamentation which neither lacks ceramic, glass nor wrought iron work. The sculptor Miquel Blay created a splendid allegory of a popular song for the angle which joins the two facades. A line of multicoloured mosaic columns occupies the first floor and in the second we see busts of Bach, Beethoven, Wagner and Palestrina.

The hall, the centre for the choir and the stage are in line.

In the hall we see natural brick alternating with green ceramic work. Consequently the lines of the arcades and the capitals which are adorned with flowers and griffin heads stand out all the more. The carpentry of the doors includes glasswork which combines transparent crystal with coloured lead.

A marvellous concave glass cupola which represents the sun and produces an iridescent light. The decorative motifs in the facades are repeated in the interior of the building: the rooves are covered in green ceramic, flowers in relief, and mosaics using the peacock feathers. The windows and the columns are repeated with infinite variations in the glasswork and the mosaics. The lighting in the hall is completed with large but light metallic crowns which support tulips. These crowns surround the columns making the most of dead space and providing a better view of the stage. The circle and boxes are finished with a railing of glass balustrades which have an aireal almost unreal appearance.

The stage, set up agist the organ, seems a little like a woodland grotto. The mouth is profusely decorated with sculptures which are asymmetrical, as though the scene would open into a natural space. The stage walls are covered with coloured mosaic in which we see the figures of women playing different instruments. From the waist up there are relieves and from the waist down there are mosaic drawings, which is a completely unusual solution.

The Palau de la Músiaca has worked without interruption since its construction and it is along with the Teatro del Liceo (this specialises in opera),the main concert hall in the city. It was restored, remodelled and extended by Oscar Tusquets and Carlos Díaz between 1982 and 1989. Part of the work consisted in shortening the nave of the neighbouring church of Sant Francesc de Paula which was planned in 1940 by P. Cendoya and which was not finished due to a lack of funds. Thus they opened a new space, in fact a small square which offered anew exit from the Palau. The offices and annexes were moved to the new wing in a cylindrical tower. Since then the two upper floors of the tower have included the library of the palau de música. Another important aspect of the remodellation effects the air-conditioning and heating system which had to be installed without altering the structural characteristics of the building, neither in the visual nor acoustic sense. In the exterior, iron and crystal have been used with great skill to integrate the new constructed parts into the ornamental whole of the original work.

Casa Martí
Address: Calle Montsió 3
Architect: Josep Puig i Cadfalch
Date of construction: 1896
Remarks: it is now a bar called "Els Quatre Gats"

Casa Martí was planned in 1895 and finished a year later. As in the case of Palacio Güell, it is a modernist work in the old part of the city, which thus reduces the visual possibilities of the facade and the general concept of the building being obliged to adapt itself to a small plot. Non of these conditions remove any of this building's charm.

It is one of Puig i Cadafalch's first important works and in it we can see many elements which would form part of his later formal vocabulary, which finds its peak in Casa Amatller (1900), De les Punxes (19059 or in the Casaramona factory (1911). The plan which was chosen for Casa Martí was neogothic but open thus permitting the easy integration of modernist neologisms. The building as a whole, within the rich ornamental characteristics typical of Puig i Cadafalch's work is relatively austere.

The ground floor houses the bar "Els quatre Gats" (The Four Cats) which was inaugurated 12 June 1897 was always a centre and meeting point for artists such as Ramón Casas, Santiago Rusiñol and Picasso before he moved on to Paris. The bar is decorated with large gothic style windows, covered in stained glass, arcades and square tiles accentuated by long walnut tables, high swivelling chairs, and medieval style glass plates and lamps. The name the four cats is owed to the painter Pere Romeu who was inspired by the bar "The Black Cat" in Paris. The bar opens to the exterior by large gothic arches with wrought iron ornamentation on the inside. It has lost the original lintel of the door which was designed by Puig i Cadafalch.

Although a late work, the Café de la Ópera is an example of the renovating interest which characterised so many bars and shops in Barcelona in 1900. On opening or renovating, they incorporated the new style interpreting it with fantasy and often with elegance.
The Café de la Ópera has its name due to its position right in front of The Gran Teatro Liceo. It opened in 1929 occupying what had previously been chocolate shops run by "La Mallorquina". The woodwork at the entrance with its floral ornaments and its paintings protected by glass are impressive. The support is pink marble. On the inside there are paintings of children carrying fruit and mirrors etched with acid of feminine figures playing the parts of different characters from divers operas. The furniture has been well conserved, the Thonet chairs, the tables, the lamps, the simple fieze ornaments which finish the walls and adorn the ceiling. Furthermore the Café de la Ópera continues being one of the most attractive places in the Rambla due to its charm and the curious people who visit it night and day.

Café de la Ópera
Address: La Rambla 74
Date of construction: 1929

Another singular example of a humble but charming modernist Café located in the old part of town at the end of the century. The wooden front piece also covers the ground floor and it possesses an attic which is spectacular. The bar which still conserves its atmosphere of that epoch is a very welcoming and tranquil place.

Bar Muy buenas
Address: Carme 63

The Casa Genové is interesting specially because of the excellent use of the narrow plot of land and the fine result of the facade, which is not in proportion to its height and width. It is located in a privileged place, in the Rambla at the height of the Plà de la Boqueria close to the Gran Teatro Liceo, and the Hotel Orient along with other famous buildings of the time. The width of the street allows a fine view of the whole, something which rarely happens with the modernist buildings in the old part of the city. The house was requested by Dr. Genové and entrusted to Sagnier, it was finished in 1911. It houses a chemists and its laboratory as is indicated in the relief of the doctor's and the mosaics. The facade is organised in various registers which correspond to the flats in which are divided apparently single opening which is formed by the windows of the upper flats. The entrance door is a large ogive arch surrounded by blue and ivory mosaic with some gold adornments this mosaic also covers the large panels of the upper floors giving life and colour to the facade. Above the arch we can see the emblem with the emblem and the snake. At the sides there are medallions with the number of the property. The upper window is very large, totally out of proportion with the facade and thus allowing a great amount of light to enter in a narrow property which would otherwise be difficult to illuminate. This solution is what gives the facade the impression of only having one window which rises independently of the floors and which lets us read the building as one object. In the centre there is a mosaic with the crest of Barcelona and in the upper part there is an ogive arch which completes the window it is framed in blue mosaic. Above this there is a floor with three arch windows. The finishing is elegant aileron which gives the whole the appearance of a tower. Within the gothic and moderate style of Sagnier this is a colourist work and an ingenious solution which offers us a different image of this architect.

Casa Genové
Address: La Rambla 77
Architect: Enric Sagnier i Villavecchia
Date of construction. 1911

Casa Genové: A middle window.

The Hotel España is one of the most charming in Barcelona. It is fortunate that it has been kept in such good condition and that its restoration was carried out so delicately, given that this is a genuine jewel of Modernisism and it is situated in a rather unusual place.
The previously named "Fonda España" belonged to Miquel Salvadó i Llorens who entrusted the reform to Domènech i Montaner. The architect did this

Hotel España
Address: Calle Sant Pau/Arc de Sant Agustí
Author of the decoration: Lluís Domènech i Montaner
Date of the decoration: 1903

with the collaboration of the sculptor Eusebi Arnau and the painter Ramon casas, who did a graphite design with a sea theme. A frieze runs all along the walls simulating waves which break against it. It evokes the Japanese engravings of the time due to its delineated form and its lively colours which were so popular at the time.

Snails shells and sea stars appear at the side of small fishes swimming everywhere. It is a paradise for sirens who move freely through the ocean. The supports in one of the rooms are also interesting they are wooden and form oblique little houses with white and blue ceramic crests which represent the crests of various cities in Spain.

The chimney is alabaster and the sculpted annex is also Eusebi Arnau's work, it is quite spectacular though it has suffered some transformations. In 1904 the hotel received the Barcelona council prize. It has recently been restored.

Hotel Peninsular
Address: Calle Sant Pau

A little further on in the same street we find another interesting hotel from this epoch. This is the Peninsular, which was created through a reformation of what was an old nuns convent. It has a patio with various gallery floors and a high skylight which offers a beautiful light dispel above the green and creme of the paintwork. Its elegance and austerity make one think of the inside of the Café Restaurant del Parc and also of some of the central European modernist buildings.

Antigua Casa Figueras/ Pastelería Escribà
Address: La Rambla 83
Decorator: Antoni Ros
Date of the reform: 1902

Shops like factories can often be perfect places for architects' and owners' expression and fantasy. In effect merchants often allow flights of fancy which they would never permit in their own homes. The Casa Figueras is a fine example of this.

Making the most of the corner to highlight its mosaics, Casa Figueras exploits the artistic language to the maximum in a splendid profusion of glasswork, wrought iron and mosaics. A peacocks tail in coloured crystal is mounted above the arches of the shopwindow. The walls are covered with coloured mosaic in which gold stands out, it is used for the letters of the name of the establishment and for some inscriptions referring to what's on sale. In the upper part of the angle there is a relief with a harvestor and the crest of the proprietor. The drawings in the mosaic show flowers and plants in an ornamental style similar to that used in the Palau de la Música Catalana. A large mosaic crest indicates that the house was founded in 1820. The lower part of the outside support is marble and has relieves.

The interior which is perfectly well conserved, houses the Escribà cake shop and a small tranquil café. One can still see part of the furniture. The present function of the establishment, similar to the original, allows us to appreciate, as no other, the flavour of the authentic establishment of the epoch.

Casa Pons i Pasqual
Address: Paseo de Gracia 2
Architect: Enric Sagnier i Villavecchia
Date of construction: 1891

In spite of its unified external appearance, this building contains two houses, that of Alexandre Pons and that of Sebastià Pasqual, relatives, who entrusted a common project to Sagnier which included both houses. This permitted the architect to complete a genuinely important work as the building occupies most of the block, with three facades and two large chamfers. These chamfers in the Eixample with their lowered angles have almost as much importance as the facades.

Sagnier collaborated with other important craftsmen such as Francesc Pastor who carved the stone. The wrought iron work was done by Emili Farrés and Josep Lagarriga. The glassworks were done by Antoni Rigalt. It is a moderate neogothic building which is symmetrical and balanced, totally distinct from the type of architecture practised by Gaudí or Puig i Cadafalch. The facades give way to the chamfers through a cylindrical tower. On the first floor which has no galleries, the windows are adorned with one or two small dividing columns (in the windows of the tower and of the facade of the Ronda de Sant Pere respectively) and three gothic rosewindows, framed within a severe rectangular window. The glasswork doesn't adjust to this size but rather continues on behind it. The tower with a conical finishes adorned with a crown with small pinnacles. The balconies have iron railings which constitute the freest element in all the building. The overall effect of the building is elegant and moderate. Its austerity and balance compensate for a certain lack of colour or imagination.

The building suffered important damage in various epochs. In the middle of the eighties a rigorous restoration was carried out which returned it to its full splendour.

Modernism in Catalonia was an immediate movement. It appeared suddenly at the end of the XIX century and grew like wild fire in the ensuing years. It invaded buildings, interiors, furniture, personal objects, clothes, graphics, and stage sets. Towards 1915 however it had almost disappeared due to the pressure of a new movement, Noucentism, which in many respects opposed the ornamentation and the fantasy which in some cases had been extremely exaggerated. This is one of the latest buildings of Modernism, planned in 1914 and finished in 1917.

The dimensions of this project were important as Bassegoda's building occupies all the block. The houses were treated as though they were part of one building though there were several doorways. The facades gained a rhythm due to the repetition of the gallery columns which rise until the fifth floor finished in a red brick cupola and surrounded by a crown of battlements and other medieval inspired adornments. In the corners a tower makes a hinge to the facades and is finished by a pointed conical helmet. All of the windows and especially those of the last floor are decorated with gothic motifs, under the pinnacles of the upper part of the building which alternate with a balustrade of gothic roses. The whole building is elegant and austere, and also well finished, especially if we take into account the dimensions of the building. As a building without wrought iron work nor glassworks, the Bassegoda houses could be considered to be a transition piece toward the rationalist architecture if it were not for the archaic medieval references.

Casas Antoni Rocamora
Address: Paseo de Gracia 6-14
Architect: Joaquim Bassegoda i Amigó
Date of construction: 1917

This house was planned in 1902 and finished four years later in 1906. This is one of the houses of the so called "the block of discord" in allusion to the three beauties between whom the mythological Paris had to choose. The other two beauties of the block are the Casa Ametller and the Casa Batlló. In 1906 the Casa Lleó Morera received the first prize in architecture from the Barcelona city council.

The house is on a corner and joins two lateral bodies with a great circular central body where the entrance door is located, as well as the square of the main floor and the two terraces of the first. We also see the square of the upper end, all of these form a continuous whole. This pinnacle was destroyed in 1937 whilst being used for military purposes and it was restored in the eighties.

The craftsmen who worked on the Casa Macaya, the sculptor Eusebi Arnau and the stone mason Juyol, elaborated a genuine stone lace for this house. Antoni Serra i Fiter did the ceramic work, Rigalt i Granell the glassworks, Escofet the pavings, Maragliano y Bru the mosaics and Gaspar Homar the furniture and interior decoration. We should point out that we are looking at one of the buildings in which the splendor of the interior decoration, specially that of the first floor is better than that of the exterior decoration. The appropriateness and the integration of all the decorative elements achieve the effect of not oversaturating, and each ornament shines in its own right without interfering with the others.

On the ground floor there were two symetrical pairs of modernist ladies with large glasses which were destroyed in the years after the civil war. The explosion of Modernism in Catalonia and the very idiosyncrasy of an exuberant style, one full of force, such as the later eruption of the severe nineties style, provoked a strong poular rejection during some decades (from the thirties to the fifties). It was something of a hiccup in Modernism. Ignorance did the rest, and Arnau's sculptures destroyed by blows were not the only victims. This time however there were two people responsible for

Casa Albert Lleó Morera
Address: Paseo de Gràcia 35
Architect: Lluís Domènech i Montaner
Date of construction: 1906

the destruction, the architect Duran Reynolds and the Loewe company, whose commerce occupied the ground floors and who requested the remodeling.

Oscar Tusquets assumed the restoration of the rest of the building in the eighties.

Casa Antoni Amatller
Address: Paseo de Gràcia 41
Architect: Josep Puig i Cadafalch
Date of construction: 1900
Remarks: It is the headquarters of the Amatller foundation

This is one of the three houses in the so called "block of discord", along with the Lleó Morera and Batlló houses. The Amatller house specially surprises us because of its imaginative use of the central-european architectural style. The building won an architecture prize from the Barcelona council in 1901 which shows the positive response to the building from the first moment.

The facade is a reform entrusted to Puig i Cadfalch of a building constructed in 1875 by the architect Antoni Robert. The owner Antoni Amatller was a well-known chocolate confectioner. The foundation which bears his name still occupies the first floor of the building.

As in the Casa Macaya, Puig i Cadafalch treated the Amatller facade as a single mansion front in spite of the fact that the building was composed of flats. Puig i Cadafalch carried out this work at the same time as Casa Macaya and there are many similarities between them which are not always apparent. The craftsmen who collaborated were practically the same: Eusebi Arnau, sculptor; Alfons Juyol, mason; Masriera y Campins, the bronzework; Casa y Bardés, the carpentry; The son of J. Puyol y Torres Mauri, the ceramics; Esteve Andorrà y Manuel Ballarín the iron forging; and Mario Maragliano the mosaics.

It is essential to observe the the sculpture in the main door in which Saint George appaears fighting with the dragon above a pilar which separates two completely asymmetrical doors. On the left handside a peddler can be seen making a bear dance and on the right a femine figure which is probably a mermaid.

The almond flower (Almond=Amatller=ametllar in Catalan) is repeated in the facade and we can also see an almond in the crests above the door.

The grafito decoration, the ceramic covering and the richness of the iron forge work are decorative elements which contribute to the magnificence of the facade.

The small windows on the ground floor have been well used by the Bagués jewellers who have created highly attractive shop windows with them, and these are in keeping with the line of the house.

Street lights in Paseo de Gracia
Address: all along the street.
Architect: Pere Falqués
Date of construction: 1906

The embankment street lights in Paseo de Gracia are one of the most spectacular achievements of Pere falqués who had a special sensitivity toward iron work and completed other street light models in the city. The sveldt lights start from a sinuous bench which are covered on both sides with white fragmented mosaic. Two strong iron pillars rise parallel to each other and curve in order to protect the street light which points toward the centre of the road. They are held together by leaf and flower iron motifs.

Street lights in the Sant Joan Hall
Address: all along the road, flanking the Arco de Triunfo
Architect: Pere Falqués

Another model of streetlight designed by the architect Pere Falqués.

Street lights in Plaza Real
Address: Plaza real
Architect: Antoni Gaudí
Date of construction: 1878

The central street lights in plaza Real are the work of Gaudí, not a widely known fact. They are next to the central fountain and originally lit all the square. Each of them holds six lamps which project in all directions. The forms are inspired by medieval armour which is specially evident in the angles of the arms which hold the lights and in the helmet which finishes the structure. This helmet has wings and is supported by two snakes engraved in the trunk. In its base, in painted relief, the city crest can be seen. The street lights are finished by a crown of arises.

The building which accomodates Montaner i Simon publishers was planned in 1879 but its construction was not begun until much later and it was not finished until 1886.
It was the first important work by Lluís Domenech i Montaner who along with Gaudí is considered to be the best modernist architect from Catalonia. This work is also interesting as a sample of the first stage of Modernism in Catalonia: in it we can see the decided break with the eclectic and classicistic styles of the XIX century. Catalan Modernism is more benevolent with the medievalist tendency in the nineteenth century architecture: some of the new modernist constructions conserve medieval elements though their presence has less structural importance.
Francesc Simon and Ramon de Montaner, the owners of the publishing company, encharged the project to Domènech i Montaner, Ramon's cousin. They wanted an extense and practical space which would cover all the necessary requirements of the publishing house. This was in at a time when publishers were largely self sufficient, each one produced, printed and distributed its own books. The aim then was to construct a building which could house a social headquarters, a publishing house, a printers, a store and office space. The plot of land designated for the building was in an unbeatable site, next to the unstaffed train station in Calle Aragó (whose circulation at that time was above ground), between Passeig de Gràcia and the Rambla Catalunya. This is a central zone which at that time was beginning to fill up with beautiful and modern residential buildings, and as consequence the construction of an industrial building represented a challenge.
The first facade planned by Domènech i Montaner was made of stone but they finally decided to have a brick facade, a characteristic which contributed to give it an oriental air. Domènech i Montaner was one of the first architects in using uncovered natural brick, a tendency which would extend in the modernist epoch and would last until our own time and be seen in many styles. The natural beauty of brick, which was then a novelty in a building of its category, harmonized perfectly with the playfulness of the arches, the windows and openings which gave the facade its characteristic rhythm. Brick was also used in the ornamentation and thus achieved totally new effects. Many of these effects were later used in the ornamentation of cheaper houses and industrial spaces due to the excellent results achieved and their low cost. For the central end piece of the facade uncovered terra-cota with cement was used. This formula produced rather beautiful results without losing the relatively functional appearance of the building. The publisher's name appears in stone letters in the voussoirs of the central arch where the entrance was located. The publisher's logo can still be seen in the centre of the building, in the central circle surrounded by another two of a smaller size in which we can see toothed wheels, a probable allusion to the machinery in the entrance. In the central circle we can see a book and a compas (related to the publisher's guild) and the progressive symbols of the eagle and the five pointed star. In the two lateral towers Domènech i Montaner placed busts of Dante and Shakespeare above columns, in the centre we can see the bust of Cervantes. Between the three busts we see some medallions with the names of famous people; Malte Brun, a French geographer who was ideologically progressive, the historian Lafuente and the astronomer Italian Secchi. The fourth medallion has still not been identified.
As in many other cases Domènech i Montaner took special care in the quality of the decorative elements, which are in agreement with the constructive innovations. The iron forging which was forerunner of all the modernist forging in Barcelona and the glassworks are also highly noteworthy.
In 1990 the restoration of the building was carried out by Lluís Domènech and Roser Amadó in order to house the Antoni Tàpies foundation. The sculpture which Tàpies completed for the roof of the building created widespread discussion, which today has been forgotten.

Montaner i Simon Publishing House
Address: Aragó 255
Architect: Lluís Domènech i Montaner
Date of construction: 1886
Remarks: It is presently the headquarters of the Antoni Tàpies Foundation.

Montaner i Simón Publishers: A view of the sculpture on the terrace against the ligt.

Casa Dolors Calm
Address: Rambla de Cataluña 54
Architect: Josep Vilaseca i Casanovas
Date of construction: 1903

The Casa Dolors calm is reform carried out on a building dating back to 1878 which was built by Josep Deu, the master of works. The request for these reforms was limited to the facade and the plans were made in 1902 with the work being finished the following year.

Vilaseca is not a well known or recognised architect. He was also the author of the Arco de Triunfo which has been undervalued until recently when the restoration underlined its better qualities. For the Casa Calm which has different floors, Vilaseca planned an enormous central gallery which, in difference to the rest of the modernist houses in the Eixample, is connected to all the floors of the house. It is an extraordinary example of the use of ornamental carpentry which is generally eclipsed by the colour and spectular glassworks, but which in this case stands out in its own right. The two balconies lateral lines stand out over a beautiful grafito decoration with floral motifs. The floral grafito decoration of the galleries plinths are also rather beautiful, with their long stalk flowers against a white background.

The unfortunate construction of floors above the end of the original house has reduced the volume of the higher part of the house. (This is a problem throughout Eixample, provoked by the francoist dictatorship and irresponsable mayors who allowed property speculation and the destruction of a large part of the architectural heritage of the city).

Much later on the ground floor Joan Prats the milliner came to live. He was a friend of the poet J. V. Foix and one of the leading figures in the Dau al Set group. Today Joan Prats' shop window remains intact in what is the Joan Prats gallery, and continues being one of the most important of its kind in the city.

Casa Fargas
Address: Rambla de Cataluña 47
Architect: Enric Sagnier i Villavecchia
Date of construction: 1904

This is one of Sagnier's freest works. In general the architect used a neogothic vocabulary rather more conservative than this work here. The facade is given a special treatment, where what stands out is the freedom in the proportions between the galleries and the whole, apart from the predominance of soft sinuous elements in the lines in the arches, the galleries and in general in all the building's ornaments.

In spite of having limited himself in the richness of the ornaments, Sagnier knew how to treat Casa Fargas as a unique object, making the most of the reduced dimensions of the plot and the narrow facade.

All of the facade is stone except for some elements of wrought iron in the balcony (which are also rather elegant) the rest of the decoration is based on the movement of the stone.

The floors begin above an entresol just above the basement. The doorway is as high as both windows, those of the basement and the entresol, with a bulls eye above the arch in order to compensate the differences in height. On the first floor, the beautiful balconies with stone balustrades are noteworthy. A line of central galleries rises until the fourth floor creating a body which runs the facade from top to bottom given a great sense of verticality. The upper finishing has three levels, two enormous lateral ailerons and a central body with a thread of windows. The house is finished by a cupola which disappeared when more floors were added.

Casa Evarist Juncosa
Address: Rambla de Cataluña 78
Architect: Salvador Vinyals i Sabaté
Date of construction: 1909

Evarist Juncosa entrusted the construction of his house and upper floors to the architect Salvador Vinyals in 1907. The house was finished two years later.

The facade which overlooks the rambla de Cataluña is a curious mixture of measurement and caprice. It is an example of how the Catalan architects, influenced by the modernist movement, knew how to integrate for good and "less" good, the exotism and fantasy with the rigid schemes of a clear thinking bourgeoisie who wished to reflect a change in their architecture not a disaster. On the ground floor various wide arches open out adorned with profuse floral ornamentation. Above the main door there are the proprietors initials engraved in stone. The door is an interesting example of wood carving, it is sober and elegant.

The gallery of the first floor is well adorned with natural, plant motifs as well as the sinuous elements of the sculpted stone, especially in the finishing. The adjacent balconies also have a rich and elegant profusion of sculpted stone with trophies and garlands of flowers and leaves.

The facade is covered with sculpted stone which gives this work a severe and regular appearance. In order to compensate the weight of the gallery, the third and fourth floors have a horizontal line of white stone running along them at the height of the plinths of the balconies. The same stone is used to finish the balconies.

The most spectacular element of this is the small circular pediment in its finishing, with a small rose hanging over the small bulls eyes and a garland of flowers carved in stone. On both sides under the two secondary sinuous elements in the finishing, we find two new bulls eyes which house the iron bars which hold the pulleys which are used to bring up the furniture.

The whole building has recently been well restored.

The plans and the construction of this building were completed in the same year. It is a building situated on a corner, the facade resolves in an austere and elegant manner without giving up any of the decorative elements so typical in Modernism. The building presents two large bodies united by a corner with

Casa Josep i Ramon Queraltó
Address: Rambla de Cataluña 88
Architect: Josep Plantada i Artigas
Date of construction: 1907

Casa Josep i Ramón Queraltó: Balconies and stone engravings.

circular galleries in the form of squares. These are supported by a giant corbel with highly suggestive ornamental plant motifs, which are situated in the structural strengthening axis.

The balconies of the first, second and fourth floors with an iron handrail, alternate with arch windows in the third flanked by small thin long columns and by an forged iron protective shields with floral motifs and stars in the upper frieze. The Venetian blinds of these windows are interesting being divided into three parts (the two sheets and an upper non mobil body). In the base of the windows of the fifth floor there is a frieze which runs along all the building giving a unity and horizontal weight to the monument.

Unfortunately the building has suffered the loss of an angula turret and various pinacles which were designed to give a verticality to the facade and to give balance to the horizontal line marked by the forementioned frieze.

All of the facade is covered with an elegant red and yellow grafito decoration whose floral silhouette reminds us of a lily.

The main door is highly interesting with a carpentry finish and with great openings finished with a light forged iron.

The building has recently been restored.

Casa Jaume Forn
Address: Roger de Llúria 82/ València 285
Architect: Jeroni Granell i Manresa
Date of construction: 1909

The Casa Forn was planned in 1904 and finished in 1909. Granell was an intelligent and moderate architect. Looking at the facade as a whole we can see this moderate, proportioned treatment in which the modernist fantasies are contained, subject to their secondary role as decorative elements. It is for this reason that some historians consider Granell to be a precursor of rationalism which would invade the Catalan aesthetic in Barcelona a few years later. The facade adapts perfectly to the angle of the chamfer. Two enormous lateral columns flank it from top to bottom preceding the two lines of the galleries. The columns follow in three registers finished by capitals in which stone decoration has been used with plant motifs.

These galleries along with those of the Palau de la Música have the most beautiful glasswork in Barcelona although their state of conservation is not up to the same level. The glass is ordered according to the drawing in large stylized and undulating pieces which represent tulips, clichés and leaves of aquatic plants which are sinuously connected to each other. Their lively colours stand out against a white background which contributes in highlighting the illumination and let light enter the the flat with greater ease. The completely symmetrical distribution of the drawings rebalances its caprichous and fantasy character and has a bearing on strongly symmetrical appearance which the building has. It is believed that the glassworks were carried out by Rigalt i Granell, one of the most important glass workshops in Catalonia.

We should also give a special mention to the iron forging and carpentry on the main door.

Granell planned a rich ornamentation in the finishing of the house, which was lost due to the addition of floors in the following years.

Casa Manuel Llopis i Bofill
Address: València 339/Bailén 113
Architect: Antoni Gallissà i Soqué
Date of construction: 1903

Without question this is the best piece by the architect Gallissà, a close collaborator of Domènech i Montaner, who died at the age of forty two.

It is a sober building in chamfer, with a rhythm achieved by the central tower and the two lateral gallery towers, crowned above the level of the roof. The end pieces of the galleries of the last floor have an arabian reminiscence. Between the towers an end piece in frieze of staggered brick produces a beautiful effect of lights and shadows which crown the arches of the last floor. While some of these arches house windows, others are blind due to wide panels covered in green ceramic.

The set of windows with the shining white of the facade is what gives it its particular charm. The use of natural brick is also interesting, which combined with the white facade evokes popular memories, specially those of Andalusian architecture and other types of mediterranean constructions. The ochre grafito decorations of the architect Josep Maria Jujol are excellent and show a light and vertical elegance with floral details. The ground floor is highly original with staggered arches made of natural brick.

Gallissà's work stands out for its use of ceramics, of which he was a passionate collector. One could be surprised by its scarce use in this facade but he had good reasons. Originally the high parts of the galleries were covered with ceramic but the bombings of the civil war destroyed them. The glassworks also had to be eliminated in the restoration as they were found in a dire state. However the conserved ceramics carried out by Pujol i Bausis are of great beauty and combine perfectly with the brick, precisely because they are found dispersed in rosewindows, and plinths in the galleries etc.
In the ground floor of the building we find the Arderiu chemists which was installed shortly after the construction of the house. It has conserved its furnishings, a superb example of modernist carpentry perfectly in tone with the buildings' decorative lines.

Casa Clapés stands out for the daring way it plays with the proportions between the openings and the size of the facade. In effect, the doors and windows are disproportionately too big and create an interesting effect in the facade. This effect is reinforced by the rich stone ornamentation of the sculpture. Casimir Clapés, an industrial textilist, chose a house in which the facade would reflect the extent of his economic power and influence.
The enormous galleries of the second and third floors make up just one body of great dimensions. It is divided in two registers of arches which are supported by high columns corresponding to the floors. Both of these are adorned with profuse stone sculpture which have plant motifs. It is finished by a relief which represents three young people, two boys and a girl, working in a weavers. The ornamentation of the first floor lateral balconies also stands out specially for the use of acanthus leaves. This is used in a most capricious way not without veiled allusions to the fantasy elements of the classical and medieval world.
There are two sinuous and capricious balconies above the two galleries which stand out. They are supported by corbels with floral ornamentation and have beautiful forged iron handrails which follow the curves of the balcony. Its noticeable forward projection produces an aireal effect and contributes in creating a light and shadow effect which is already important due to the size of the central windows. There are small gothic windows with mullions at the sides of both balconies.
We can see a niche which houses the figure of a woman in the end piece of the building, she seems to be holding a spindle and is flanked by folded woven cloth.
In the ground floor we can see three doors beneath gothic arches which have stone floral ornamentation. The carpentry of the main door also stands out as does the cabinet work and the marquetry and the brass work.

Casa Casimir Clapés
Address: Diputació 246
Architect: Joaquim Bassegoda i Amigó
Date of Construction: 1908

Casa Casimir Clapés: Gallery on the first floor.

The Casa Thomas was completed three years after the plans were finished. These date back to 1895. Thomas was a publisher with an important art section and like Montaner i Simon stood out for his progressive spirit and his keeness to renovate. Thomas also carried out lithographs and photoengravings of an extraordinary quality. Given that today the publishing sector has so many difficulties to expand it is surprising to look back and see that it was two publishing houses which were able to afford the luxury of of building their headquarters in the centre of the city. These were times of expansion in the publishing trade, not only because of the importance of the printed letter in communication but also because of the renovating, cultural and internationalist spirit which existed in Catalonia at the end of the century.
Domènech i Montaner constructed the press and the proprietors' house in the same building, which was made of two floors, two turrets and as an unusual element a lower ground floor above the basement. The facade is made of stone and alternates with polychrome ceramic ornaments which are located in the plinths of the balconies and in the friezes which finish the buiding. The glazed glass wall lights are very beautiful which rivet like adorn the lateral turrets. The running gallery of the last floor also stands out for its elegance and harmony.
The Casa Thomas is also unusual for fact that its reform has been well run. It was undertaken in 1912 by the architect Frances Guàrdia at the request of

Casa Josep Thomas
Address: Mallorca 291-293
Architect: Lluís Domènech i Montaner
Date of construction: 1898

Josep Thomas' sons Eudald and Josep and with the express consent of Domènech i Montaner. They added three floors which were newly crowned by the existing turrets.

The ground floor is completely covered by a low arch which is closed by an important bar. A special entrance to the lower ground floor and the basement allows independent access to the neighbours' businesses which is gained through the other door.

Palacio Ramon de Montaner
Address: Mallorca 278
Architect: Josep Domènech i Estapà, Josep Domènech i Montaner
Date of construction: 1893
Remarks: It houses the headquarters of the Spanish government delegation

The plans were completed by Josep Domènech i Estapà in 1889, and had been ordered by Ramon de Montaner, one of the owners of the Montaner i Simon publishers who had ordered the centre from Domènech i Montaner. Francesc Simon also requested his house from this architect in a plot of land situated in front of Ramon's palace. Unfortunately Simon's house was knocked down. However, there were serious problems between the owner and the architect once the works had begun, and as a consequence of this Montaner decided to give the job to his cousin, Domènech i Montaner, who had already succesfully completed the publishers building. The design of the last floor and the decorative elements were carried out by Doménech i Montaner and in these he permitted himself certain whims and liberties which had not been possible in the publishers facade. Eusebi Arnau (who was also the author of the sculptures in the Casa Macaya), was in charge of the stone work, Antoni Rigalt carried out the glassworks for the doors and the windows, and Plans i Tort did the carpentry.

Gallissà, also an architect was in charge of organizing the decoration of the building as Domènech i Montaner's first assistant. It is worth pointing out the beautiful glass mosaics which tell the story of the invention of the press by Gutenberg, on the last floor of the buiding. Its finishing is perfect and the motifs are of a great beauty and elegance. We can see human figures whose bases are converted in plant forms, a resource which was later used with great frequency in the figured ornamentation (remember the sculptures in the stage in the Palau de Música). The glazed pottery combines perfectly and in contrast with the smooth and austere stone of the facade. In the main body we can see a stone eagle flanked by two shields where the year of the buildings construction can be seen. The formal game of the eagles silhouette repeated in the stylized form of the shields is very interesting.

The garden is defined by a barred wall. The forging of this is elegant and austere. There is a predominence of stylized iron forms which combine with flowers in interpolated stone and which is regularly reproduced. The railings are finished by two magnificent gates. The street lights with an eagle from whose beak hangs an oil lamp also stands out. This beautiful building by Ramon de Montaner which is surrounded by a garden is only mansion-house in the Eixample neighbourhood which has survived until today as as a testimonial example of a house in the middle of the city. In this case, the facade corresponds to a genuine house and doesn't hide floors as in other occasions in modernist architecture. The palacial appearance fully satisfies the aspirations of the owner in evoking old sumptuary buildings belonging to the Spanish and Italian nobility without falling in the trap of being an imitation of a specific construction. Being situated on the corner the mansion was freed of being imprisoned between party walls and other often higher buildings, as is the case with the majority of the modernist houses in the Eixample. This characteristic allows us to contemplate a most singular building in the centre of Barcelona.

In 1980 the facades were restored and the interior was reconditioned in order to house the headquarters of the Spanish government in Catalonia. This work was carried out by Marc Carbonell.

Casa Ramon Casas
Address: Paseo de Gràcia 96
Architect: Antoni Rovira i Rabassa
Date of construction: 1899

Ramon Casas, the painter, encharged this house to Antoni Rovira in 1898 in a place near to which La Pedrera would be built a few years later. Casas' family possessed a considerable fortune and the painter always moved within innovative environments which were close to the new style and the wish to investigate which characterized it. That said, this work can not be said to be particularly innovative: it stays within certain measured limits in which there is little assumed risk. The results are good.

The facade is of stone worked in small pieces with a delicate bolster in which some veins within irregular distribution stand out. It is an austere and elegant work in which the decorative elements near the windows and doors play a rather limited role. The galleries have wide windows and the balconies are profusely adorned with stone sculptures. The decoration of the Casas' flat was carried out by Josep Pascó. Josep Oriols carried out the ceramic works which can be seen in the Vinçon shop which today occupies the ground floor. The forging which is extraordinary is the work of the Flich brothers, who were acredited craftsmen with many clients in Barcelona.

The entrance door is a really extraordinary element. The carpentry, studded with floral styled brass ornaments opens to six glass openings protected by iron forging. In the upper part we can see five magnificent flowers (one of the six that was there has disappeared) The doorhandle is also exceptional. Stylised versions of the stone carved acanthus frame the upper part of this work of art.

Casa Ramón Casas: Entrance door.

Casa Pere Serra i Pons
Address: Rambla de Cataluña 126
Architect: Josep Puig i Cadafalch
Date of construction: 1908
Remarks: Headquarters of the Diputació de Barcelona

Casa Pere Serra i Pons: Upper part of the main door.

"Can Serra" as this house is commonly called in Barcelona ends the Rambla de Catalunya and is one of the houses which has experienced many mishaps at the hands of famous modernist architects in Barcelona.

It was encharged to the architect Puig i Cadafalch by Pere Serra in 1903, thus allowing the first to complete his dream: to reproduce the Gralla mansion, a renaissance work which had been knocked down in the middle of the previous century. The main door and the ornamentation of the large windows are a faithful reproduction of the lost mansion. As in almost all of Puig i Cadafalch's works we find Eusebi Arnau, the sculpture, and Alfons Juyol, the stone mason colllaborating. We can see a saw within the stone crest which is an allusion to the proprietor's surname. A circular tower unites the two facades. This is "Remarada" by a little roof with attics recovered with green and red ceramic work. The curious and archaic doorhandle on the main door is Puig i Cadafalch's own work who, like the French architect Viollet-le Duc, enjoyed working with these details. However, it is not original given that it was robbed in the restoration works carried out in the eighties.

The building remains unfinished in its details and consequently lost the 1908 architectural prize awarded by the Barcelona council. Shortly after it stopped being used as a private home and housed a school. Later it served as the republican Ministry of Health offices during the civil war before becoming the nuns school again. In 1943 a wide reform was started which finished two years later. After the building suffered from a general lack of interest and was nearly knocked down in the ferocious decade of the seventies when each plot of land only meant money and speculation. When the Diputació de Barcelona planned their installation in the building there was a proposal for the destruction of what had been built in the fourties. This was a topic which generated a rather angry discussion. The widespread restoration carried out by Federico Correa and Alfons Milà in the eighties has been heavily discussed and the solution would seem to be uncommon. The house has been respected but behind the facade there is a totally new building made of iron and glass.

Casa Sayrach
Address: Diagonal 423
Architect: Manuel Sayrach
Date of construction: 1918

The architect Sayrach planned this house for himself in 1918. It is a building which belongs to late modernism and clearly shows Gaudí's influence. The facade and the end piece are conceived as a single piece which reminds us of Casa Batlló in which the idea of construction where one sees each piece is substituted by a more sculpted concept. The facades undulated and sinuous forms reinforce this effect which to a large extent aims at creating a sharp contrast of shadow and light. The beautiful corner tower stands out and this offsets the horizontal and undulated forms which run along all the facade with its vertical line. The inside of the doorway is a spectacular example of the modernist "horror vacui".

Casa Fuster
Address: Paseo de Gràcia 132
Architect: Lluís Domènech i Montaner
Date of construction: 1911

The Casa Fuster was finished two years after the plans had been completed by the brilliant Domènech i Montaner. This was a request from Consol Fabra de Fuster when Domènech i Montaner was in the most prestigious moment of his career and the zenith of his maturity. In fact the Casa Fuster is his last work in the city and in it we see all his experience and moderation revealed. The architect knew how to make the most of this plot of land, located on the junction of Passeig de Gràcia and Gran de Gràcia, a narrowing which follows a lenghthened garden. This garden allows a view of the house which is unusual in the buildings in the Eixample. It was planned by Plà Cerdà.

Two wide and beautiful asymmetrical facades meet in a gallery-square which includes all the floors of the building. The square projects in such a way that its volume is daringly apparent and thus reenforces the effect of the corner. Many windows of different forms and sizes combine in a most daring manner in the facade producing a fine result. The combination of white and pink marble contributes to livening up the facade. The scrolls in the capitals and in the balconies are far removed from the first delicate floral ornamentation which characterized incipient modernism. We find here more somber adornments which whilst not seeming to do so, herald the changes which would come later. Neither ceramics nor stained glass are used in this construction.

89

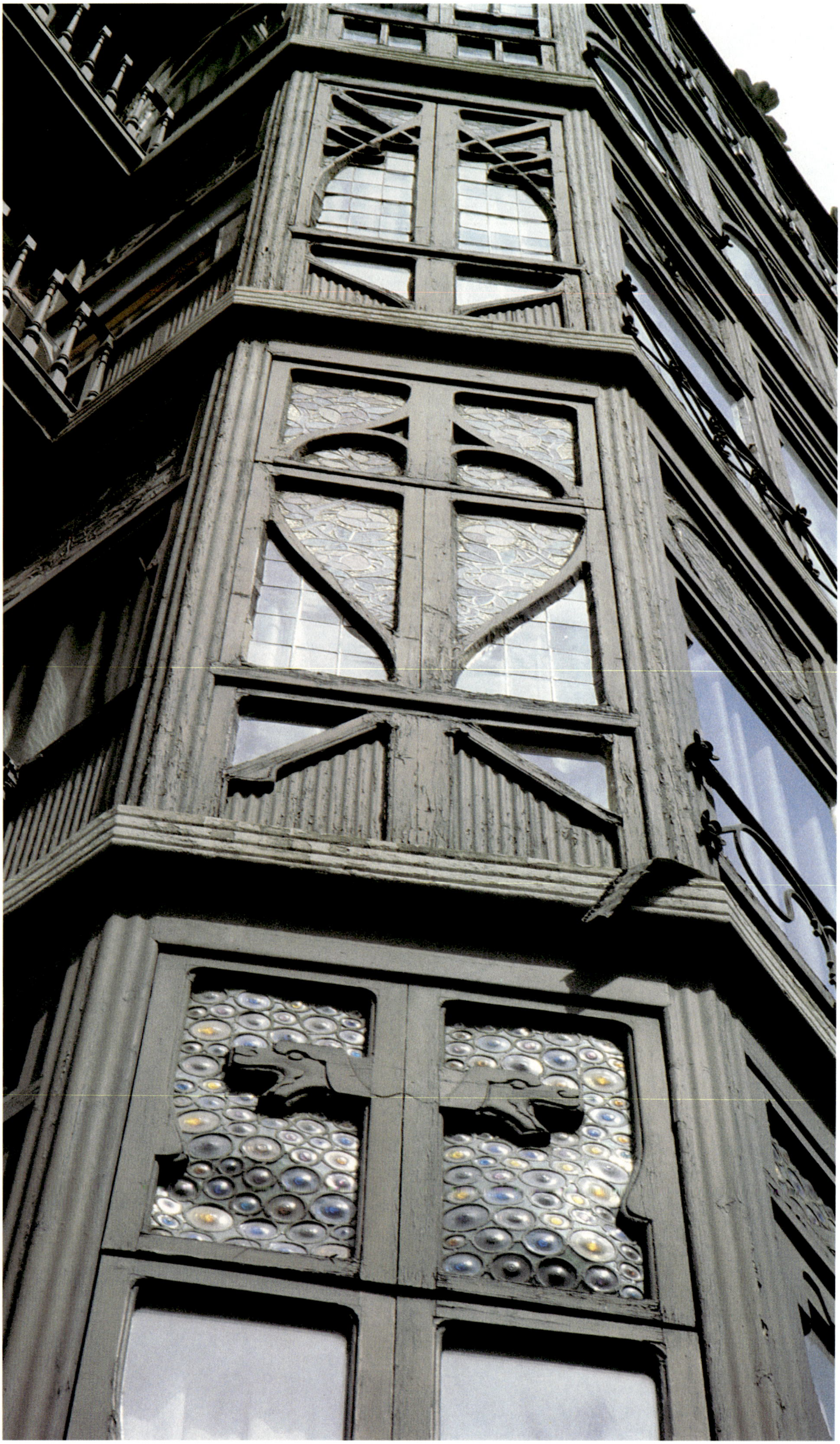

91

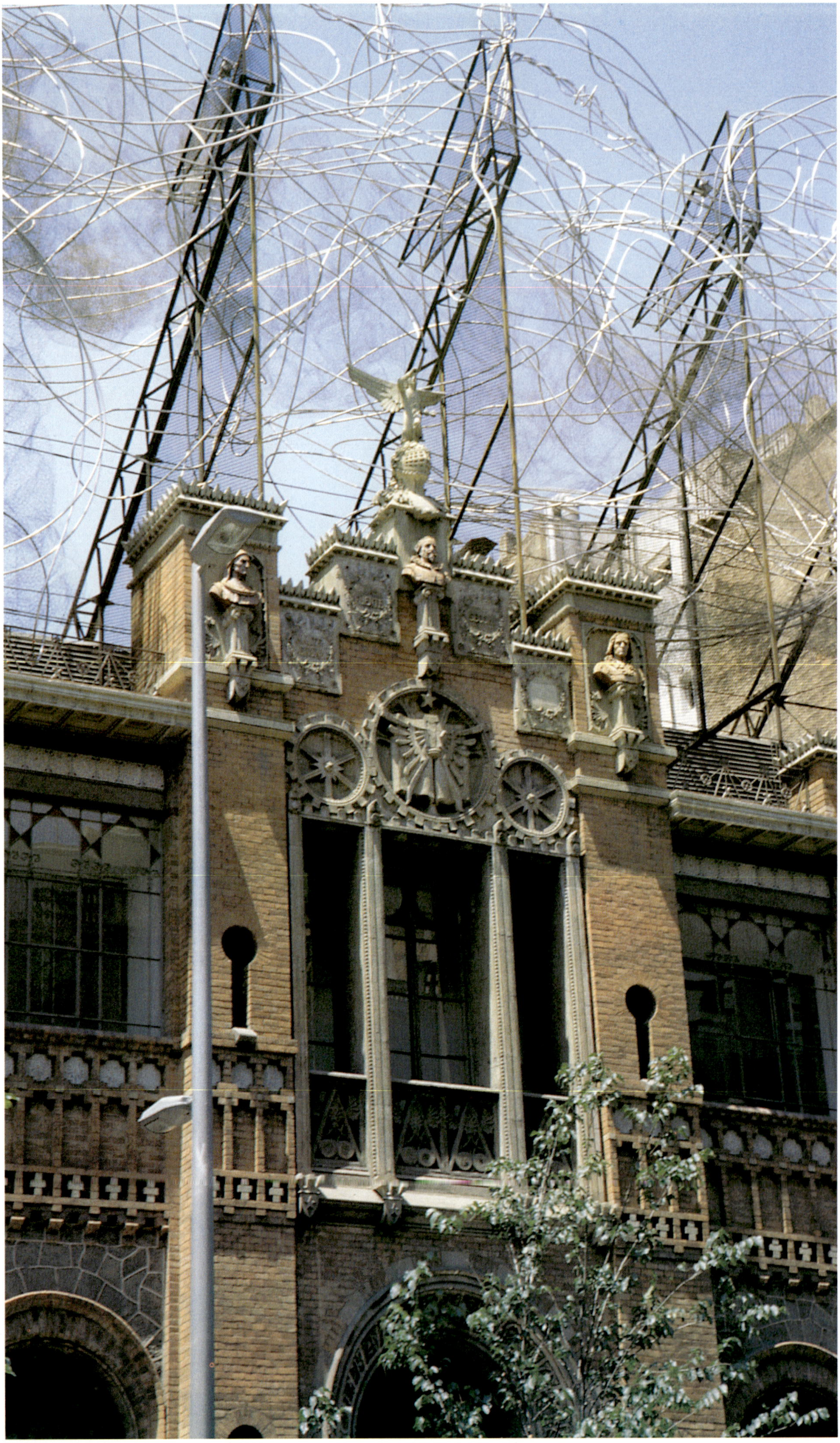

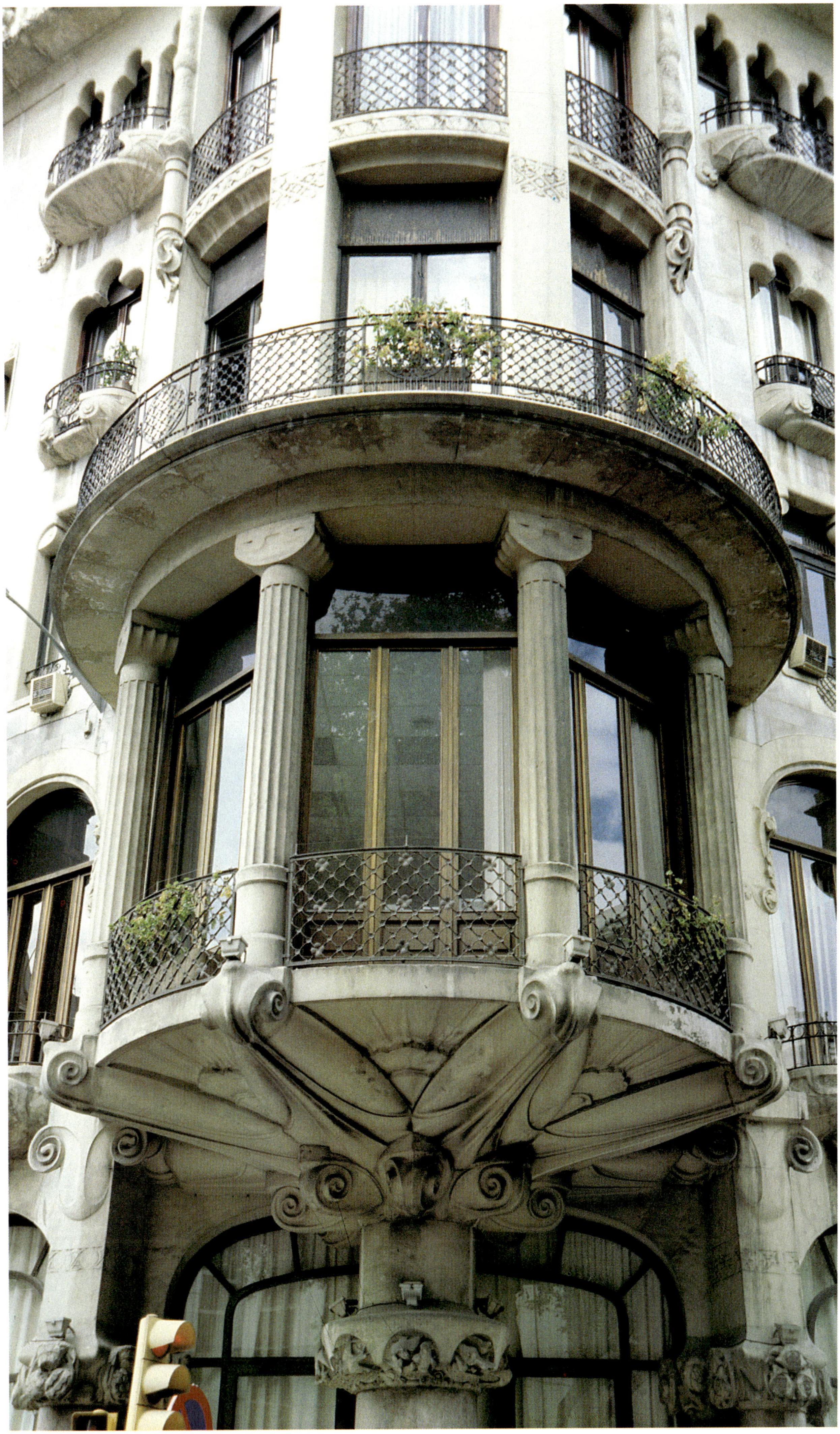

94

95

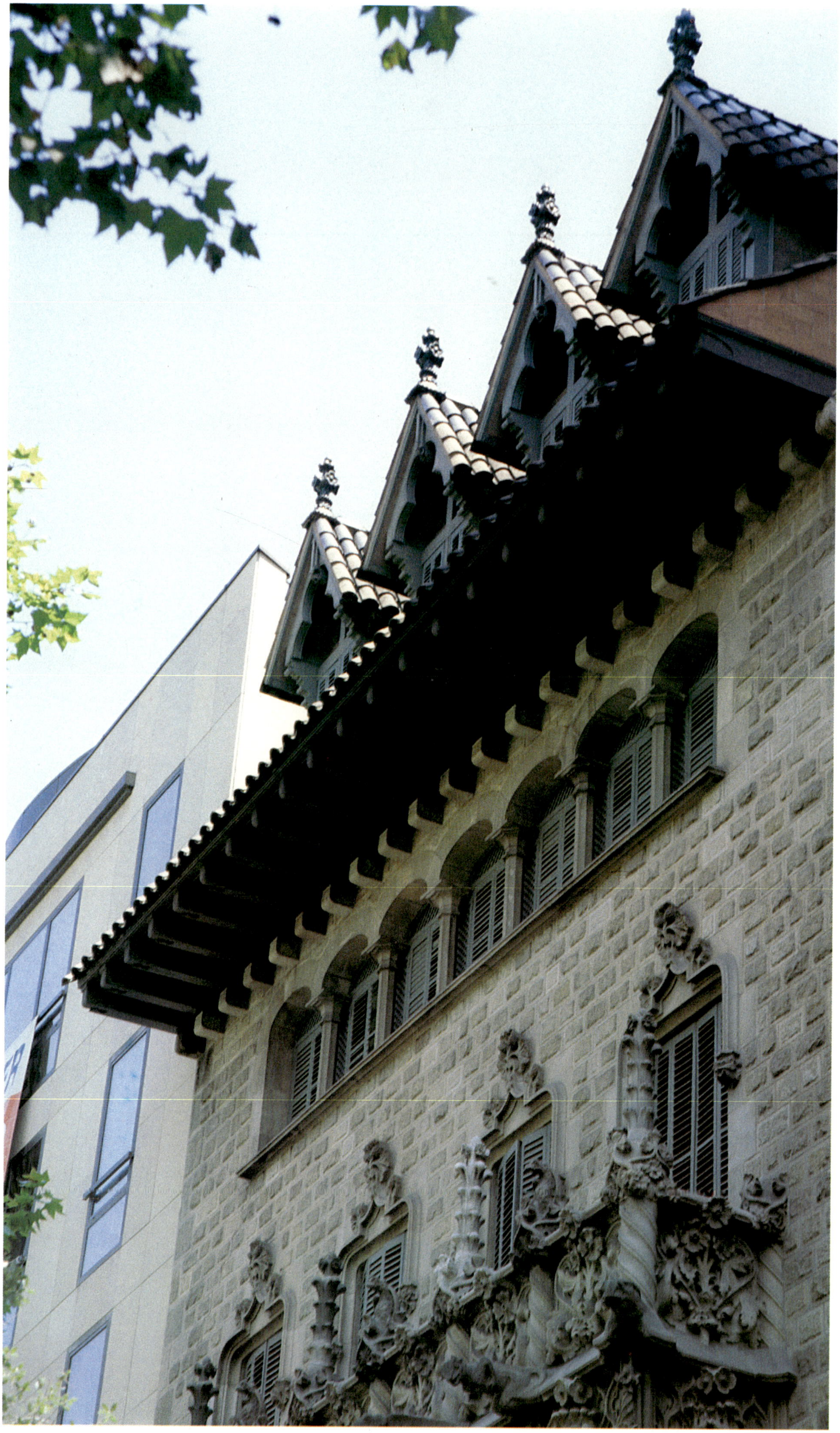

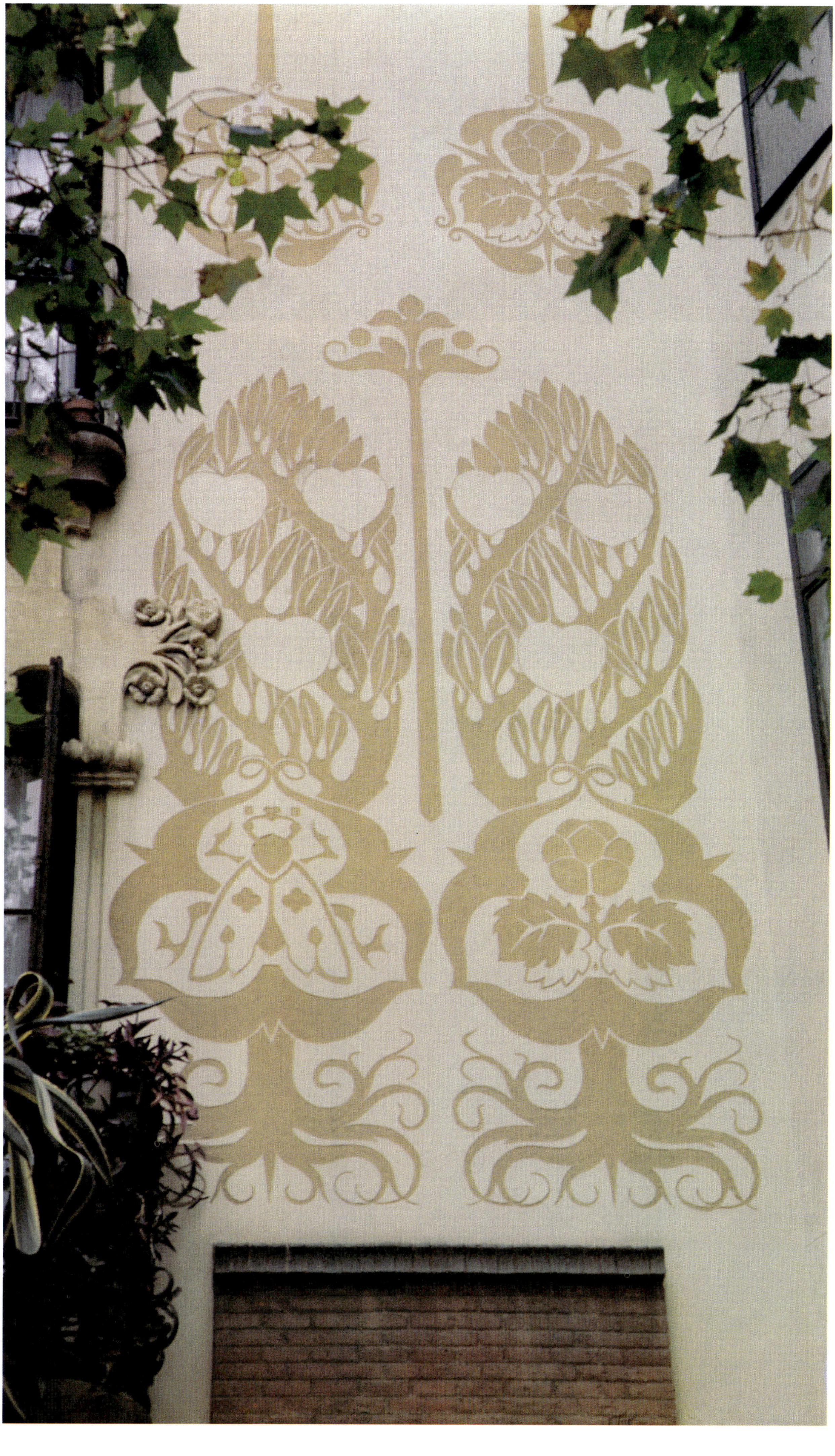
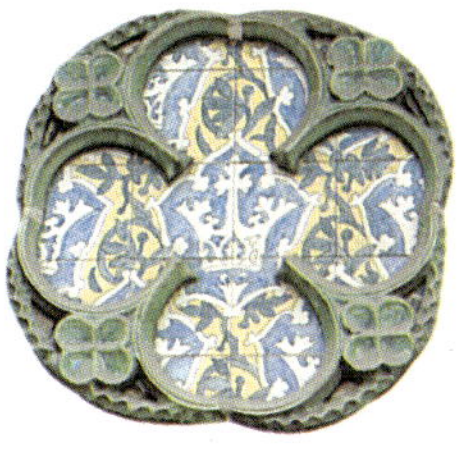

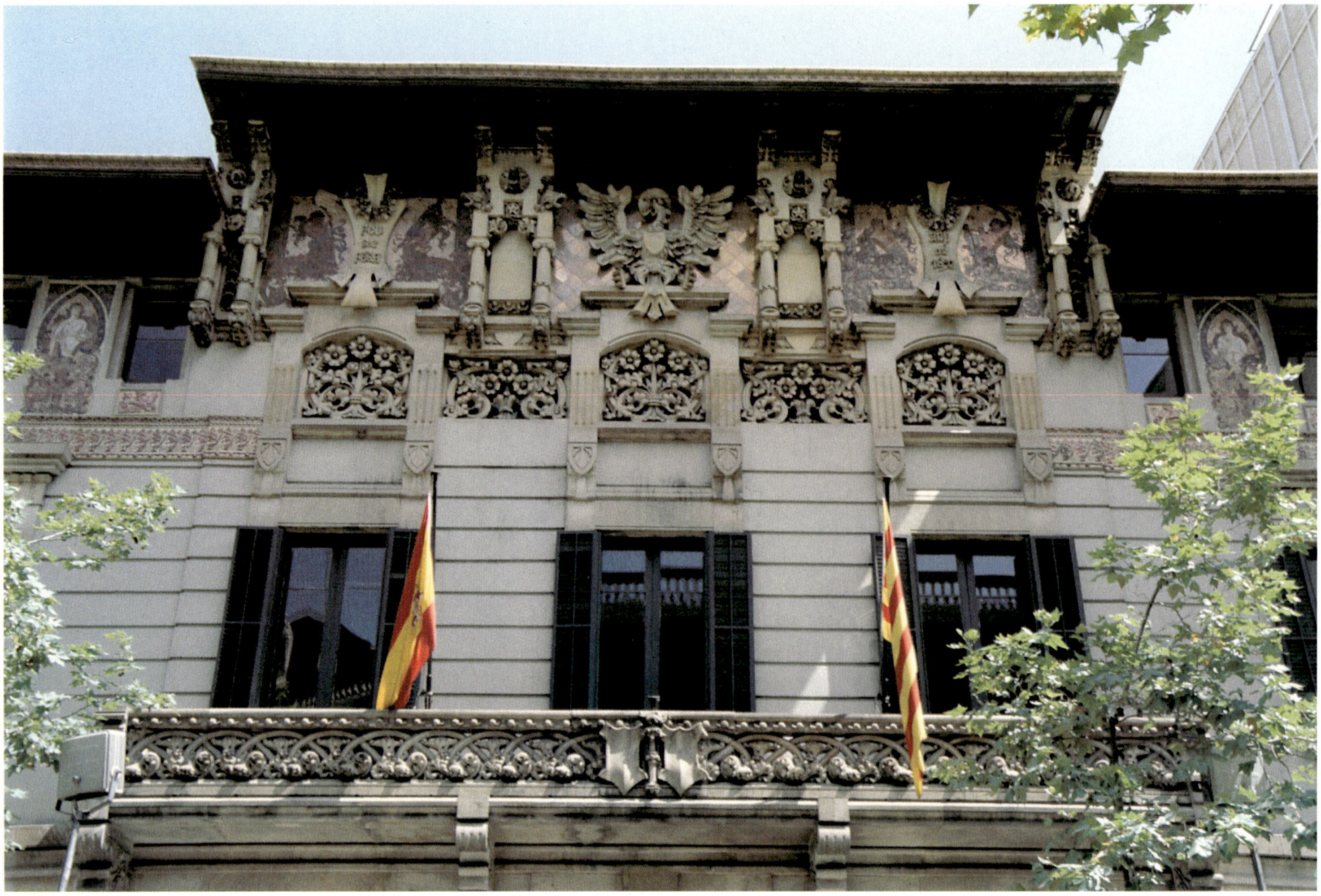

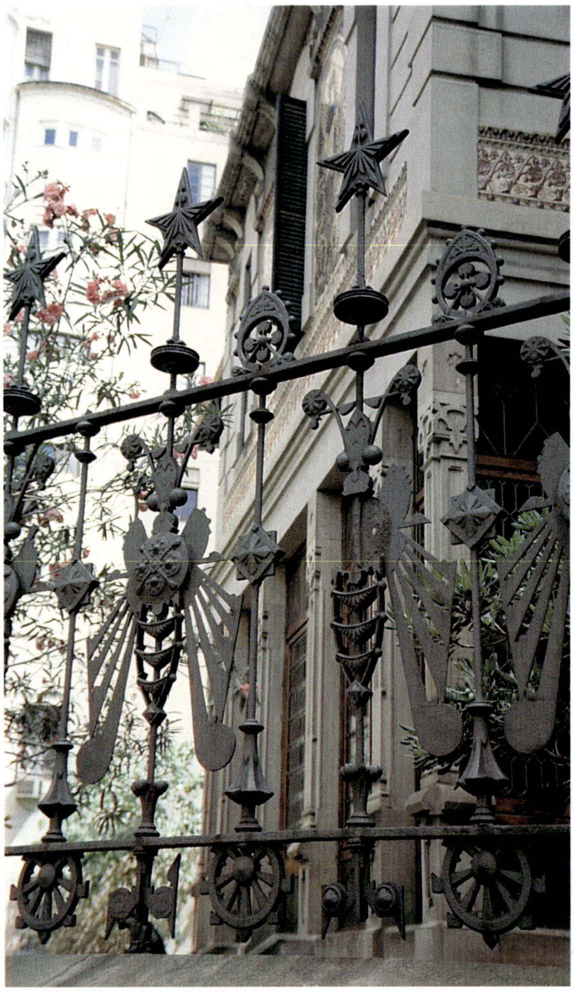

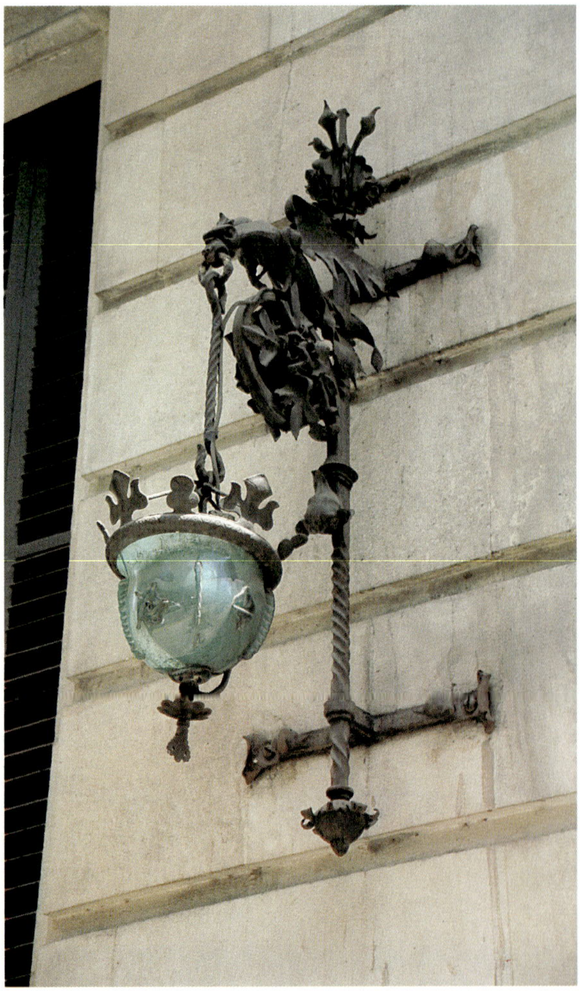

99

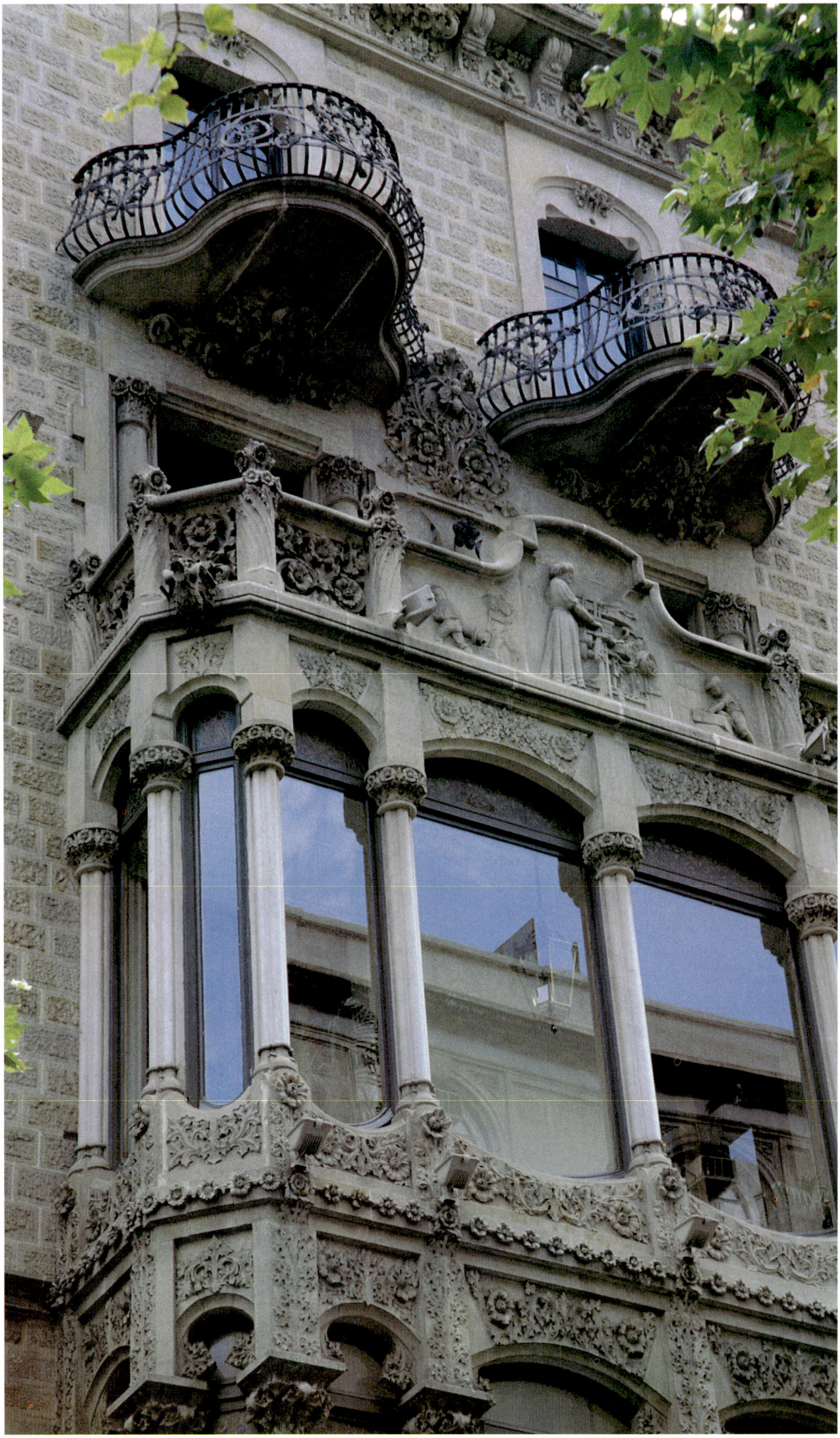

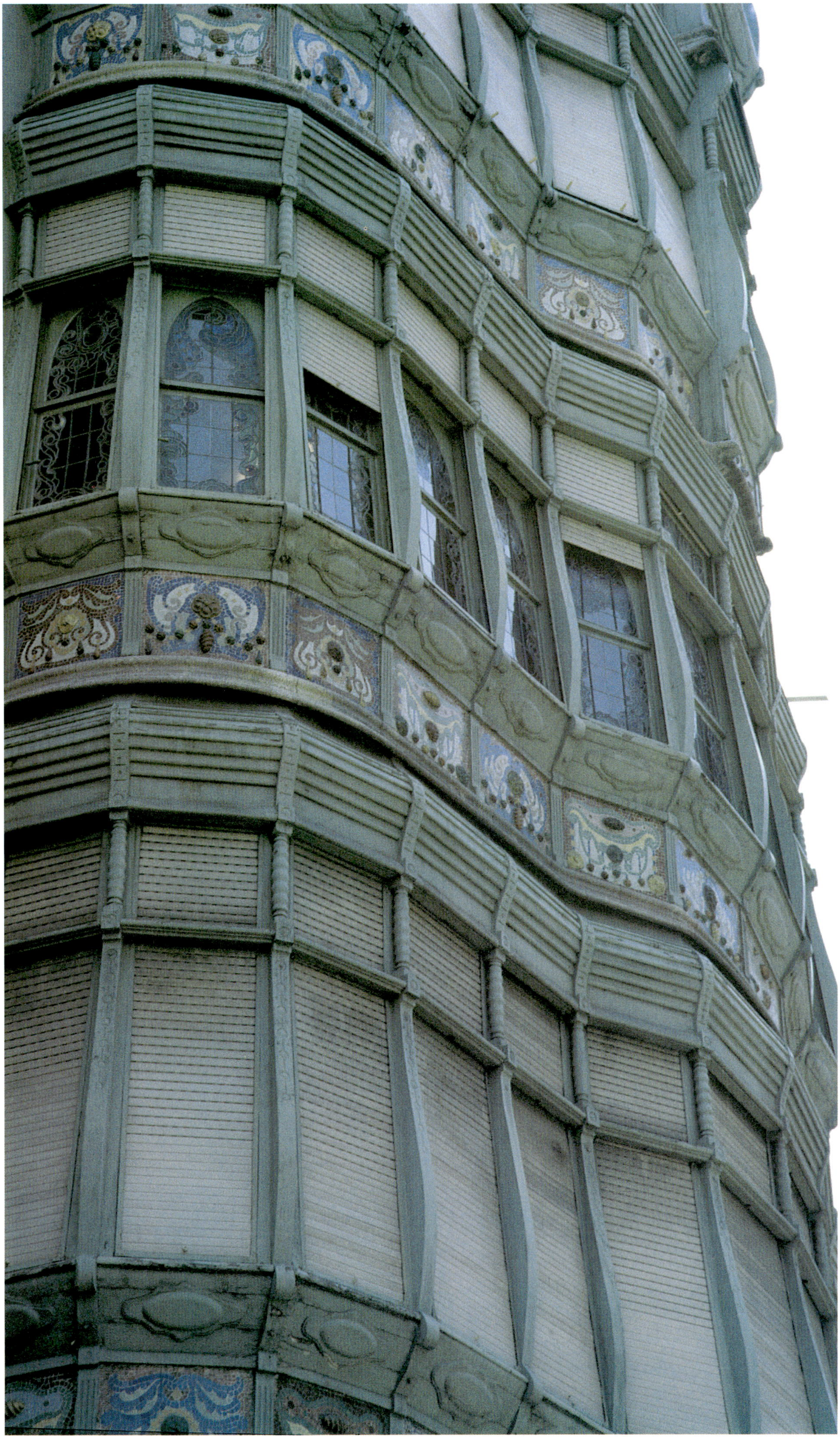

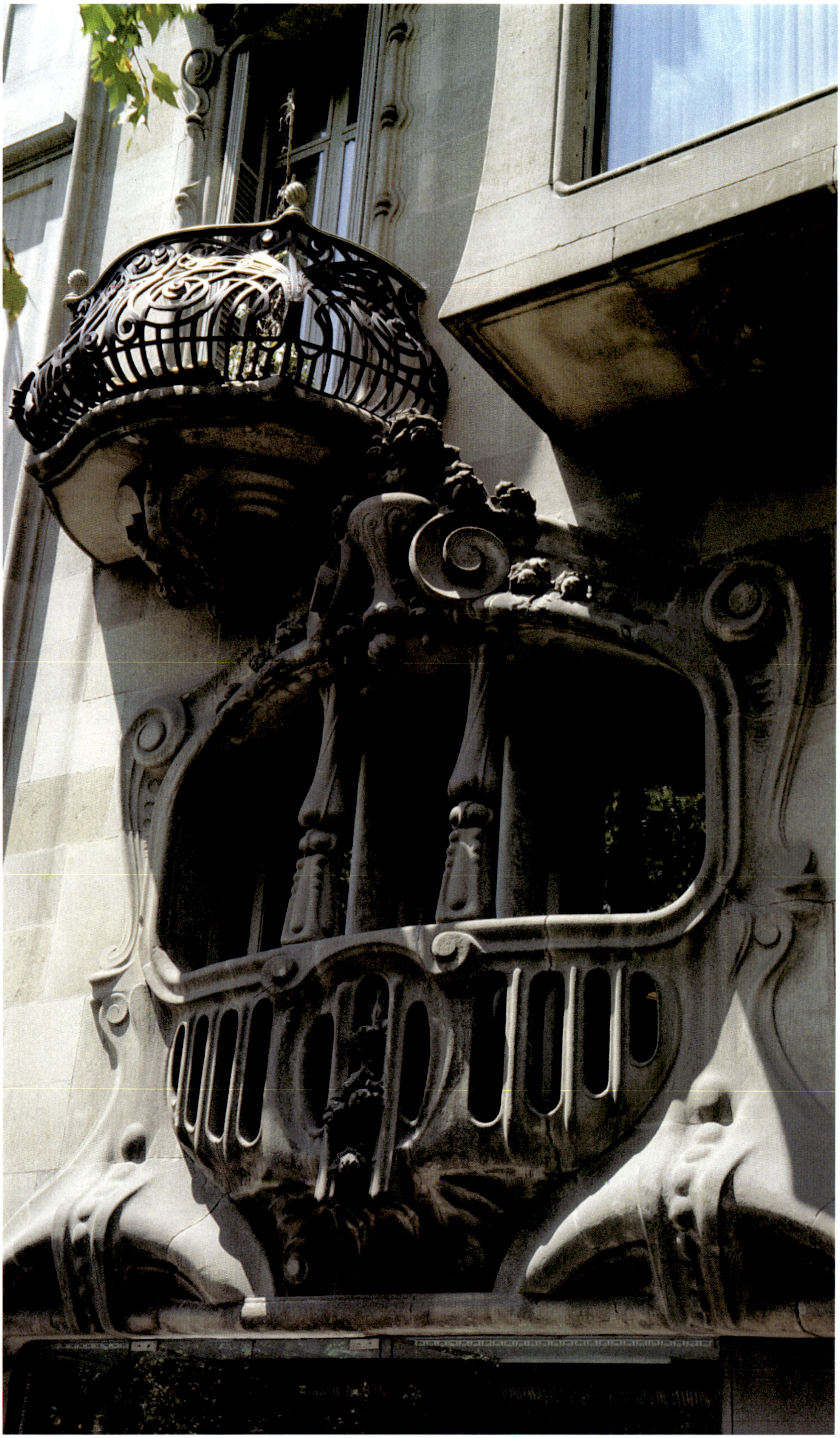

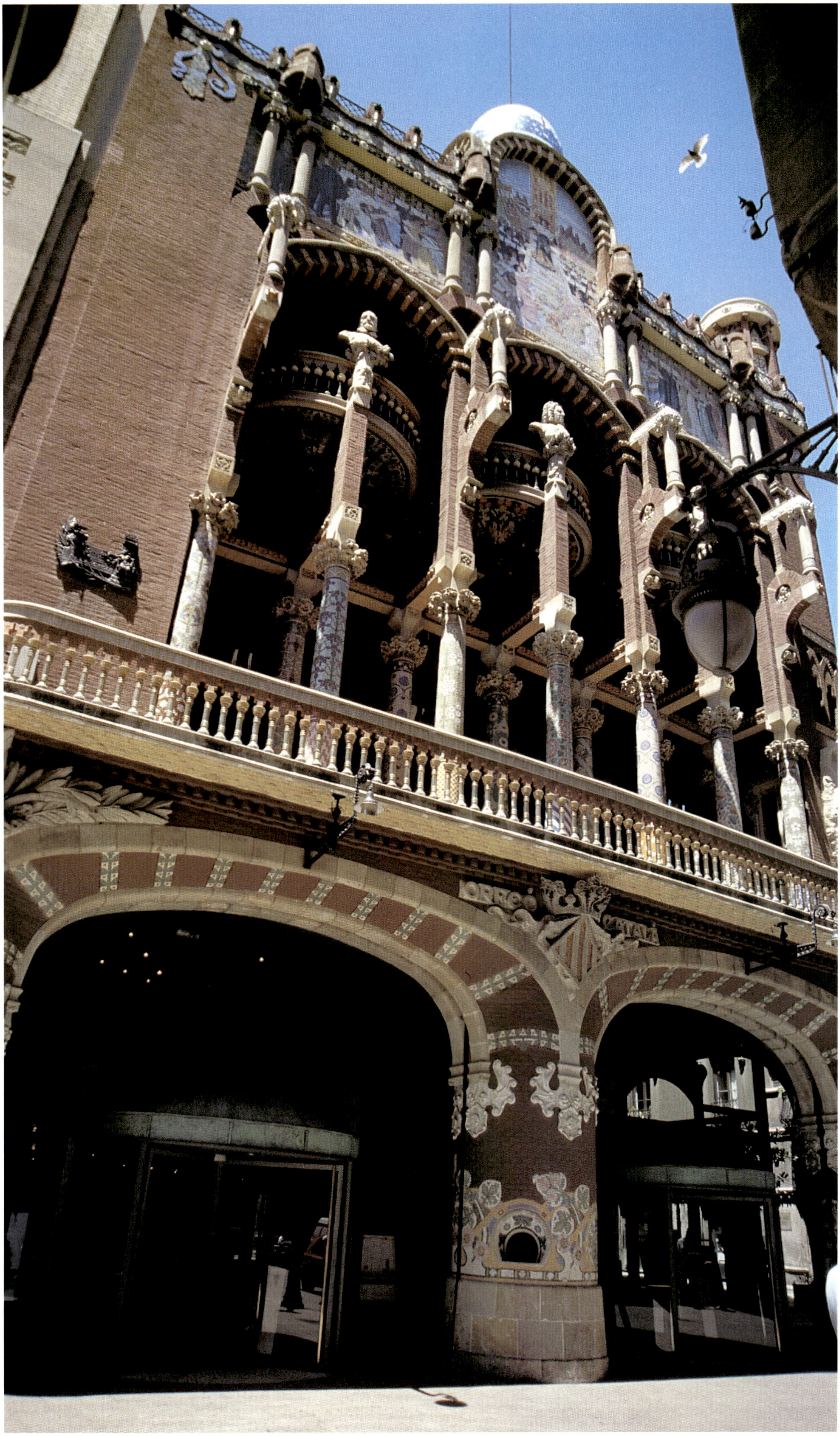

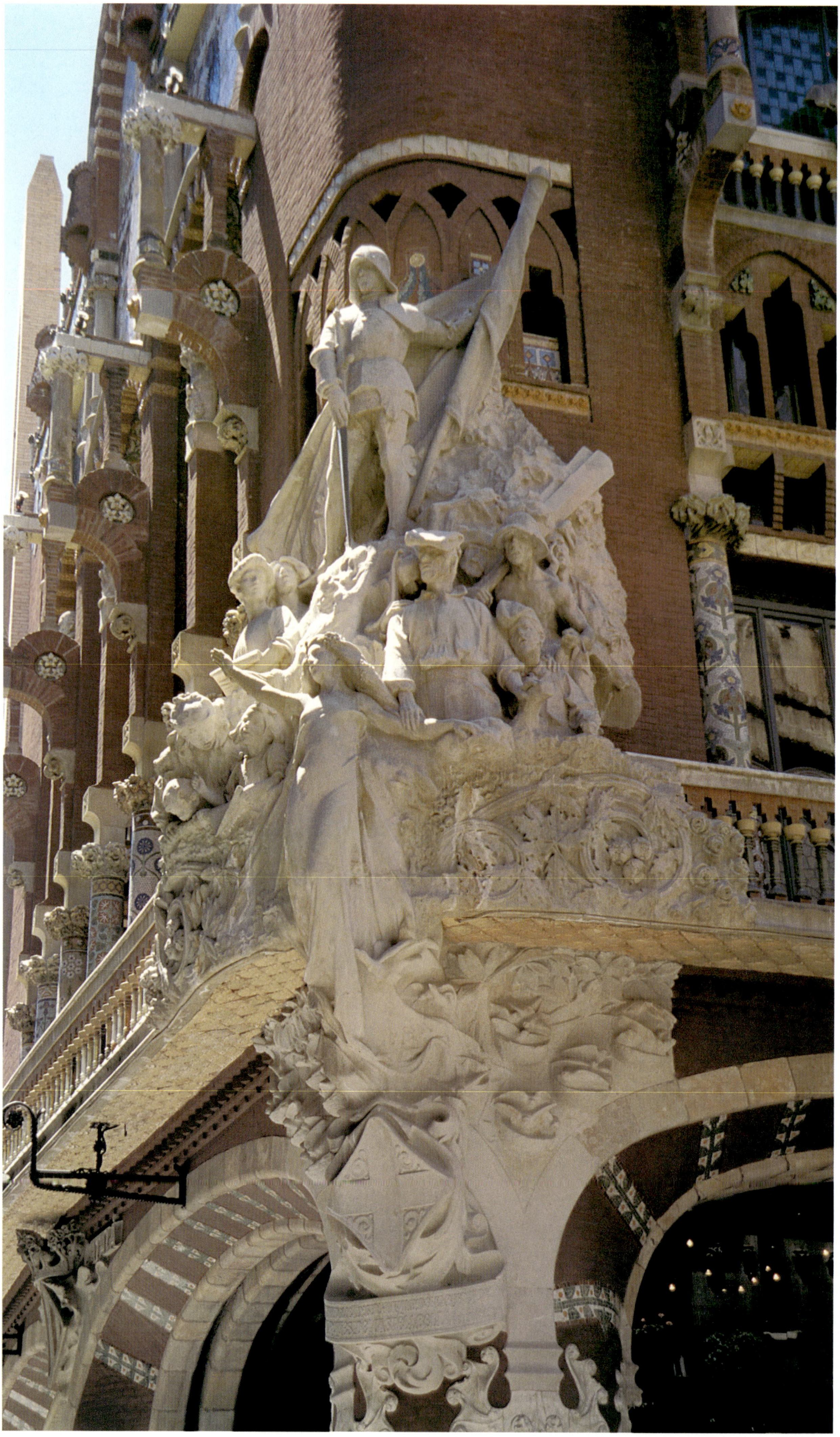

The building is finished with beautiful balustrades alternating with attics. There are pinacles at regular intervals finished with the Catalonia crest.

The building has a third facade which looks onto a narrow side street, La Calle Jesús. This more modest facade renounces the great projected spaces of the previous two and develops a highly elegant decoration which has an incisive character.

Although the building was finished in 1911, the plans were completed six years earlier. Salvador Valeri carried out few works in Barcelona and this is of the greatest magnitude of those which can be seen in the city. It is a building with two facades of unequal importance, one which looks onto the Diagonal and the other onto Calle Córsega.

The house belongs to an advanced period in Modernism and is noteworthy because of its decorative abundance in its facade, and specially in that which refers to the treatment of the doors and windows.

In the most important facade, that of the Diagonal, the stone ornaments stand out as do the central galleries and the doorway flanked by balconies possessing curved and plant forms. The continuity of the main door toward the galleries of the first and second floors is achieved thanks to these forms, which in the shape of trees and stone ivy creep upwards. The gallery in the second floor is finished by an enormous pinacle overmounted in relief in the same wall. The arrangement of the windows also accentuates the sensation of verticality, as they appear to converge in ascendant borders. All the lateral balconies sat on great stone curved corbels have important forged iron handrails. In the end piece there are five staggered openings below which there is a beautiful relief in the form of a garland of flowers which covers all the building. The other part of the facade is finished by a pine kernel covered with green ceramic.

Valeri completed one of the most spectacular works in Barcelona Modernism in the Calle Córsega. Making the most of the corner and its irregularity, he carried out various horizontal curves in the balconies, thus imprinting an undulated, almost liquid, rhythm in all the facade. This is similar to Gaudí's Casa Milà. In the finishing we can see a gigantic tear which falls. The singular persian blinds and the delicateness of the colours of the mosaic with its infinity of motifs and details also contribute to this sensation of malleability, totally opposed to the idea of construction and building.

Casa Comalat
Address: Diagonal 442/Córsega 316
Architect: Salvador Valeri i Pupurull
Date of construction: 1911

Casa Comalat: The upper part of the facade and its end piece.

Barón de Quadras had already encharged Puig i Cadafalch with the rehabilitation of his house in the region of la Selva (a province in Girona). He consequently didn't suffer any unfortunate surprise as had been the case in other buildings encharged by the bourgeoisie to other modernist architects.

The work consisted in the reform of a house. The facade facing the Diagonal was treated as that of a single small palace or mansion whilst that which looked onto Calle Rosselló denotes clearly the flats/floors which exist inside. The work on the facades is very interesting given that it makes the most of the reduced dimensions of the plot of land, by creating elements with a sequential rhythm which are well proportioned.

The work on the Diagonal facade was carried out completely with carved stone. A beautiful gallery of eight openings creates the delicate rhythm to which we refer. The arches are loaded with stone ornamentation which have floral motifs and paired sculptures. The gallery is finished by the balustrade of the upper floor, also containing stone ornamentation with floral motifs and which also has light pinacles which finish the inflection points of the columns. Four beautiful balconies with gothic inspired arches occupy the terrace this floor. On the upper floor we find a new gallery, this time with seven windows. It is finished with a sharply inclined roof with attics which remind us of the architecture of the Europes' mountainous areas. The roof is covered in glazed glass. Its vertical and dark appearance contrast strongly with the gallery of the first floor and contribute in giving weight and gravity to the whole building. This palace is a good example of the interrations of Neomedieval and Modernist architecture which, whilst often producing succesful results, also occasionally led to less fortunate ones.

The entrance door shows an imortant example of iron forging and glass work:

Palacio del Barón de Quadras
Address: Diagonal 373/ Rosselló 279
Architect: Josep Puig i Cadafalch
Date of construction: 1906
Remarks: The headquarters of the Museum of Music

it is well worth the time to ponder on this. The facade looking onto Calle Rosselló is more modest and it is adorned with floral grafito decorations. The door made of iron and glasswork is also interesting.

Casa Terrades "La Casa de les Punxes"
Address: Diagonal 416 - 420
Architect: Josep Puig i Cadafalch
Date of construction: 1905

The building was entrusted to Puig i Cadafalch by Mrs. Ànglesa Brutau, Terrades_ widow, who wanted to build three independent houses with their separate doorways and porters_ rooms, for their three daughters Àngela, Josefa and Rosa. Making the most of a rather irregular shaped plot, the three houses formed one single exterior and have a majestic and harmonic appearance, similar to that of a castle. The small towers wich crown the roof and the numerous iron lance adornments have gained the building its nickname of "La Casa de les Punxes", The house of Spikes.

As usual many craftsmen of prestige worked on the project: Alfons Juyol the stonemason, Manuel Ballarín was in charge of the iron work, and Masriera Campins did the metal work on the doors.

One of the highlights of the building is the use of natural brick wich has been combined excellently with Calafell stone and ceramic. The buildings forms remind us of medieval Central European architecture due to its verticality. The ornamental elements are gothic and the galleries are overlaid and the towers stylised. One of the most striking aspects are the lateral galleries of the façade overlooking the Diagonal, wich form triangles and seats on an upside down pyramidal plinth. In the centre of the façades there are some beautiful ceramic designs. One of them is a sun dial with the engraved inscription "Nunquam te crastina fallet hora" (let time not fail yor tomorrow). One of the others represents the patron saint of Catalonia with a spade, in the position of fighting the fierce dragon under the orange tree. In the base of this we can read the sentence written in Catalan "Oh patron saint of Catalonia, return our freedom to us". This inscription upset the non Catalan nationalists of the day who wanted to remove this phrase. Lerroux went as far as to publish an article in El Progreso on the 10 December 1907 in wich he accused Puig i Cadafalch of committing a crime against the nation. Finally this plaque was not removed as it was in the finish of the building and the inscrption was illegible for anyone who passed by in the street.

Casa Romà Macaya i Gilbert
Address: Paseo de Sant Joan 108
Architect: Josep Puig i Cadafalch
Date of Construction: 1902
Remarks: In the present day it is the Cultural Centre of the Caixa Foundation.

Puig i Cadafalch received the assignment of constructing the Casa de Romà Macaya in 1901. The plans were finished the same year and the house in the following one. Although the Casa Macaya was a building made up of flats, Puig i Cadafalch used the mansion-house style for the facade which had produced great results in other houses. As a consequence, the external appearance was that of just one building and could easily evoke the idea of a "casa pairal", a house-mansion, castle or palace which maintained each familiar lineage through the years. This justifies the rural appearance of the house with its windows in "donkey's back form" but given a monumental appearance by the grafito decorations, the ceramics and the iron grilles. As in other cases, Puig i Cadafalch surrounded himself with excellent collaborators and craftsmen in order to carry out the job. The sculptor Eusebi Arnau worked on all the capitals and all of the window and balcony decoration of the first floor flat. On the left capital of the main entrance Arnau sculpted a person on a bicycle, as an affectionate allusion to the director and architect of the work. Arnau, who at that time was also directing the construction of the Casa Amatller, travelled daily, and often more than once, from one building site to the other by bicycle. Arnau worked with Alfons Juyol who was in charge of the stone ornamentation. The ceramic works were entrusted to the expert craftsman Pujol i Bausis, the grafito decoration to Manuel Ballarín y Esteve Andorrà.

The house was well received by both the experts and the public and gained a special mention as one of the best houses built in 1902.

One of the secrets of the beauty of the Casa Macaya is the restraint in the use of the ornamental elements which are limited to the doors and windows and which combine perfectly with the white and gold splendor of the grafito decoration. The glazed pottery in the hall is a colourful element of contrast which contributes in giving light and happiness to the whole. Puig i Cadafalch was very keen on using the skill of the decorating craftsmen, and of playing with the more Mediterranean colour and lighting effects in the ceramics, glassworks and paintings, without ever overusing them.

*Casa Romà Macaya i Gibert:
A balcony.*

The construction of the Hospital de la Santa Creu i de Sant Pau began in 1902 thanks to a donation by the banker Pau Gil i Serra. In 1911 the money ran out when the hospital was not yet finished, in fact three quarters left to be completed. The directors of the hospital managed to get the rights on the invested money in exchange for a commitment to finish the whole building as had been planned.
Lluís Domènech designed various pavillions with brick cupolas, which were profusely adorned with carved stone and ceramic. On his death Pere his son took over the work, and in spite of respecting many of his father's plans he introduced many innovations. The convent, the chemists, the kitchens and above all the conralescing house are a testimony to his eclectic taste and his taste for rich ornamentation.
Lluís Domènech carried out a genuine master work with the hospital. The concave entrance is organised above a great staircase, uniting two faces of the building in a large thin central tower, it finishes with a clock and a pin-

**Hospital de la Santa Creu i de Sant Pau
Address: Avenida P. Claret 167-171
Architect: Lluís Domènech i Montaner, Pere Domènech i Roura
Date of construction: 1902**

nacle as though it were an arrow pointing to the sky all the facade is richly adorned with stone and ceramic sculptures, which combine naturalist and plant resources with elements from the gothic vocabulary. It is worth mentioning the masterly control of the natural colours of the materials used and the lighting effects in these. On no more than entering in the hall we are impressed by the decoration in the vaults in which the stone , brick and mosaic alternate with a particular richness. The name of the benefactor is written into the vault and dated 1910. The initials of Par Gil can be seen in the mosaics outside the pavilions, above the windows. We also can see the names in mosaic of famous and prestigious men from the world of science and medicine.

All of the hospital is designed on the base of not very large pavilions which are situated in the garden. There are some extraordinary ceramic ornaments, some mosaics and beautiful stone sculptures finishing the columns of the pavillions let us neither forget the great round cupolas with enormous windows, the games of shadow and light in the lighting of the basement. We should also remember the small and capricious towers and above all an extensive game with brick, a genuine lesson of making the most of such a simple and humble material, which, as we see, has so many possibilities.

The pavilions which were planned for service are independent but they are connected by underground passages. This intelligent distribution allowed hospital services to be shared but leaving each pavilion autonomous, something very useful from a therapeutic point of view, as well as from a hygienic and human one it also was a great solution to give the maximum light and ventilation giving the hospital a happy and healthy air. This was so much so that the underground passages were functioning until recently and in spite of the radical changes in contemporary medicine and of having housed the Faculty of Medicine de la Universidad Autónoma de Barcelona since the seventies. However the interior reforms of the thirties and sixties were totally inconsiderate toward the decoration and destroyed it to a large extent some of these disasters were reduced with the restoration which took place in 1980 in which the recovery of a national heritage was combined with the demands of a modern hospital, in fact it is one of the largest and most important in the city of Barcelona.

Hospital de la Santa Creu i de Sant Pau: Ceramics, sculpture and a brick wall.

Estación de Vallvidrera
Address: Calle Queralt 20
Architect: Bonaventura Conill and Arnau Calvet
Date of construction: 1905

The people in Barcelona have moved toward Tibidabo since the XIX century, with the opening of the road to Arrabasada in 1868. In 1900, Doctor Andreu, who was famous for his cough tablets, founded the Sociedad Anónima Tibidabo which took on the responsibility for the construction of the "Tramvia Blau" and of the Vallvidrera funicular. A little later, in 1902, the church of the Sacred Heart was also founded. This was a work by Enric Sagnier and built at the highest point of the mountain and in 1904 the Marquis of Alella donated the magnificent Fabra Astronomic Observatory which was the work of Josep Domènech i Estapa, located half way towards the funicular. The following year the Mentora Alsina cabinet of physical sciences was inaugurated, thus completing a complex that in 1900 would become an agreeable summer location, a place of recreation for the citizens of Barcelona.

The station of Vallvidrera, neighbour to Tibidabo, was built in this epoch and within the most sober but advanced modernist style. It is a small white cube adorned with towers which emerge from a sinuous stone base in which the entrance door opens like a giant palm leaf. The window and the arch of the passage reproduce this capricious arch in the form of a parabola which belongs to the Vienese Jungendstil. In effect, the whole evokes some examples of Vienese architecture of the epoch, especially those outskirts stations planned by Otto Wagner. The lines of the windows and doors are reinforced by vertical and horizontal adornments in the finishing of the facade and towers. In the starting point of these there is a simple detail of green and yellow ceramic tiles. Delicate and austere iron work in the railings and the towers finishes a rather beautiful and harmonious building which gives us the most European image of Catalan Modernism.

The building called "La Rotonda" at the beginning of Avenida Tibidabo, which is next to the station of the typical "Tramvia Blau" is currently on a rather bad condition. This is a pity, given that we are talking about a really beautiful building and one that was highly representative of the recreational and residential Tibidabo and the Collserola mountain. The most note worthy aspect of the building is that which gives it its name, the upper rotund or roundhouse in ceramic and mosaic. Eight thin columns covered with mosaic designs and which have an elegant ring in the centre and in the capitals, support the ceiling of the roundhouse. Each column is finished by a thin pinnacle supported by a stylised green ceramic gargoyle. The pinnacles surround the central column which is much taller.

There are many interesting mosaics in the building which reflect the sports that were practised around 1900. Unfortunately these mosaics have been lost.

It is rather agreeable to catch the "Tramvia Blau" at this point which goes up Avenida Tibidabo until it comes to the funicular station square. If you walk up the avenue then you can contemplate the beautiful houses built at that time.

The funicular which goes to the top of Tibidabo is a moving viewpoint. It has an intermediate station at the Observatorio Fabra (Josep Domènech i Estapà, 1904) and the Mentora Alsina cabinet.

The expiatory temple of the Sagrado Corazon (Sacred Heart) is a neogothic work by Enric Sagnier and his son. The fairground attraction park conserves some of the attractions from 1900, such as the puppets in the Museo de Autómatas. Some of these small elements allow us to get an approximate idea of the milieu in Barcelona at the time of the modernist explosion around 1900.

La Rotonda, El Tramvia Blau (Blue Tramway) and Tibidabo

La Rotonda
Address: Paseo de Sant Gervasi 51
Architect: Adolf Ruiz i Casamitjana
Date of construction: 1906

The Catalan bourgeoisie which sponsored Modernism, and made its expansion across Barcelona possible, requested not only the building of houses but also shops, factories and workshops. It is arguably in these buildings where they practised their new materials more daringly as well as new building procedures which could satisfy the needs of industry. These were large spaces with few subdivisions, which had the possibility of opening large windows so as to work longer with sun light, thus saving electricity. There was easy access for loading and unloading and the construction prices were reasonable for the large factories.

The Casaramona factory is nowadays completely surrounded by the city, so that we have the opportunity of seeing the outside of a large factory without having to go far out of the city, it is five minutes from Plaza España. It is a later work by Puig i Cadafalch, built on a plot of the Cerdà plan. It fits in to this plan as it has large work spaces divided by chamfers. These spaces are roofed with brick and supported by light iron columns. The large windows allow the maximum quantity of light to enter. These windows are lined in rows of one or two depending on the facade, and are flanked by pillars which are finished by pinnacles. These give a vertical rhythm to the building which contrasts with its extensive length. Two high towers give the building the air of a medieval fortress or even that of a late gothic Italian convent. The building stands out for its elegance and shows that Puig i Cadafalch is a maestro when dealing with ornamental richness and the profusion of decorative elements which characterise many of his houses.

Fábrica Casaramona
Address: Calle Mèxic 36-44
Architect: Josep Puig i CadaFalch
Date of construction: 1911

Although the large waterfall in Parque Ciutadella is not a prototype of modernist constructions, it is interesting as a precedent of what must have been the Catalan version of this movement, and because the young Gaudí collaborated in it. This was another construction requested for the Universal Exhibition of 1888, and one finished ahead of time in 1875. Josep Fontseré conceived one part of it as a romantic English garden with winding paths. In order to get to the fountain square you may walk along the first of these paths which continues by a terrace where Vilaseca built a monument in honour of Aribau, the poet who began the romantic epoch and the renaissance of Catalan literature. The path leads to the square where the waterfall can be seen in all its splendour. Fontseré planned it as one of the jewels of the park. The stone chipping,

Gran Cascada de la Ciutadella
Address: Parque de la Ciutadella
Architect: Josep Fontseré i Mestres, Antoni Gaudí i Cornet
Date of construction: 1875
Remarks: some parts can be visited

the iron bars and some of the decorative motifs are attributed to the young Gaudí, then an Architecture student. We may also suppose that he collaborated in the plans for water supply coming from Calle Wellington.

At the time Fontseré was accused of having copied his waterfall from Neobarroque forms which Esperandieu designed for Marseilles. Today he has regained his well earned prestige, which has increased due to Gaudí's participation.

From an imposing triumphant central arch two stairways descend toward a semi circular lake which dominates the whole. Apart from the severity of the arch we can appreciate the fantasy of Venanci Vallmitjana's sculptures, the winged dragons, with a chariot as the finishing touch, the mythological figures and the aforementioned stone chipping with plant designs, as well as sinuous stone lines and irregular ornamentation. The view from the square is perfect in order to appreciate the sculptured details and the ornamentation which is a precedent of a modernism which is full of life and fantasy.

Casa Vicens "Casa de les Carolines"
Address: Calle de les Carolines 18-24
Architect: Antoni Gaudí
Date of construction: 1888

The house of Manuel Vicens i Montaner, which was planned in 1878, was finished ten years later. The work was originally Fontseré's but Gaudí took charge of it. He was only 26 and had just finished his studies. Vicens was a brick and ceramic maker and the house was intended to be a summer residence. The plot lay to the north of Gràcia (next to the present day Plaza Lesseps). It was not very large given that it had a spacious garden. In order to make the most of the plot, Gaudí placed the house in one corner so as to leave the rest for the garden, this was later sacrificed when the house was enlarged. The traditional elements used are very eclectic: we can see medieval references next to Islamic and Arabian ones. The most characteristic element of the house is the white and green ceramic work which is found throughout the house, the little towers, the balconies and the end pieces. The materials evidently come from the owners own factory and so appear to be a catalogue of his production.

The ornamental richness is quantitative given that the variety of motifs is small. Here lies the real secret of the beauty of the house and the key to its originality. The way the light falls on the brilliant ceramic colours creates the impression that the house is much bigger than it really is, and gives it an unreal air, one of a fantasy palace. As is typical in this architect, the interior of the house is richly decorated with designs which were specially thought out for this house. The craftsmanship of the dining room, with its branches of cherries is quite out of the ordinary. The main room with its embroidery on the walls and ceiling appears to be a part of an oriental palace.

In 1925 the architect Serra Martínez carried out an extension to the house which respected Gaudí's style.

Casa Vicens, "Casa de les Carolines": Wrought iron work, ceramics, and brickwork.

Gaudí began the plans for the Palacio Güell in 1885 on the request of Eusebi Güell i Bacigalupi. The plot (18 x 22 metres in the Nou de la Rambla, a perpendicular street to the Ramblas) was not the ideal location and created problems which the architect resolved the best he could. The street is too narrow to appreciate the beauty of the facade, but fortunately the present use of the house gives us the chance to visit it and see the inside.

Eusebi Güell, a man of humble origins, had made his fortune in America and gained an aristocratic title. As an entrepreneur, innovator and progressive thinker he sympathised with Gaudí and became his first client. Later he would become his maecenas and friend.

Gaudí drew more than twenty designs for the main facade. Finally the client chose balanced symmetrical and serene solution which had a Venetian air.

From the main door we go down to the stables, a basement with vaults supported by short thick columns with enormous capitals in the form of cone trunks and inverted tetrahedrons. The snail stairs for the horses and the pedestrians seem unreal. The way the light falls changes what is a humble

Palacio Güell
Address: Calle Nou de la Rambla 3
Architect: Antoni Gaudí i Cornet
Date of construction: 1890
Remarks: it can be visited

Palacio Güell:
A detail of the interior patio.

Palacio Güell: Pinnacles and tower.

space into something that seems to come from "A Thousand and One Arabian Nights".

The beautiful parabolic arches on the ground floor catch our attention, these were one of the specialities which made Gaudí a genius in architecture. Between these two arches we find the Catalan four bar crest forged in iron and full of fantasy, it seems more like a jewel than an architectural element. The rest of the facade is much less daring. The symmetry of the facade hides the extreme complexity of the arrangement of space inside. The ground floor houses the entrance hall and offers access to the lounge on the first floor. The quantity of arches, windows, columns, passages, bedrooms as well as the great height of the ceiling, reduce the liveable area of the house. The craftsmanship on the ceiling is extraordinarily rich, combining medieval elements with other Islamic ones. The wrought iron work is superb, outstanding in some parts of the house and the carpentry, with its logical adaptations to the work also is quite excellent. In various places the walls are covered with ceramics, an element which Gaudí always used, combining it with light and showing a masterly use of colour and reflection. In this sense, it is important to point out the intelligence of the architect in the way that he made the most of the little light that there was especially in the facade. The windows are so skilfully arranged that one wouldn't think one was in such a narrow street. In general the whole building breaths an enigmatic combination of free historicism and personal fantasy, using past resources and the architect's compositions which are freely carried out.

The lounge is crowned by a copula with a conical tower on top which is only visible from outside. Small openings in this allow light to pass through creating the effect of a celestial vault or evoking the beautiful reflections of light on the Mediterranean wells, and these have metal covers and also small openings.

Eighteen distinct pinnacles covered with colourful mosaics accompany the tower on the roof, as chimney ornamentation's and ventilation shafts. These are a precedent of the famous sculpted chimneys on the roof of Casa Milà.

The back facade is very simple, it gains its effect from the carved stone and has some galleries with oriental inspired wood decorations as its only form of ornamentation.

Casa Andreu Calvet i Pintó
Address: Casp 48
Architect: Antoni Gaudí i Cornet
Date of construction: 1900

The house was planned two years before and won the prize in the first held Barcelona council architecture awards.

It was the house that Gaudí constructed in the Eixample in Barcelona, and it was made using stone from Monjuic, a mountain in Barcelona. The facade is one of the most austere by our imaginative maestro, and due to the material and size it reminds vaguely us of one of the Tuscany palaces of the XIV century which were so appreciated at that moment.

The central hall is quite original with its different stone columns, exotic capitals and and central "remate". In the plinth there appears a cypress, a traditional Catalan symbol of hospitality. The ram of olives signifies peace, the initial C is for Calvet and the shield for Catalonia. The iron forging is extraordinary in the form of wild mushrooms. Calvet was a botany fan, a pastime shared with Gaudí who was alsways fascinated by wild mushrooms and popular mythology. The mushrooms combine with beautiful stone flowers.

In the entrance door two of the columns in the form of textile bobins remind us of the owners' industry.

Lluís Badia carried out the forging and Casas i Bardé the carpentry.

The symmetry of the facade arises due to the organization of the windows and balconies, as well as from the arches of the ground floor. The iron handrails are shaped elegantly above the Tuscany stone.

The detail of the little balconies which support the pulleys above the last floor is charming. We should remember that these pulleys were used to bring in furniture from the balconies given that it was very tiring and at times impossible to do so using the stairs.

Two semi circular pediments finish the facade, crowned by busts which represent Saint Peter (in honour of the proprietors' father) and secondly Saint Ginés, the notary and comic, citizen of Vilassar, the village where the proprietor was born.

Casa Calvet is the most conventional of Gaudí's works, but it has the charm of being an austere and elegant work.

Casa Andreu Calvet i Pintó: Upper pediment and balconies.

In 1875 the architect Emili Sala i Cortes completed this house whose reforms were entrusted to Gaudí in 1904. The requested reform essentially referred to the facade, the caretakers' room, the stairs, and the first and second floors.

The architects Josep Maria Jujol and Joan Rubio i Belver collaborated in the completion of this reform. The glassworks were carried out in the Pelegrí workshops, the iron works in the Badia brothers workshop. The carpentry was done by Casas i Bardés and the ceramics which cover all of the facade (an unusual work) by the Fills de J. Pujol i Bausis and Sebastià Ribó workshop.

Some people think that Casa Batlló is the prettiest house in Barcelona. Its facade is quite unbeatable, an explosion of colour and fantasy which is conserved with all its elegance.

What did Gaudí want to suggest by giving these strange forms to the Casa Batlló? This is a mystery.

Some experts beginning with the particular roof end piece believe that it was inspired by the hat of a carnaval harlequin. The balconies would be the "antifaces" and the rain of colours falling all across the facade could evoke tradi-

Casa Josep Batlló i Casanovas
Address: Paseo de Gràcia 43
Architect: Antoni Gaudí i Cornet
Date of construction: 1906

Casa Josep Batlló i Casanovas: A detail of the facade.

tional confetti. There are those who oppose this interpretation pointing to Gaudí's religiosity, but it is certain that in the history of the Church, Carnaval and Lent have been inseparable companions, and many artists, of a religious background who have worked for the Church, have represented and evoked as much the spiritual aesthetic as the colourist and at times even the grotesque party in hell in their works.Gaudí used many fantasy elements in the Sagrada Familia, in Parque Güell, and in the crypt in the Colonia Güell...so why shouldn't he have done so in this case?

Other experts have wished to see the back of a dragon or lizard in the winding end piece (remember the lizard in the fountain in Parque Güell). The tower in this case would represent Sant George's lance,(Sant Jordi/Saint George is the patron saint of Barcelona), in its fight against the dragon trying to free the princess. The lance which is driven into the dragon enters in the red stained wound on the right. The roof and the facade would thus be covered by the colourful scales of this ferocious and gigantic animal. The balconies would represent the bones of monster's previous unfortunate victims.Thus we could see skulls in the upper balcony and in the first flats, tibias and fibulas used as columns and lateral ornamentation. This second

interpretation is the most popular among Barcelona's citizens, some of whom call the Casa Batlló, the "house of bones".
The house suffered some damage during the civil war: the paintwork in the balcony, ceramic damage, and accumulation of dirt. The restoration carried out in 1984 returned the original splendor to the house.

La Pedrera is the most emblematic modernist house in Barcelona, although it hasn't always been appreciated with the same enthusiasm as at present.
The house encharged by Pere Milà soon received its nickname of La Pedrera, as the people saw a type of evocation to a stone quarry in it. It was constructed above Ferrer Vidal's knocked down chalet and the plans included a basement, a lower ground floor a ground floor, five further floors and two attics. The building was in danger once completed as it was reported as taking up more space than the municipal ordenances allowed. Fortunately the beauty of the whole, though not seen by everyone, saved the exceptional construction. The following intervened in the decoration of La Pedrera: the architect Josep Maria Jujol, Badia the blacksmiths, the Manyach foundation, the plasterer Joan Beltran and the builder Josep Bayó.
Gaudí conceived this building as a great sculpture trying to avoid all the divi-

Casa Pere Milà i Camps (la Pedrera/the Quarry)
Address: Paseo de Gràcia 92
Date of construction: 1910
Remarks: The seat of the Fundació Caixa de Catalunya

Above: Casa Pere Milà i Camps (La Pedrera):
Terraces and interior patio.

Below: Casa Pere Milà i Camps (La Pedrera):
Balconies.

sions between the floors and vertical lines. Consequently long horizontal curves run all along the house, marking the corner which separates the two sides of the facade, that of Passeig de Gràcia and that of Provença. La Pedrera doesn't have one straight line or angle, not even on the inside. This obliged him to change the form of the rooms and design special furniture for the house, given that traditional orthogonal furniture would have fitted really badly. As a result, the interior sems more like an exterior and one would say that nature had invaded the rooms, given that the walls and the roof, supported by columns seem to be trees.

The stone blocks brought from the Garraf quarry are lightly carved in order to give a sensation of naturalness, something which doesn't impede the delicateness of the work. Some writers see reminiscences of the unfinished sculptures of Michelangelo in this treatment of the stone. The building really appears to be a mountain or a stone quarry and the idea also arises of a mountaian that had been transformed into a water current. Gaudí proposed finishing with golden bronze sculpture of the Virgin Mary to the owner, to be carried out by the sculpture Carles Mani. This was rejected by Pere Milà. As a substitute Gaudí sculpted a mystic rose in the facade and the inscription "Ave Gratia Plena Dominus Tecum" with the M for Maria in the centre. The balconies' metalic railings are owed to the architect Jujol, genuine sculptures which border on the abstract. Jujol had stood out for his extraordinary abstract decoration in the facade in Batlló house and was a pioneer in the execution of iron sculptures. This also produced great results later for the sculptures Julio González and Pau Gargallo. The lower ground floor had barred windows which later disappeared on being used as shop windows for the successive businesses which occupied them. Two of these remain however next to the main door. Perhaps the most impressive part of La Pedrera are the chimneys, ventilators and protruding from the flat roof. These have recently been opened to the general public after their restoration and cleaning. There is also the colourful stone garden in which Gaudí used the famous "trencadís", a mosaic of broken ceramic work arranged in irregular forms which had given such good results in Parque Güell and other constructions.

This is adored by some and rejected by others Respected or not depending on the styles and fashions, La Pedrera has always made its presence felt. It is a house which goes beyond the classifications of whichever style and beyond the schools. It is a gigantic work of fantasy which emphasizes the genius of the architect but the boldness of a bourgeoise self made man who had achieved power due to his own effort. This was a class that did not look to the past but rather only desired one thing: to invent their future.

Parque Güell
Address: Entrance via Calle Larrard / Calle d'Olot / Calle Ramiro de Maeztu
Architect: Antoni Gaudí i Cornet
Date of construction. 1914
Remarks: it is possible to visit the Casa Museo Gaudí in the park grounds

Gaudí completed this project for his friend and maecenas Eusebi Güell. Originally it should have been an important city garden of 60 plots, a com-

Parque Güell:
Hall of a hundred columns.

mon square and various lines of communication. However the plan was not well received, the plots didn't sell and only two houses were built so Güell chose to build the park instead. It passed to the council in 1922.

It couldn't be better located, lying at the foot of the Carmel, a mountain which along with those of Creueta and La Montanya Pelada, separate the old town neighbourhoods of Gràcia and Horta. The lower entrance opens to a stone wall flanked by two pavilions whose polychrome mosaic ceiling is highly attractive. These were designed by Gaudí to portray the story of "Hansel and Gretel". On the right is the house of a witch crowned with a poisonous mushroom, and on the left the house is crowned by a cross. Many of the parks mosaics are made in a traditional way using fragmented irregular shaped pieces of ceramic, some of which were recycled and others especially made for the occasion. The fragments are broken randomly, and from there comes their name in Spanish which translates to "fragmentary". On crossing the threshold we are greeted by a large lizard in a fountain.

Some stairs between two mosaic decorated walls lead us to the hall of a hundred columns, one of Gaudí's most famous works, and not without reason.

Parque Güell:
The ceramics at the entrance.

Eighty-six Doric columns support a mosaic ceiling which is full of undulations. It is splendidly adorned with polychrome rosewindows where we can see all sorts of strange objects: porcelain dolls, crystal glasses, fragments of plates and cups, pieces of glass...The outside columns are bent which brings the halls curves together producing a sensation of controlled instability which increases the magic and the charm of feeling oneself to be in a space which is almost oneiric. The architect Jujol, in charge of the decoration, was able to express himself to the full in this hall.

Surrounding the hall, there are two paths which lead to a circular square, which is no other than the terrace of the area with columns, delimited by a continuous curved line of fragmented mosaic covered benches which use all sorts of colours and drawings. In these Gaudí's fantasy helped by Jujol reached unsuspected limits and heralded, as Alexandre Cirici points out, the imminent arrival of Abstract Art.

In the high part of the square, the containing walls have capricious forms which mix with the natural elements which surround them: stones, trees and insects. We shouldn't ignore a totally bent tree which, with the years, has taken the random example of the architect and appears to have with the express intention of paying homage to the man who in his moment paid tribute to nature. A path winds until the high part of the garden passing various beautiful fountains, of different forms, and offering us from time to time some remarkable views of the city. This was something that Gaudí was always conscious of. The constructions made of large pieces of stone seem like pebbles given the way they were put together and with the years they seem almost natural. At the top there is a place with three crosses, called precisely "the three Crosses". The other slope of the mountain is almost wild, an ideal compliment which contrasts with the maestro's work.

Parque Güell is a place where architecture and nature meet and work together in a way that is infrequent in our western architecture. Gaudí's constructions put the most irrational and primitive part of our sensibility into relief, and accentuates what civilisation still has in common with the earth's elementary forces. It is not strange that in 1984 it was declared part of the world's heritage by UNESCO, along with Casa Milà and Palacio Güell, also works by Gaudí.

The Expiatory Temple of the Sagrada Familia
Address: Plaza de la Sagrada Familia
Architects: Francisco de Paula Villar Lozano, Antoni Gaudí i Cornet
Date of construction: 1882-1883, 1884-1926

The Sagrada Familia (Holy Family) is the most challenging work taken on by Gaudí. Francisco Villar, the architect, began the project in a Neogothic style but shortly after Gaudí received the request to remodel it. This church marked a large part of Gaudí's life and XX century architecture.

The work took over 40 years of slow progression, only interrupted by the First World War. The style reflects the mature phase in Gaudí's work, using a consolidated vocabulary. Flying in the face of orthodoxy Gaudí began the works without any definitive plans and remodelled as he went along. This procedure which is rooted in the medieval way of constructing cathedrals would be used for the last time in the west here in the Sagrada Familia. Today it would be totally unthinkable to build in this way. Conceived as a sculpture, the temple was built day after day following the creativity of the brilliant architect, who made a great number of models and partial models as an alternative to a conventional plan.

The towers of the Sagrada Familia are not inspired in the typical modernist way, but rather remind us of the clay architecture in the North of Africa. The structures which support the temple correspond to Gaudí's research in the application of natural resources to architecture, in areas such as weights, the organisation of large spaces with important openings, the use of light, the relationship of tension and force of the different natural forms, the staggering assembly of organic structures. All of these elements are present in the facade of the Sagrada Familia, which should be looked at not only from the outside but also from the inside of the towers, in order to appreciate the snail stairway and the effect produced by looking at the multiple windows as one goes down the steps, and the tree of life which holds a central place.

When Gaudí died in 1926 only the facade which shows the birth of Christ was finished. The work was continued by the architect's disciples. However, it has been impossible to follow his work faithfully. This is not only because of the personal characteristics of the followers but also because of the lack of plans, and the fact that the day to day work demanded the free creativity of the author, and not all architects have the same brilliance. The works became complicated due technical and budgetary reasons. The economic hardness of the post-war situation paralysed the works, even more so because Rationalism had now replaced Modernism. The over ornamentation had produced a reaction against the modernist movement, and the generalised opinion of the 40's and 50's was highly critical of aesthetic standpoint. In the sixties the continuation of the works was heavily criticised and the cathedral was referred to as "the Cathedral of Kitsch".

The revaluation of the building didn't happen until the end of the sixties. Since then popular donations and institutional grants have helped continue the works, although the architectural and aesthetic problems have still not been resolved.

In 1986, the sculptor Josep Maria Subirachs received a request to carry out some sculptures on the facade of the crucifixion. Subirach's work

The Expiatory Temple of the Sagrada Familia: The ornamental richness.

has been heavily questioned and although he has his supporters he also has felt rejection, not only from those who reject his work but from those who are simply in disagreement with the idea of finishing the temple.

None of this however has been an obstacle for the Sagrada Familia to become the most emblematic building in Barcelona.

The Expiatory Temple of the Sagrada Familia: General view.

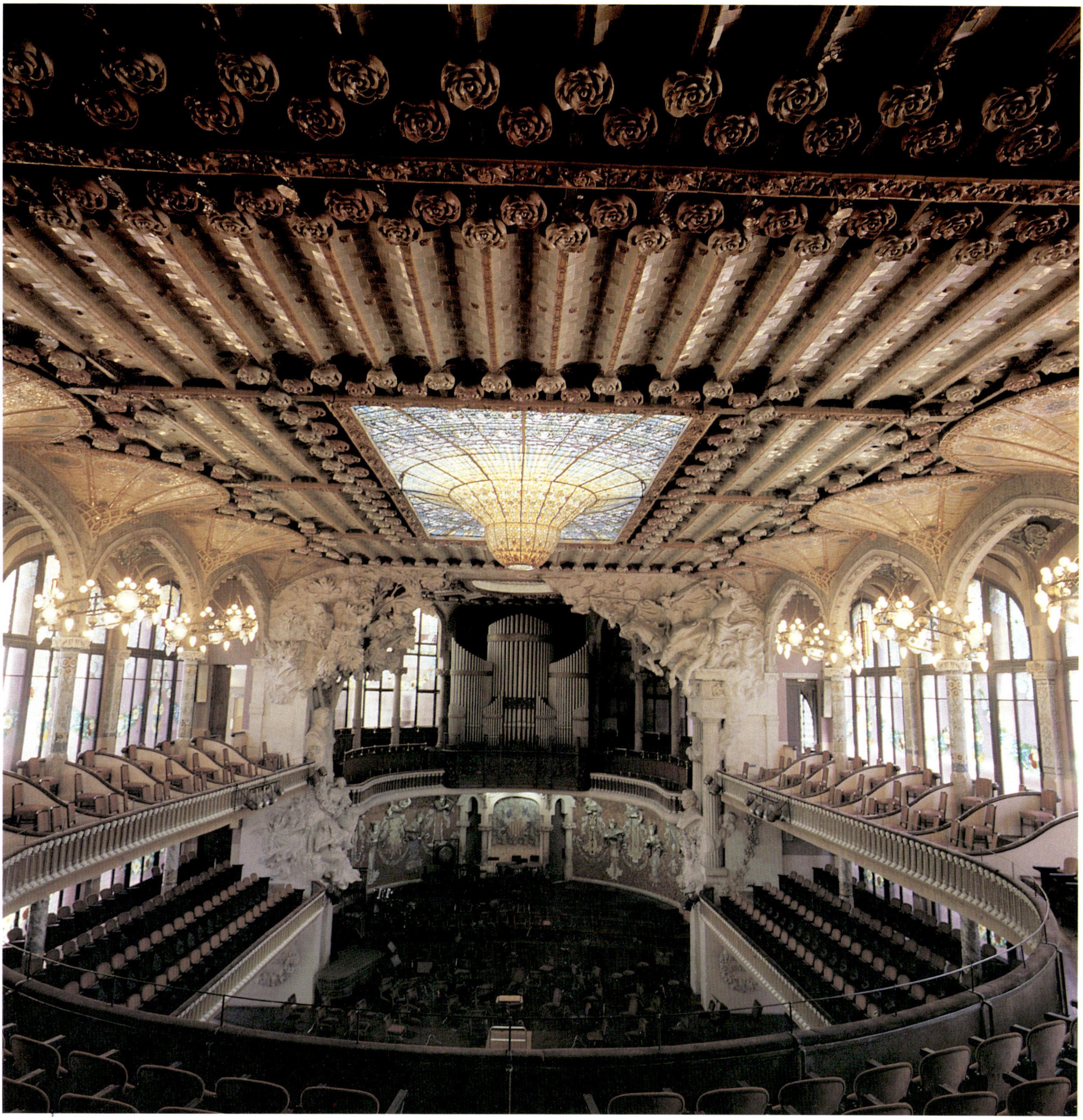

122

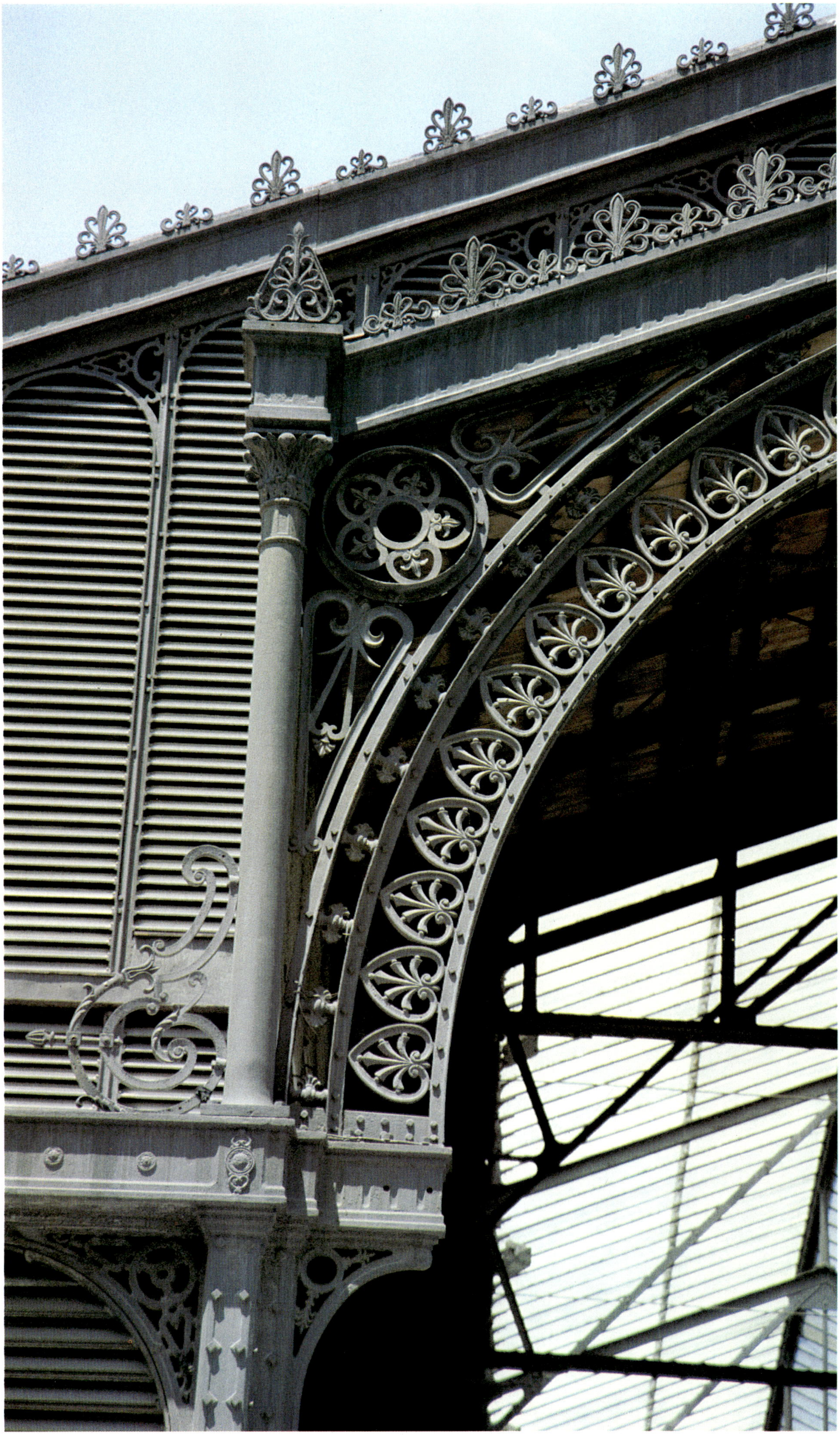

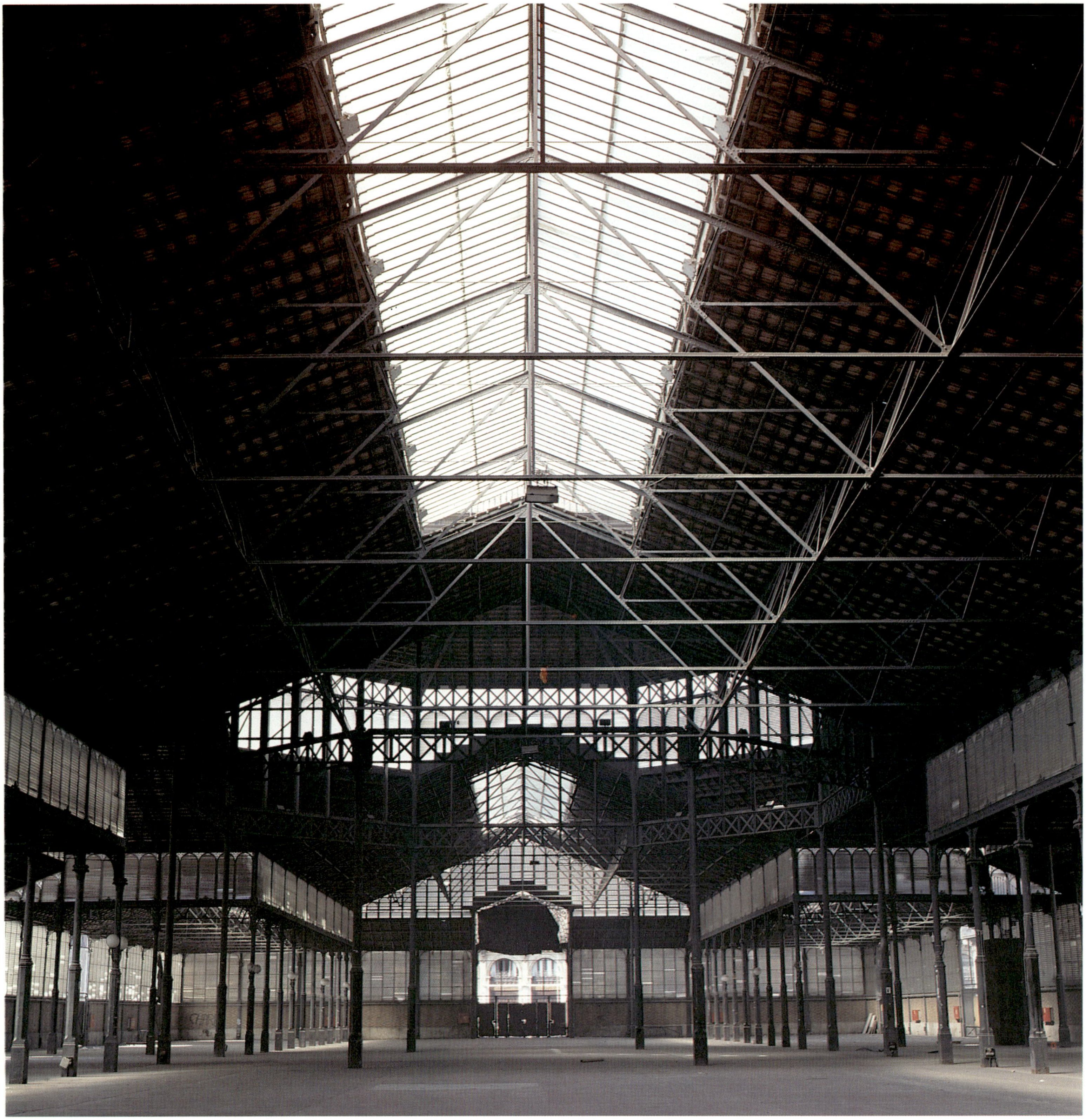

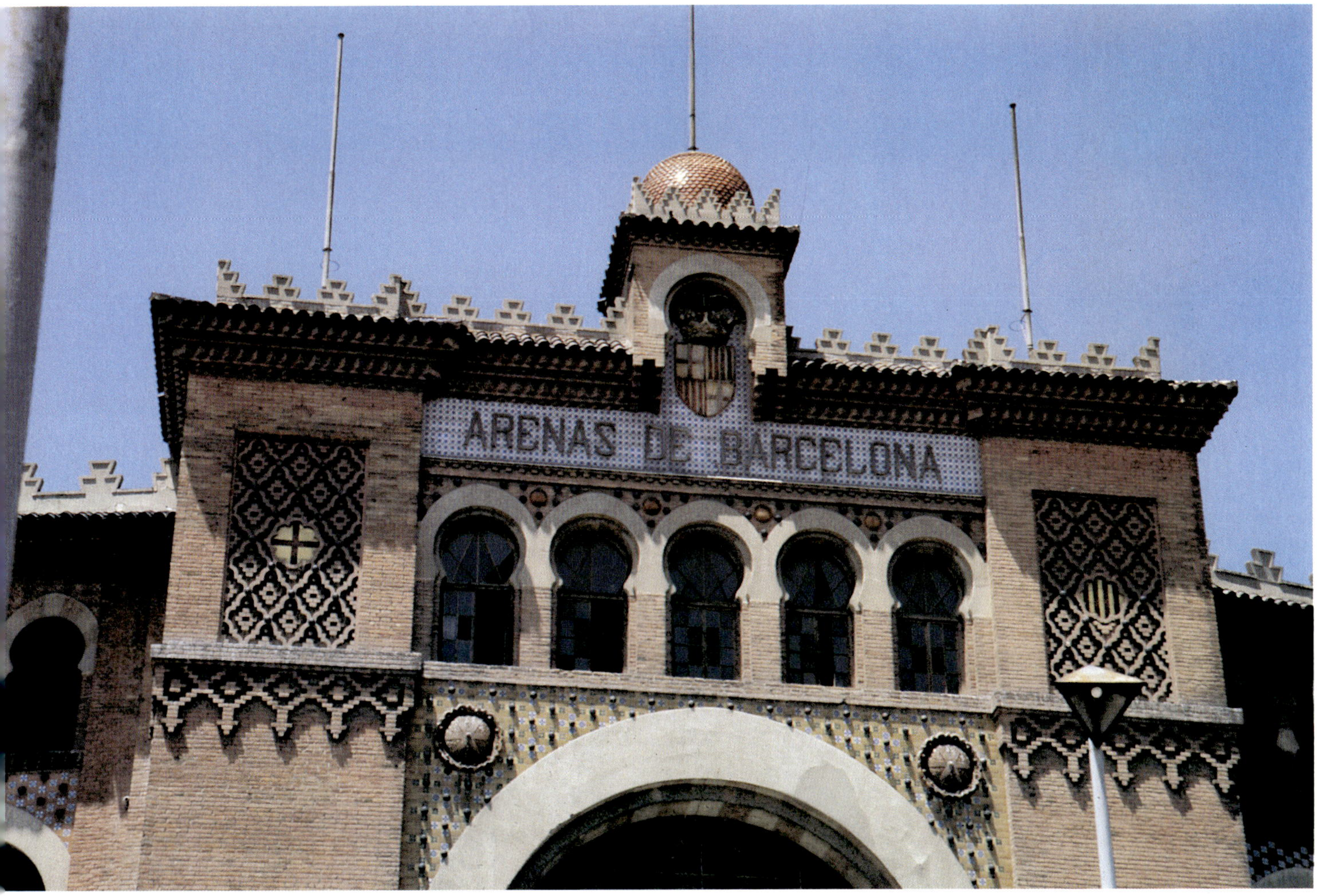
ARENAS DE BARCELONA

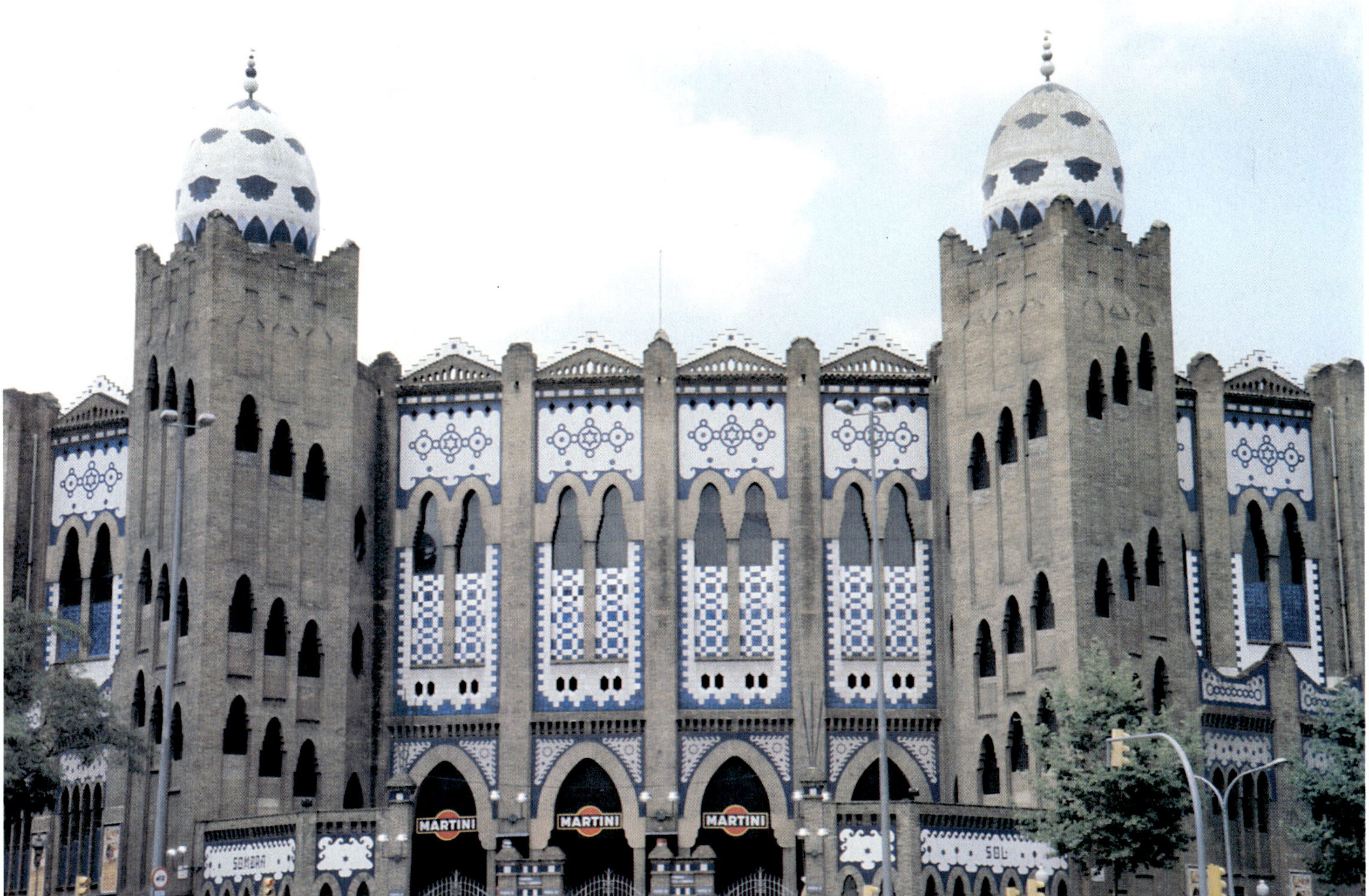
MARTINI
MARTINI
MARTINI
SOMBRA
SOL

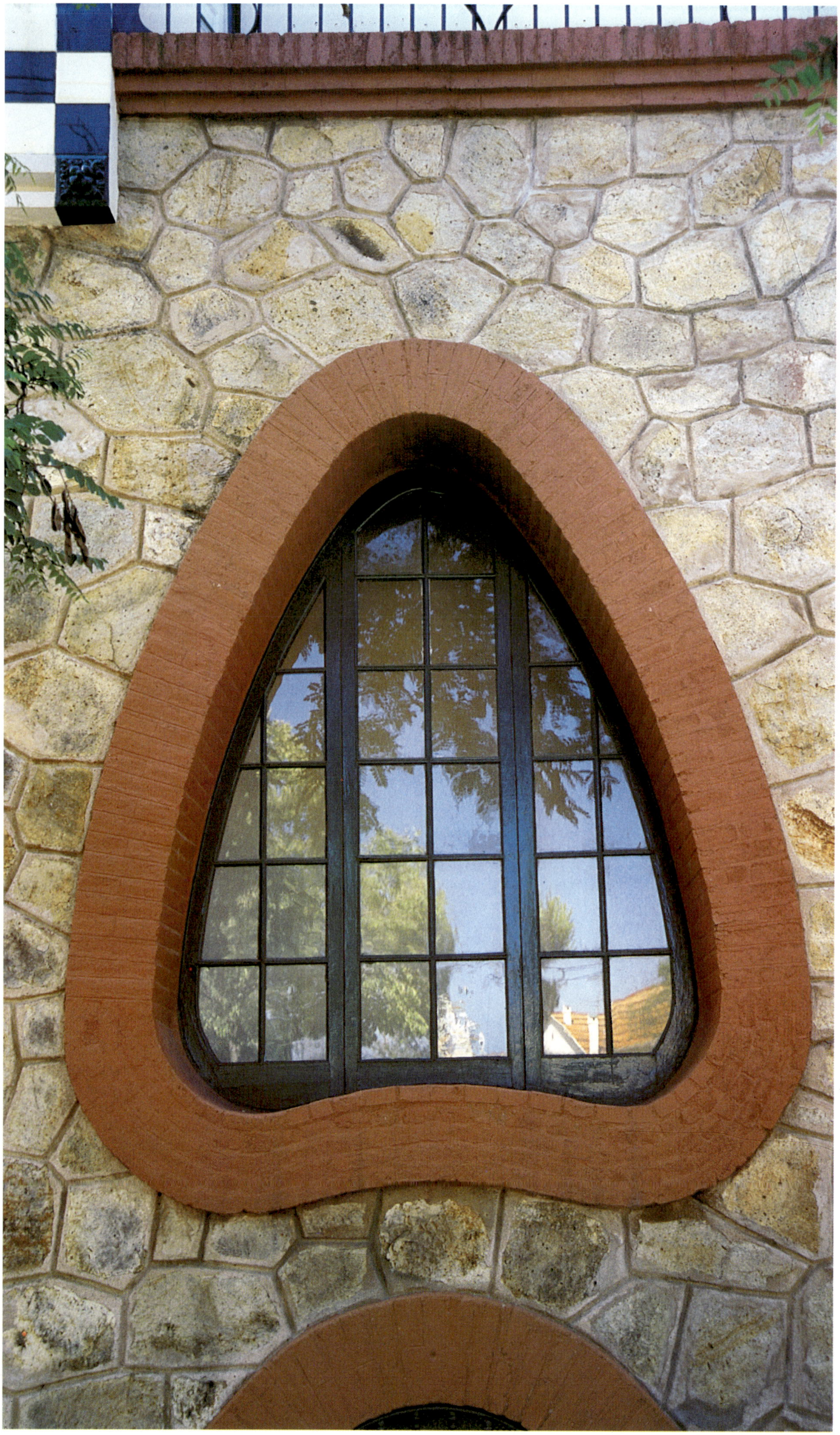

127

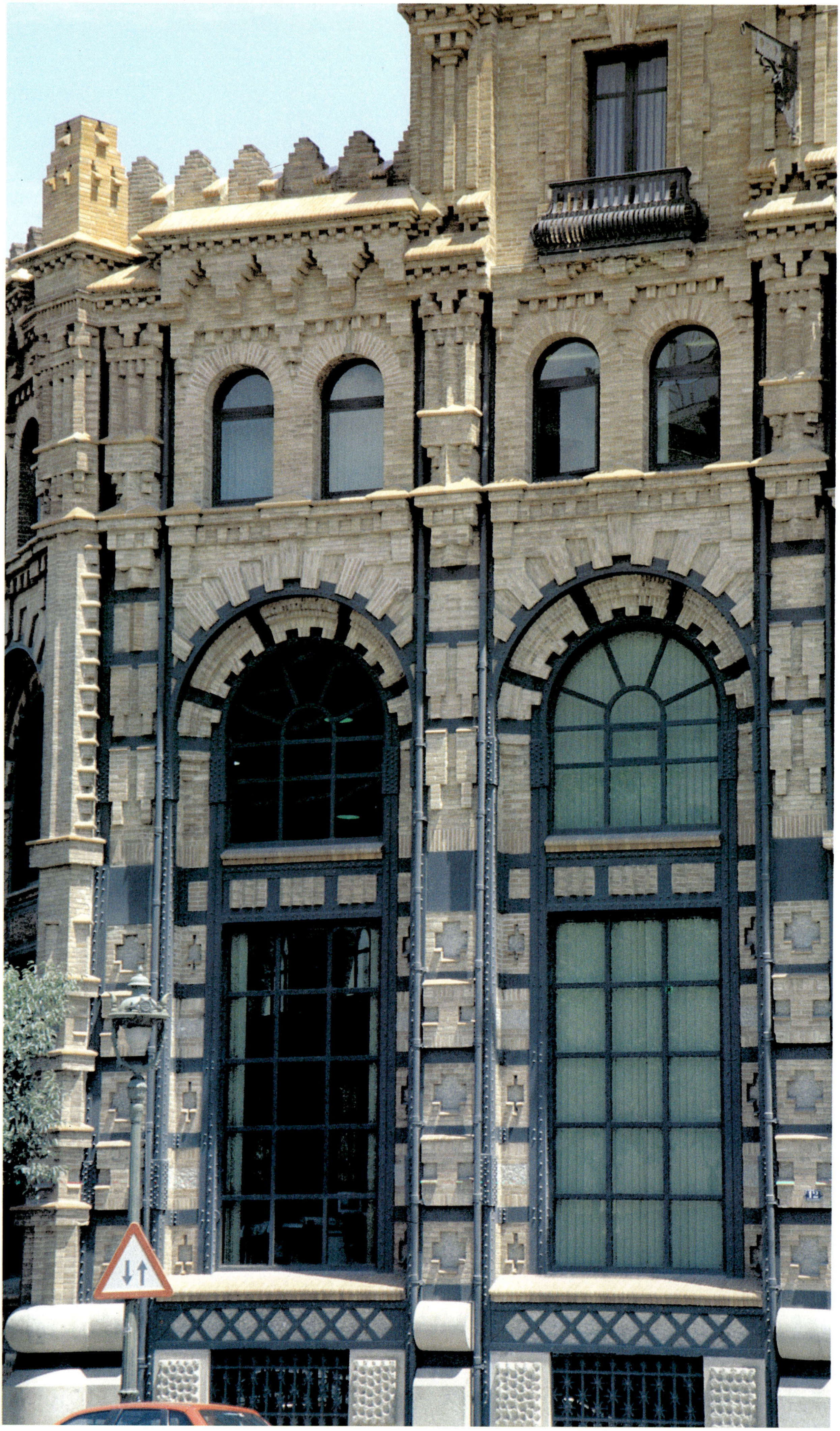

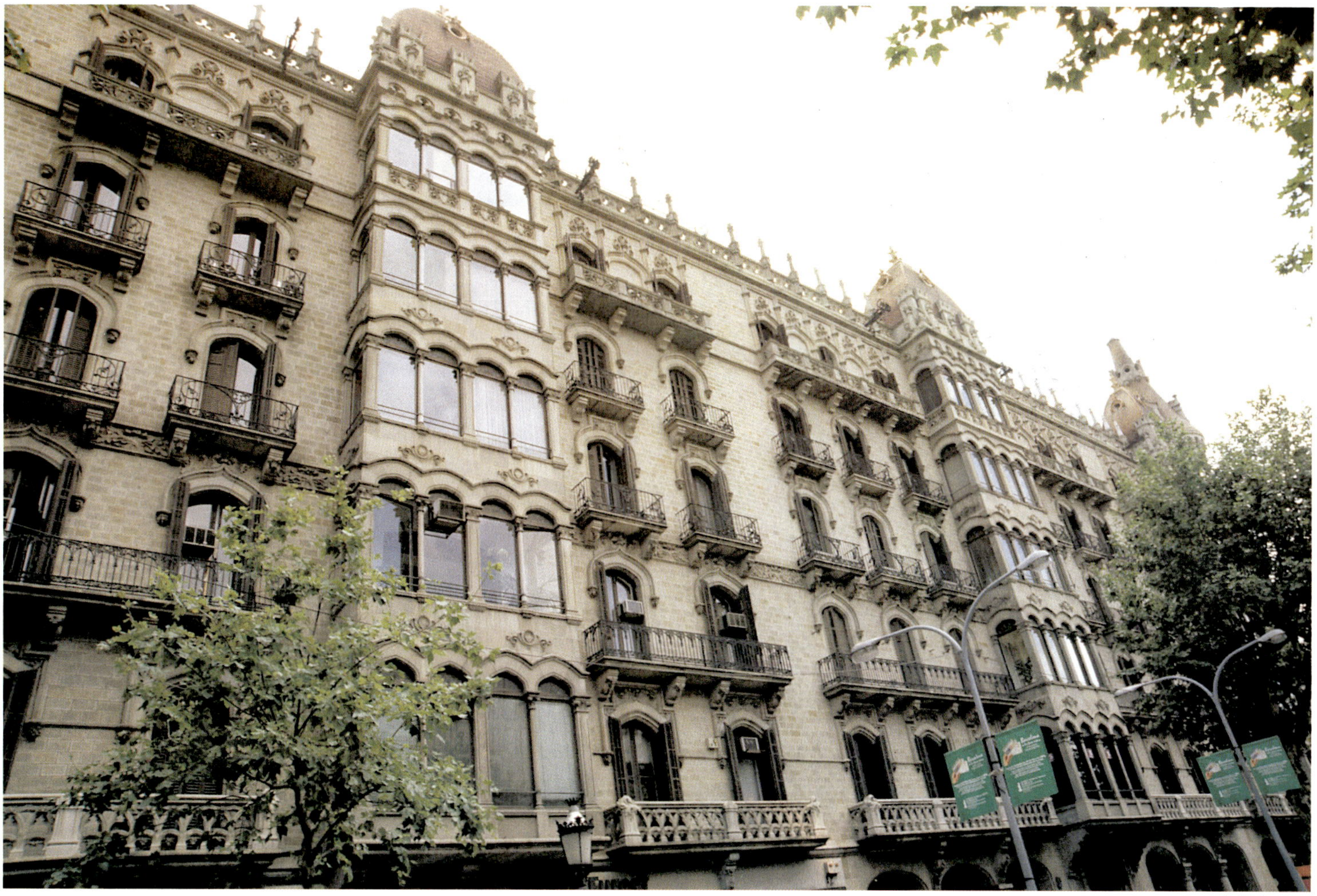

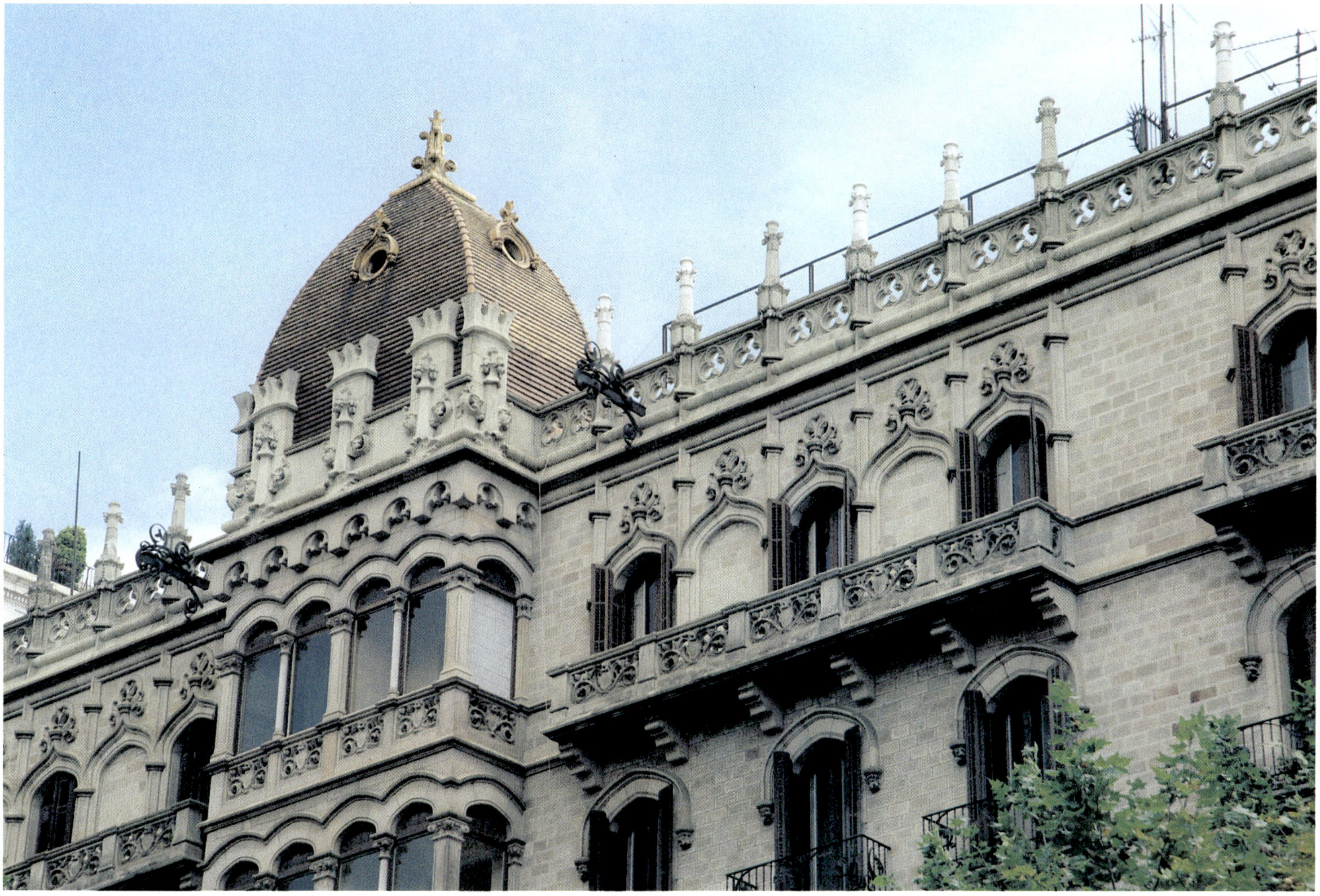

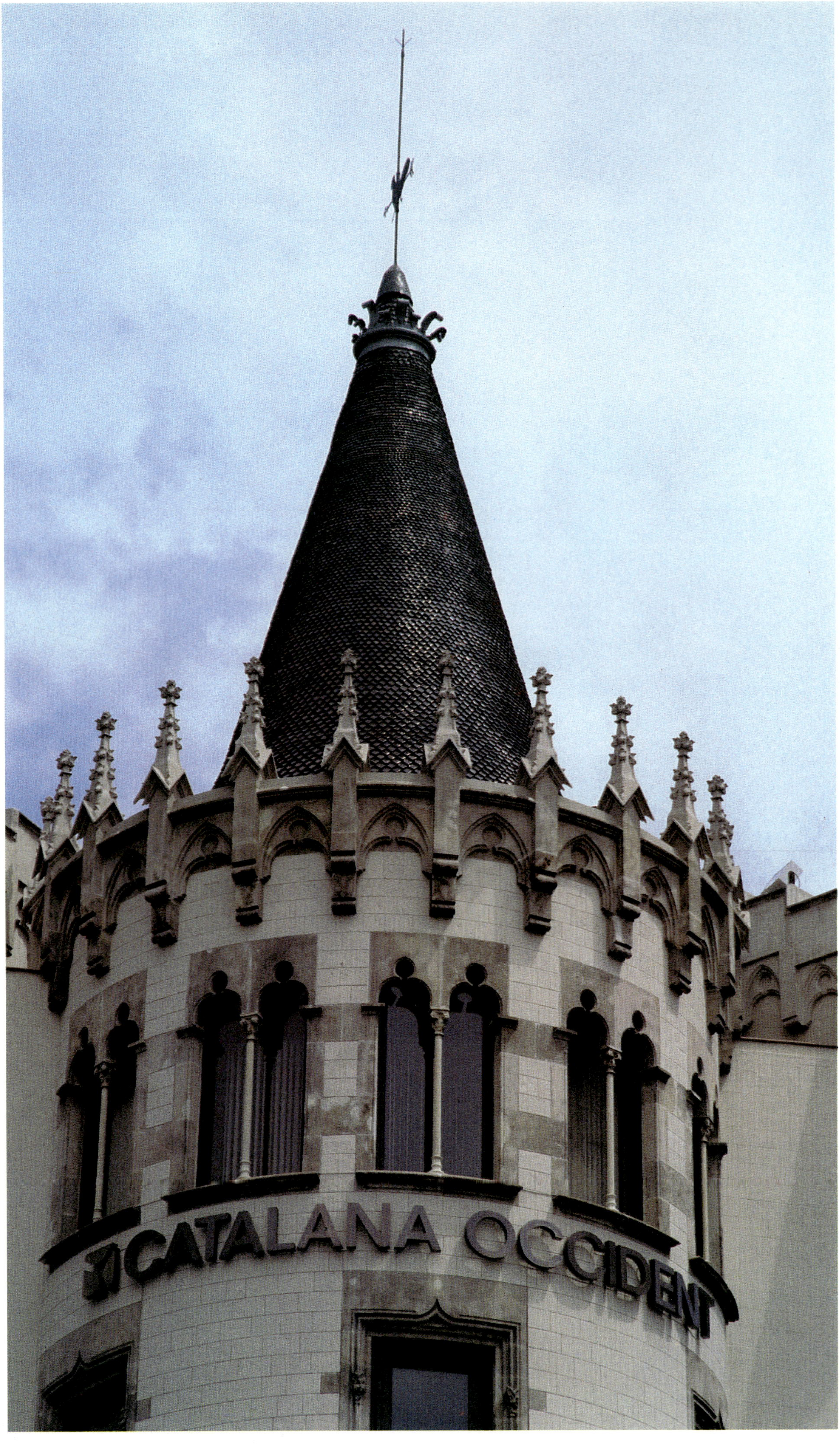
CATALANA OCCIDENT

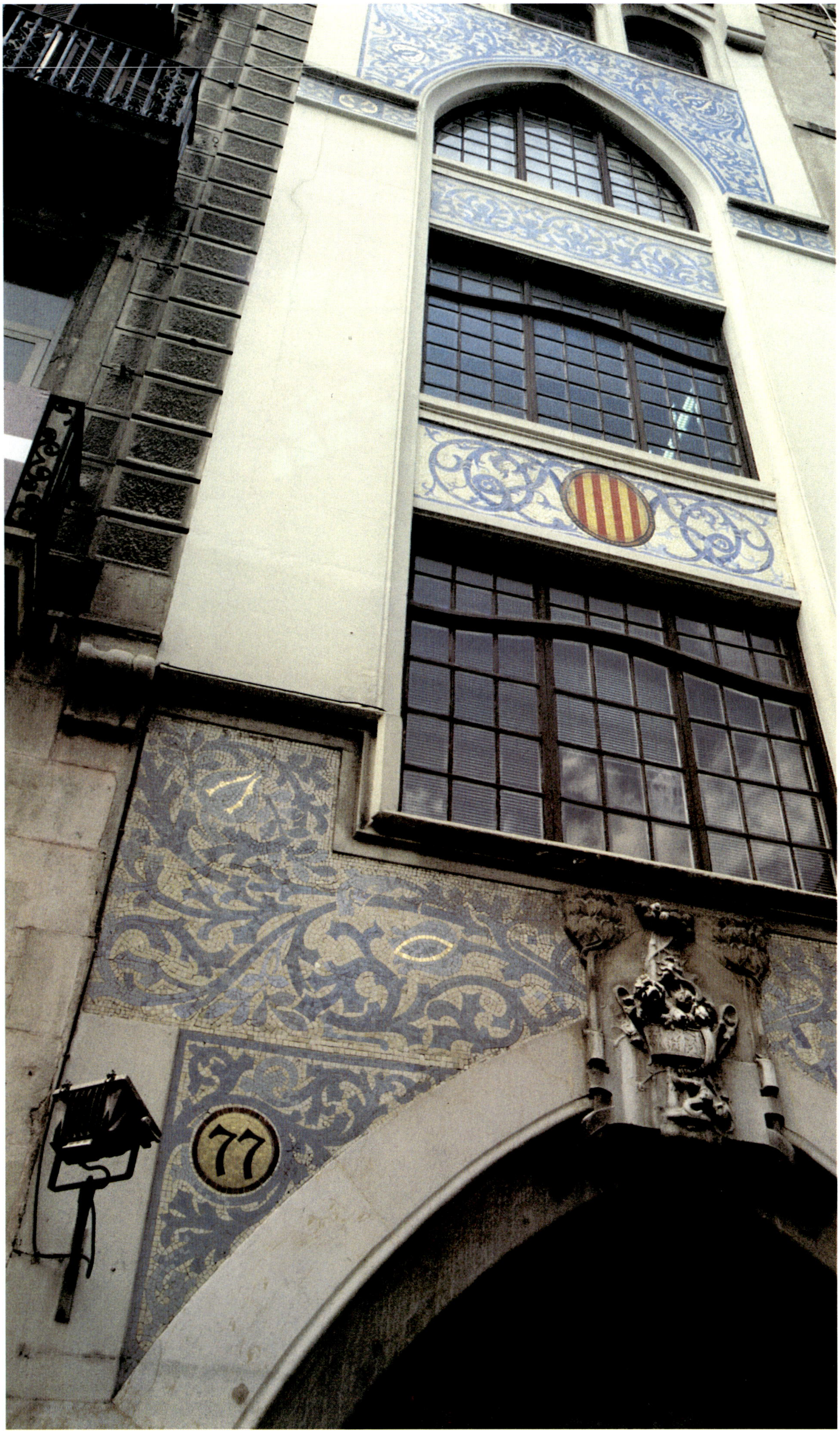
77

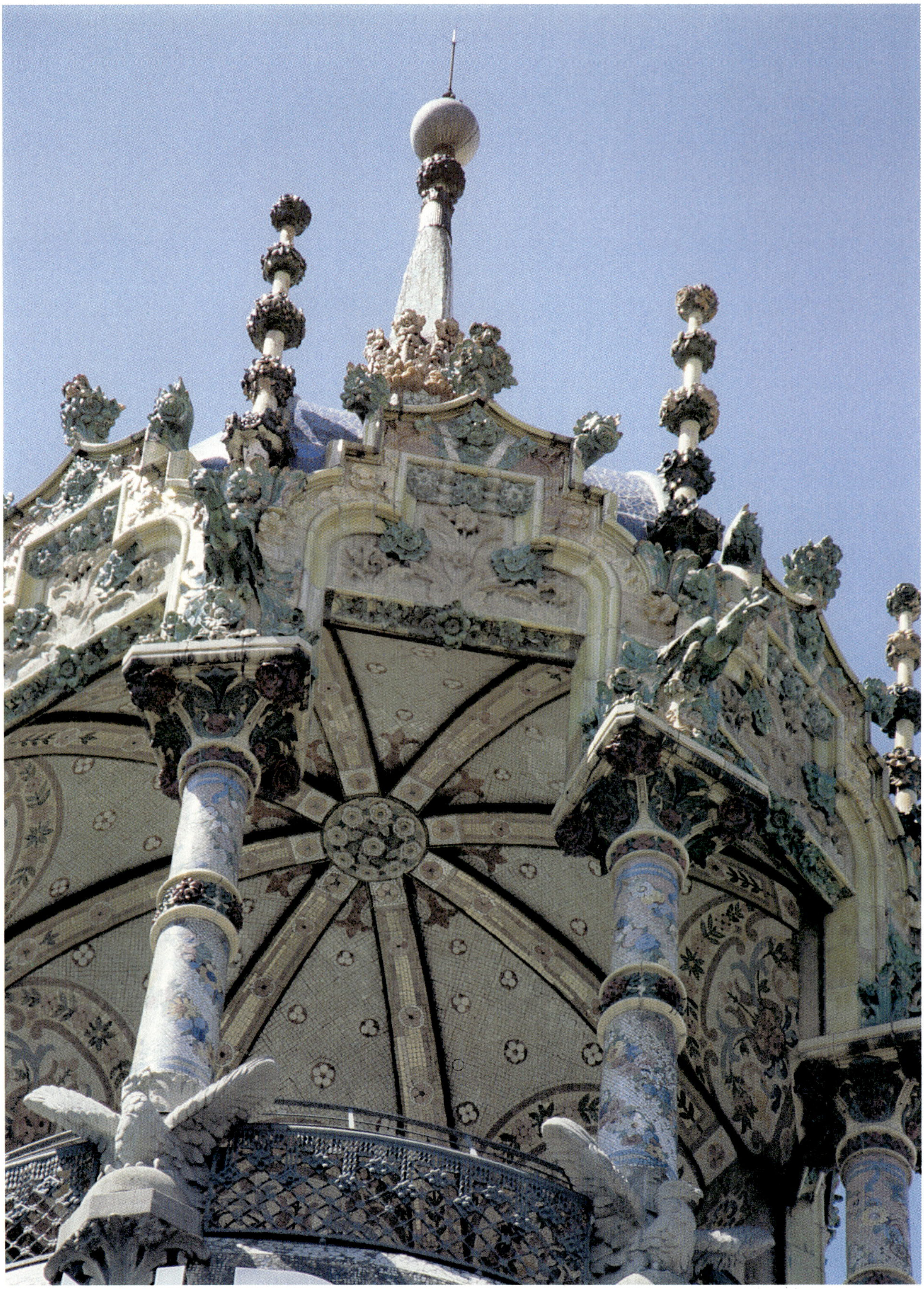

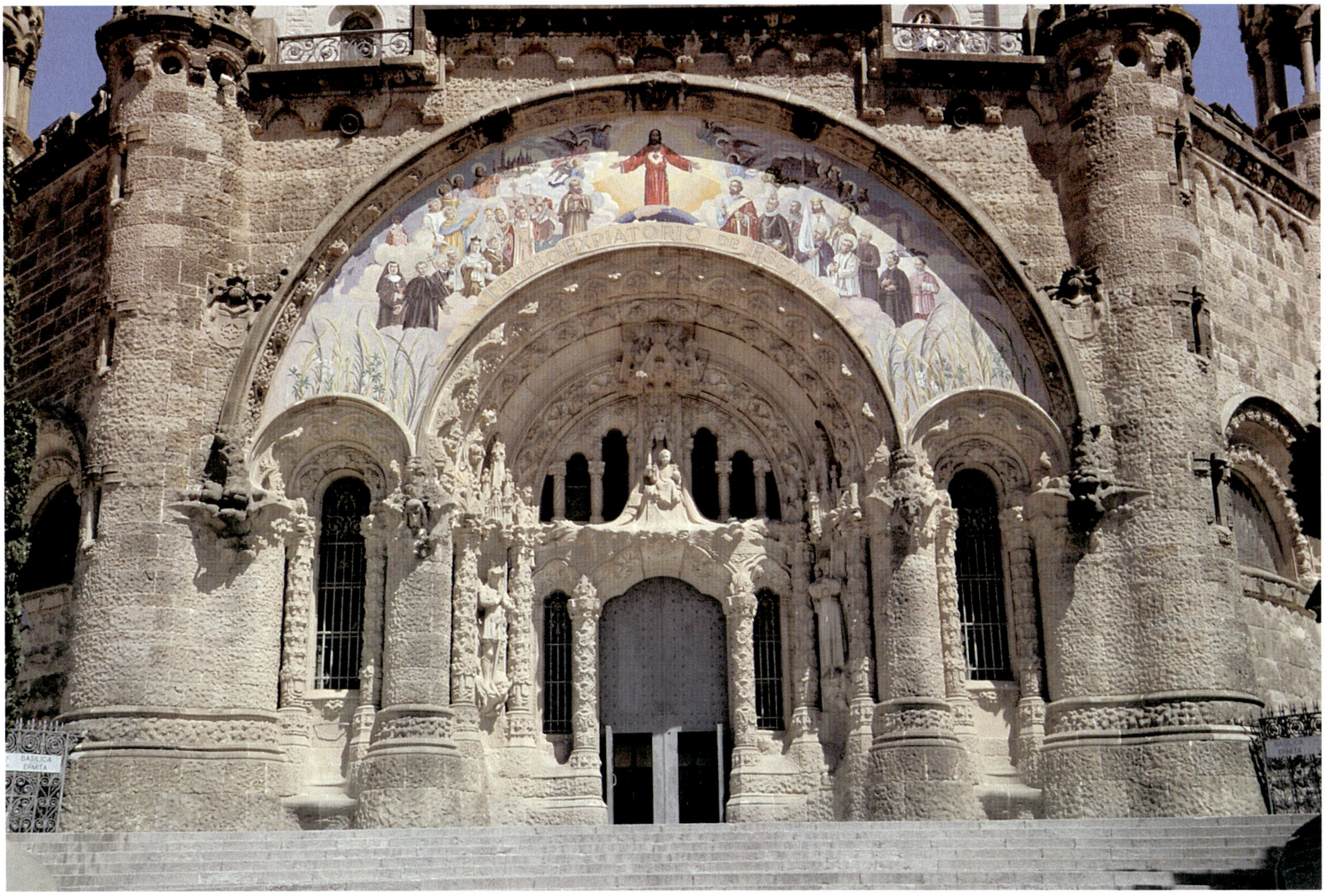

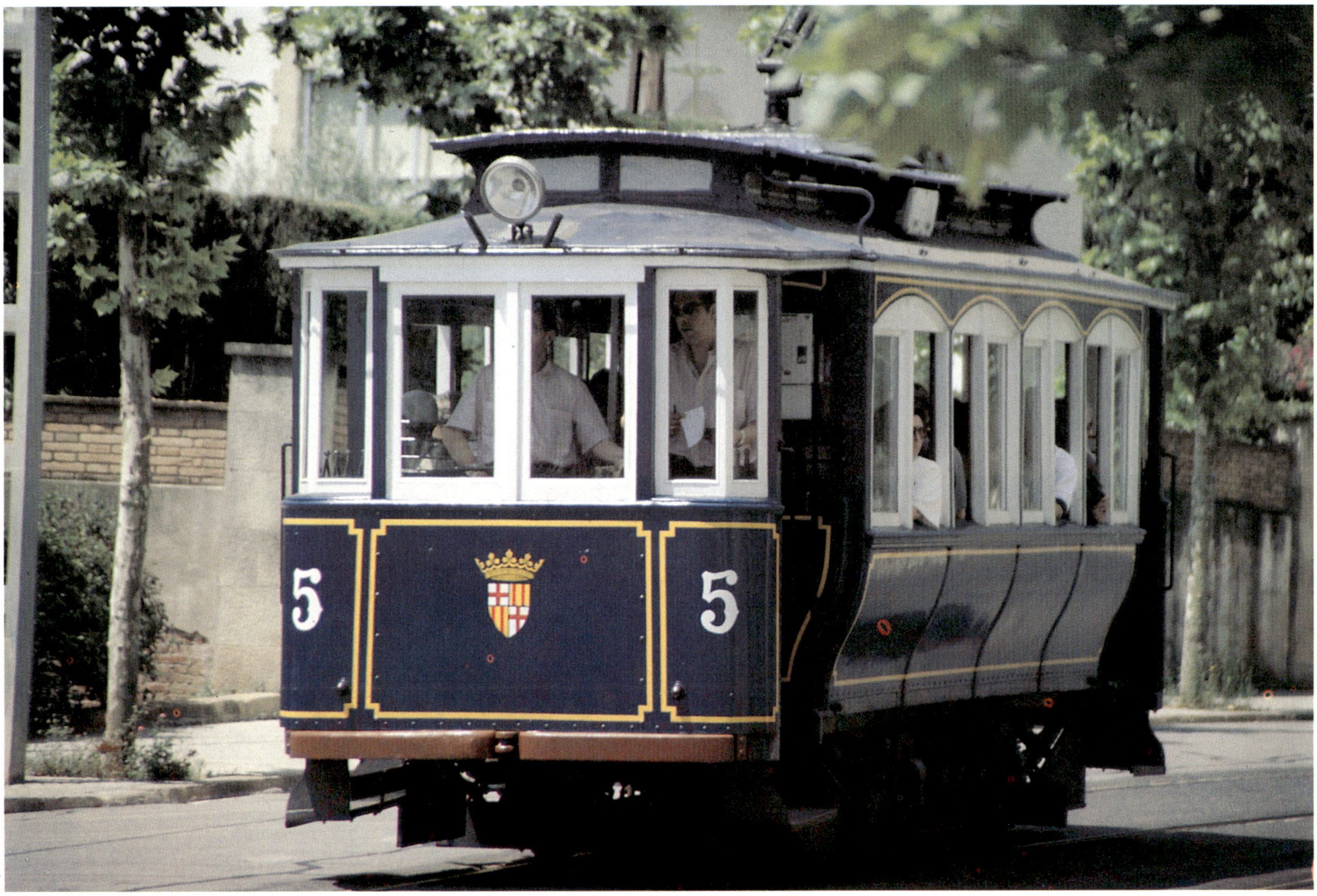
5
5

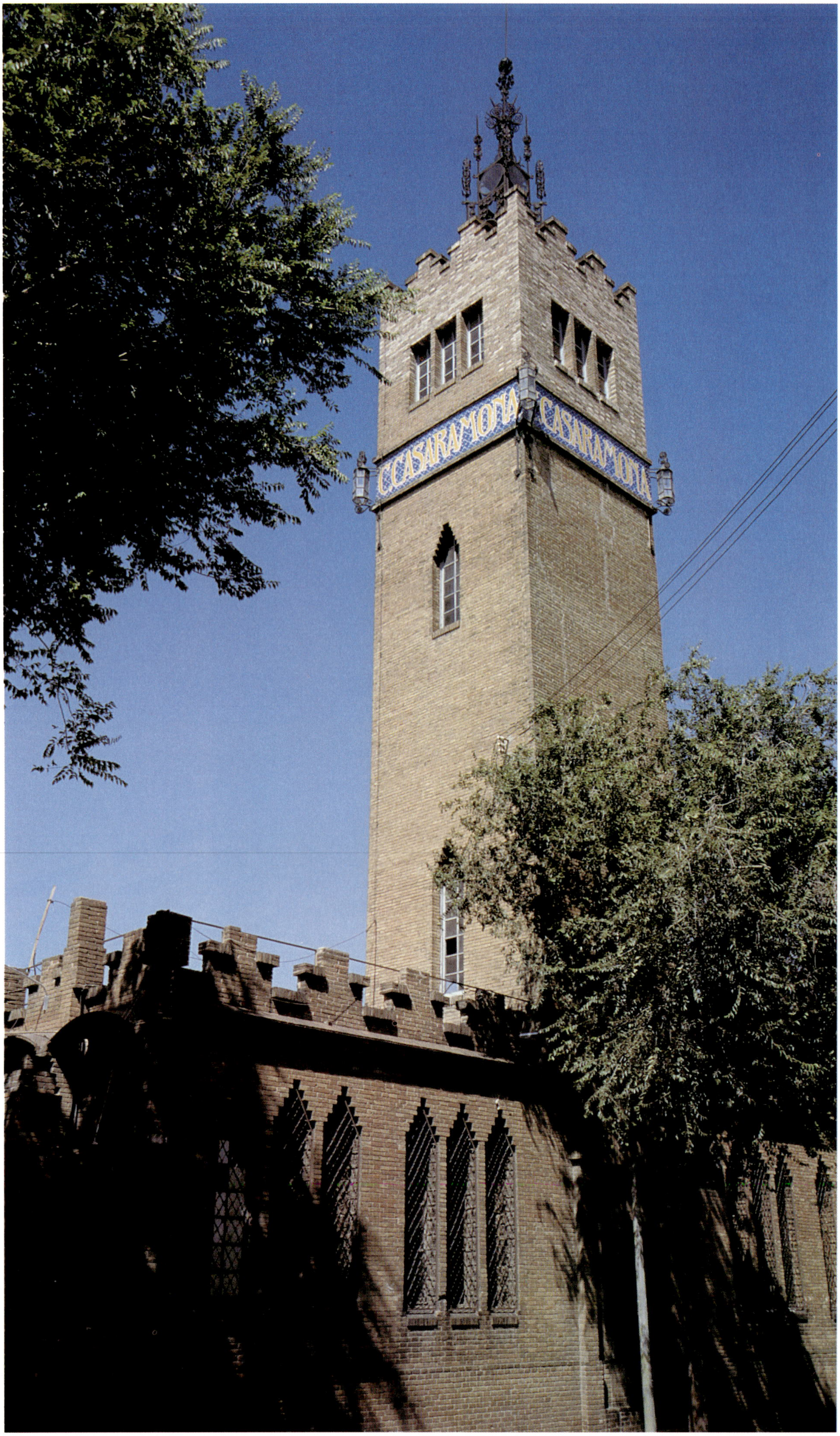
CASARAMONA
CASARAMONA

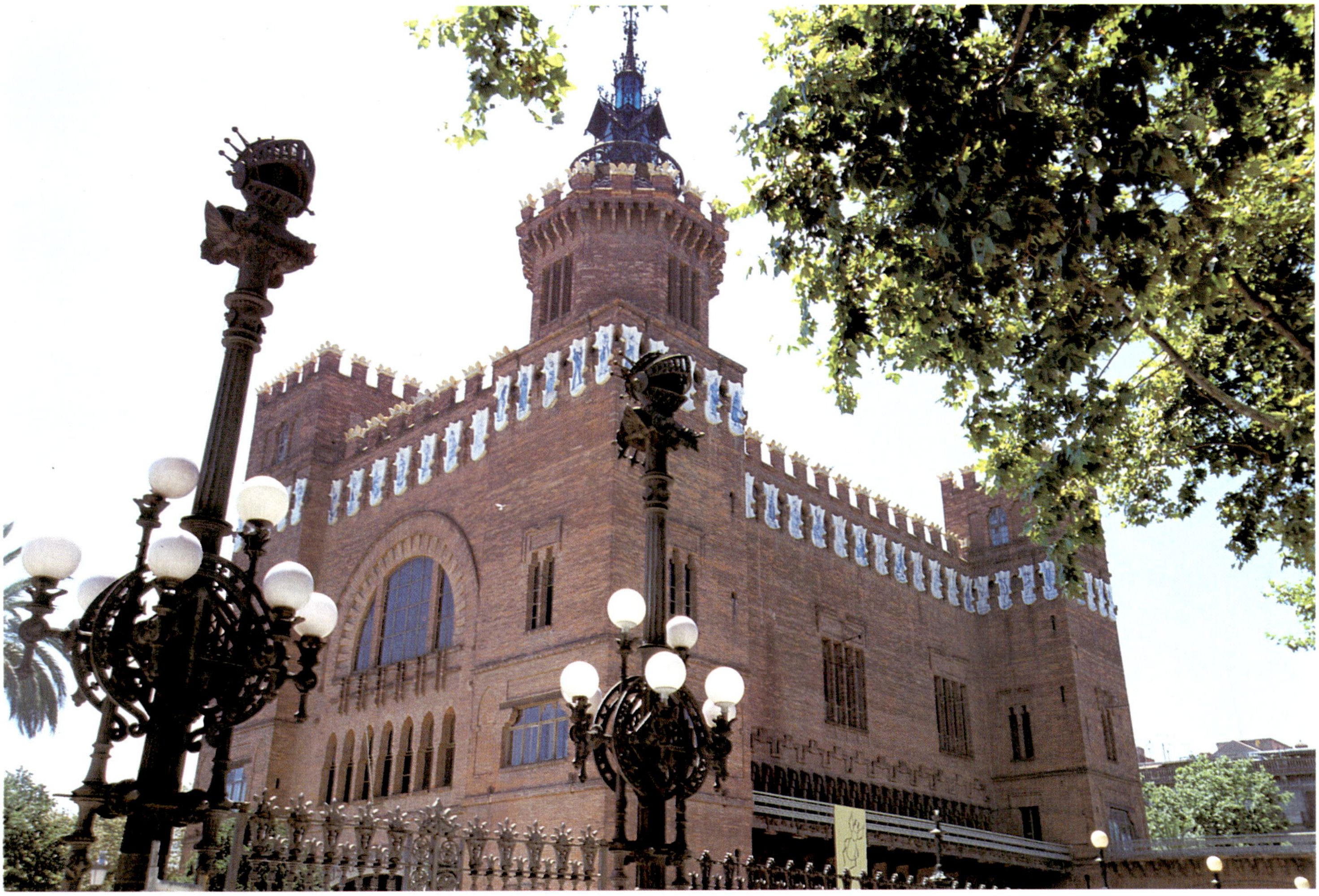

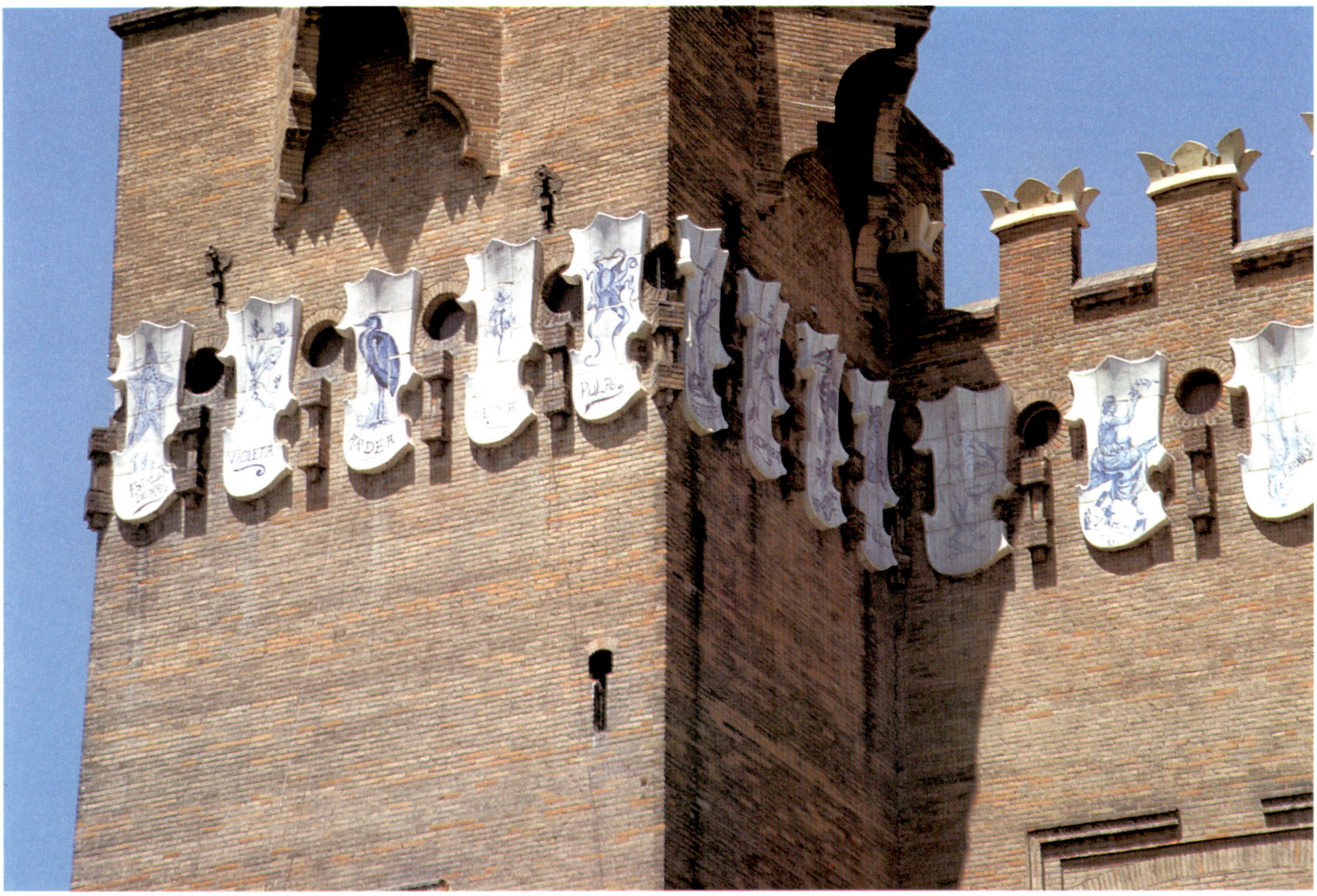
VIOLETA
PULPO

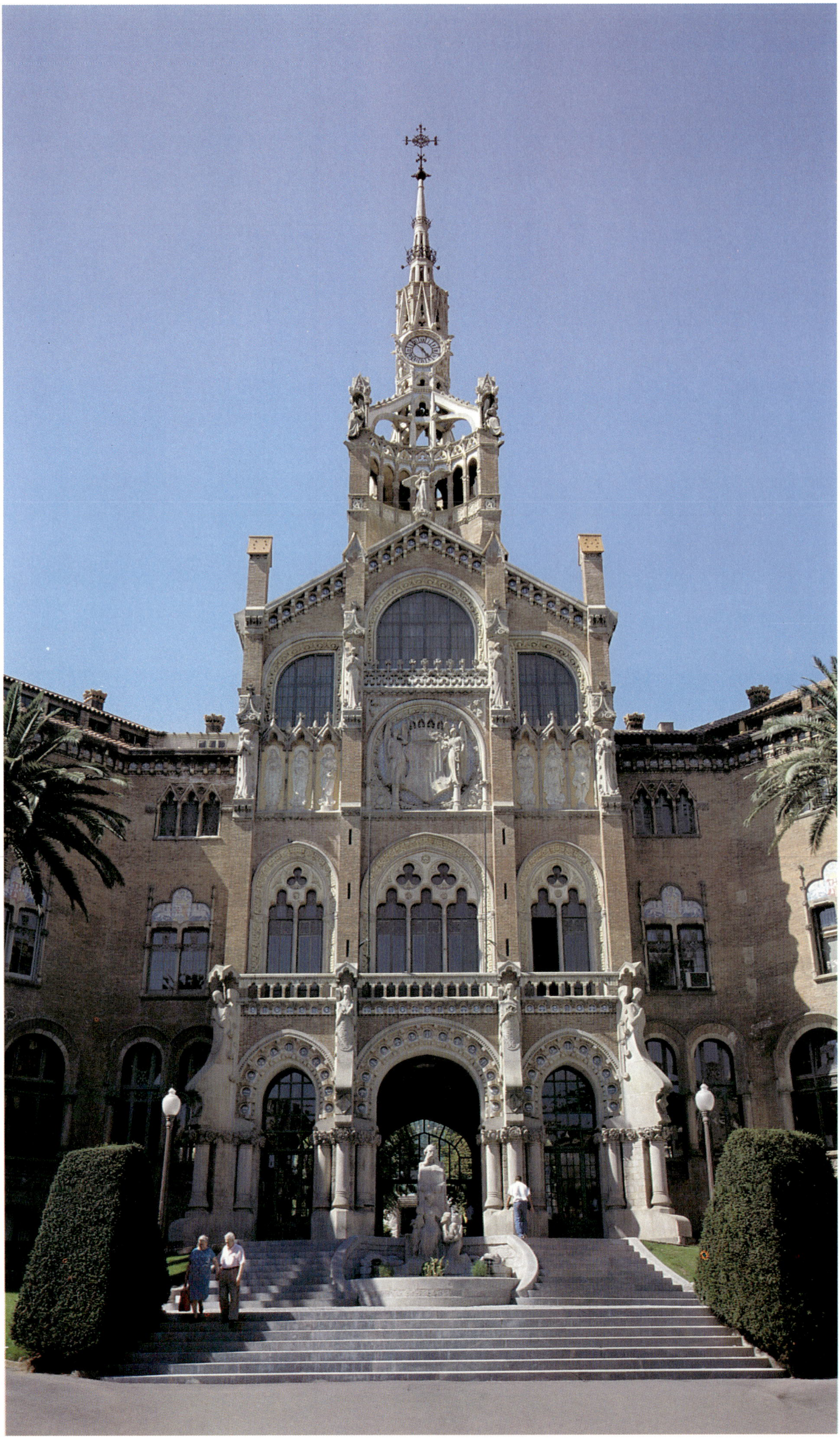

HISTORICAL VIEW OF MODERNISM

Between 1890 and 1910 a wave shook the worlds of architecture, interior design, publishing design and graphic art as well as the world of fashion throughout Europe and North America. Never before had an artistic renewal been produced that was so sudden, drastic and simultaneous. There wasn't even time to become aware of what the movement meant, or to theorise about it, or to come to an agreement as to what should be the common name to designate this style. It was Art Nouveau for the English, Modern Style for the French (although it would seem to be the opposite), Modernismo and Modernisme for the Spanish and the Catalans respectively, Jugendstil for the Germans, Sezession for the Viennese, Floreal for the Italians; and yet it was a single movement which knew no frontiers, unified under a flag of freedom and progress as well as a natural formal invasion of the urban and civilised world.

In spite of this unit we can speak of European Modernisms to the extent to which the movement had its own peculiarities in each country, all the more so given that Modernism was an extraordinarily open and eclectic style. In it there was space for the craftsmen, and for the artists, for the progressives and the most conservative as well as for Functionalism and luxury and waste.

Catalan Modernism was one of the most characteristic in Europe and was marked by the resurgence of Nationalism as well as by the insistence in the formal repertoire of Gothic art and the Medieval inspired motifs which reminded the Catalans of glorious moments in the past.

Characters as unclassifiable as Gaudí had no difficulty in finding sufficient space to express themselves in this new wave, and of course, they definitively left an indelible local and universal stamp on the style. There was also space for moderates and historians such as Sagnier, who was faithful to the Neogothic style, and above all to balance and symmetry. Between these two extremes we can find the work of more than eighty architects, and that is without counting on the indispensable work of the builders, the foremen, the craftsmen, iron forgers, the glassworkers, sculptors and ceramic or glazed pottery workers who made the city of Barcelona "The Athens of Modernism", as was said in the "L'Esquella de la Torratxa" magazine in 1909.

Modernism, an international hurricane

Modernism, of which Architecture was the maximum form of expression, aspired to being a total art. The modernist building encapsulated the techniques and skills of the craftsmen and those jobs which must be carried out in order to complete a work in which strange structures and ornamentation are associated with difficulty: the glazed ceramics, a frequently used recovering for exterior facades and interior walls, and not only gives beauty and colour but also protects against rising damp and erosion caused by atmospheric elements and also keeps the bathrooms, kitchens and laundry rooms clean. Other

Total art, social art

coatings such as the plaster work, the marble work, the worked stone and brick also show this ornamental-functional duality which so interested some of the architects of the epoch. The wrought iron work, normally used as a means of security in bars and balconies also acquires anew impulse; its forms are freed in order to draw the most unusual fantasies and whims, which range from medieval inspiration to that of the imitation of wild forms and those of nature. The coloured or transparent glasswork is used to make the most of the entrances of light which used to present an important construction problem as they were conditioned by the form and dimensions of the building sites in the city. The mosaics cover the floors with truly beautiful colours and substitute the old and traditional wood floors with polished pavements which were easier to clean and conserve. The woodwork and carving was used as much to embellish the windows, arches and rooves as to integrate beams, windows and cross pieces in to the building.

Modernism also invaded the world of furniture. At the beginning it took over the design of the furniture which appeared following the new customs of the society at the turn of the century: ladies dressing rooms, washbasins, umbrella stands and hat stands. Slowly however, table and chair design also became fashionable, (remember the famous Viennese chairs Thonet, using curved wood, which entered history and even today are endlessly imitated). Beds, bookshelves, desks also became the object of this movement. The curves and the peculiarities of the walls , doors, windows and stairs of these buildings demanded furniture that suited them and integrated perfectly into the spaces as required. Architects such as Gaudí or Puig i Cadafalch, aware of the importance of interior design and decoration, designed superb furniture for the houses which they had planned.

The new design also effected objects which were in common daily use, crockery, kitchen and bathroom utensils, paper, books, pamphlets, clothes, especially those of the ladies. In the same way that this new wave reached the smallest object it also extended to embrace the largest: the gardens, the fountains, the squares, the theatres, even the temples felt the renovating impulse of Modernism.

There is another characteristic through which the new art showed itself to be the precursor of all the architecture of the twentieth century, and that is the free and uninhibited use of poor materials (such as plaster and brick) with the new building materials such as iron. Precisely one of the charms of Modernism resides in having known how to combine the most luxurious materials such marble, ebony, crystal and gold with the most simple and common ones. Paradoxically, in spite of this exuberant taste for luxury and for the sensuality of the precious materials, the modernist artist also sought visual truth and hid from mediocre imitations in which lateromantic and eclectic art had all too often fallen in.

The flexible and innovating spirit in the treatment of the new building techniques as well as the lack of prejudice at the time of mixing luxurious materials with poorer ones responds to another totalizing element of Modernism: the opening and expansion which led its architects not only to plan houses for the rich or great public buildings but also normal houses for people to live in.

Modernism is an art which was born of, by and for the European bourgeoisie of 1900. Families which had gained wealth as the fruit of constant hard work along with saving and austerity, emigrant families which returned home having made their fortunes, industrialists who knew when to automate their factories at the right time, entrepreneurs, who commercialising small products such as refreshments, zips, oil lamps forged great companies. They were producers of new services of entertainment and communication, a middle-class which looked for the legitimacy in their fortunes and power between the romantic eclecticism, historical architecture and Modernism, without finding any obstacle in mixing any or all of these tendencies.

Modernism went further though. Its speech about the use of simple materials and the application of the new resources allowed the development of an ornamental and aesthetic repertoire which could be produced at a low cost. This was how modernist art invaded the humble houses of the craftsmen, or the wine cooperatives in fields of Tarragona, the advertising boards or even the dance cards of the young ladies of a marriageable age, and this is just to give a few examples of what happened in Catalonia. The factories (for which the best Catalan architects showed no disdain at all to plan or in which to use their creativity and professional knowledge) were a field of extraordinary tests as they were conditioned by functional aspects but were totally free of the ideological restrictions found in building houses, in which the family was inevitable more conservative. Along with the great factories, Modernism also intervened, though with much more discretion, in the small houses of the workers, which were often built at the same time as the factory in order to house the site workers who were nearly always made up of immigrant rural workers.

In this aspect, Catalan Modernism was a forerunner and even revolutionary. It was influenced by the ideas of artists such as John Rushkin or the English socialist William Morris who in the middle of the nineteenth century had fought for total art and the social and political potentialities of architecture and especially those in design. The Catalan modernists made a valuable contribution to the social renewal in urbanism, architecture and design which went beyond the frontiers of the city or even the country.

The plan by Cerdà and the Eixample (known as Ensanche)

In 1854 the city of Barcelona gained governmental authorisation to pull down the walls which imprisoned the city and which with the new demographic growth were generating important health problems in the city. The walls ran all along what is now the Ronda de Sant Pau, Universitat, Sant Pere and el Paseo de Lluís Companys. Four years later in 1859the Ministry of War authorised, at last, the construction of a great space understood as being between the city of Barcelona and the villages of Gràcia, Sants, Les Corts, Sant Gervasi de Cassoles and Sant Martí de Provençals, an area with a two kilometre radius (the distance which a canon ball would travel) and one which until this date it had been prohibited to build for reasons of security.

Both the pressing need which the city had for houses in this moment and the size of the land in which this new city was to be built demanded an urban plan of great vision and expansion capable of ordering the building in a progressive way, and of responding to the needs of circulation which were becoming increasingly complicated as well as foreseeing the public mechanisms which would grow along with the city. The government in Madrid, in an attempt to control the urban expansion after the city walls were pulled down rapidly adopted the development plan which had been put forward the same year by Ildefons Cerdà. However this quick decision upset the Barcelona authorities who looked badly at the meddling of central government in the developing of the municipal development in answer to this they held an urban planning competition in which all the most important architects in Barcelona entered and which was won by Antoni Rovira i Trias who presented a concentric radial plan of the city. The experts of Queen Isabel II rejected this plan which they considered to be far inferior to Cerdà's plan and they didn't allow their arm to be twisted in this question this question created a large discussion. Given that each project implied a totally different vision of the development of the city. While Rovira's plan tended to focus on the centrality of the old centre of Barcelona, maintaining its structural role, Cerdà forgot the old city and designed another which was simply next to it and open to the outside and based on a homogeneous serial repetition. One must recognise that this last plan was far more innovative than that presented by Rovira. There were also other interesting plans, specially that of the group of Catalan artists and engineers for the progress of Contemporary Architecture, GATPAC, which was a nationalist influenced group.

Cerdà proposed a plan which moved the centre of the city toward The Plaza de les Glories and in which there would be equal square blocks of 113,33 metres with the corners cut in 45º thus drawing a small square at each crossing, and making it easier for the "steam machines" to turn. This also allowed parking without interrupting the flow of the traffic on either side of the road. The streets would have a minimum width of 20 metres, at times up to 30 or 50 metres. A diagonal street crossed all the land from one side to the other and today is called the Avenida Diagonal. The houses were built in blocks in such a way that each had an large internal patio permitting gardens and parks, though speculation would render this unworkable. Cerdà foresaw a density of 250 inhabitants per hectare, which was quickly outdated due to the demographic growth and the waves of immigration into the city: already in 1890 there were 1400 inhabitants per hectare in the Eixample and in 1925, 2,000.

Although the previsions were not fulfilled exactly as they had been foreseen, Cerdà's plan was one of the most positive urban decisions which Barcelona has taken in its history. The urbanistic order found in the Eixample constitutes not only a plan which has remained valid until the present day but has also offered much to the urban landscape. The regular formal structures of the blocks created a model which was full of harmony and one which allowed the juxtaposition of houses with large public buildings. The speed with which a large part of the land was developed gave a stylistic unity to the facades and the unity of the area and this gives it one of its greatest charms. It is precisely in these charms that Modernism stands out.

Barcelona, the mirror of Modernism in Catalonia

Catalan Modernism has remained unquestionably marked, as we have seen, by the inspired figure of Guadí and by the artistic personality of two or three more architects. However, one shouldn't forget for one moment that these figures are only the tip of the iceberg; constructors of buildings which would have been impossible without the creativity of these forgers, sculptors, glass and ceramic workers. Standard bearers of a style which whilst having its stars also had an anonymous multitude of foremen, craftsmen technicians and engineers. It id for this reason that today we visit some of the signed jewels, La Pedrera, the Casa Batlló or the Casa Lleó Morera, which shine in a city of small anonymous treasures and which are found in all the streets in the Eixample, and in the little houses which remain in Sarrià and Horta, and in the old workers areas in Sants, Poble Nou, Sant Andreu and La Sagrera and in that which was an area of artists and is nowadays Gràcia. Catalan Modernism which had so many authors and so many maecenas, was above all quantitatively speaking an art without signatures and an art without classes.

Modernism in Catalonia survived longer than in other countries. The first manifestations which can be considered modernist, though varying according to the experts, are placed between 1875 and 1888. The last oscillate between 1907, for the most restrictive experts, and 1930.

At the end of the XIX century Catalonia was in full economic expansion, and in the process of industrialisation, experiencing an extraordinary social mobility and demographic growth. It was a good time after centuries of economic crisis and political difficulties. The Catalans looked back to their glorious medieval past and taking this as a base whilst warmed by the romantic historicism which came in from Europe rebuilt their fervent nationalism whose signs of identity, whilst born then, can be seen easily today. The "Indians" as those were called who had emigrated to Cuba returned pressed by the dangers to the independence of the colony, but loaded with gold and a wealth which they could invest as well as their wish to show their recently acquired wealth and power to society. Many rural property owners throughout Catalonia left the fields and set up in Barcelona entrusting their lands to agents or administrators. The majority of the new bourgeoisie were less conditioned by their past than the aristocracy; many of them were open to the new tendencies in art and culture, and ready to protect contemporary creation. Some buildings such as the publishers Montaner i Simon de Domènech i Montaner, or the Casa Vicens by Gaudí were the forerunners of what would be the great modernist boom. The Universal Exhibition in 1888 contributed decisively to the renewal of the city and to the expansion of Modernism, especially to public buildings.

The route of Modernism in Barcelona is marked out by houses requested by moneyed families and completed by the famous architects of the time. But as we have already observed this was only the top of the iceberg.

The majority of the houses built prior to the modernist phase in the Eixample area were built with the idea of being flats. Often there would be a first floor, then a second with its own stairs in which the buildings owner would install himself and live. In this flat the windows were larger and it had bigger balconies and galleries. As the flats rise so the exterior appears more simple, this is because the higher flats were colder and there were more stairs to climb and consequently they were cheaper than the lower flats the facades were generally 14 metres wide and these had three or five balconies, of little depth, of about

80 cm. On the ground floor apart from the main door there were other doors for service or coaches. Many had lower ground floors and basements and sometimes a floor placed 150 cm above the floor called the mezzanine or entresol. The roof is normally a flat roof finished with a balustrade. The modernist innovations in these were radical. A quick drive around El Paseo de Gràcia would make us immediately aware of the fact that many of the modernist facades were conceived as small palaces, castles or mansion seven when these corresponded to houses of flats for various families. The unitary treatment of the facades contributed to the monumentality of the buildings and to their beauty and harmony.

Another renovatory characteristic consisted in the integration of applied arts as much to the exteriors as to the interiors. Barcelona always had a union/guild network which was important and in the centre of which traditions were maintained as was professional solidarity and the transmission of knowledge. However, the Catalan decadence of the XVI-XVIII centuries had also had its effects on the professions and in the transmission of craftwork techniques, many of which had been dormant or were being lost. After the Universal Exhibition in 1888, the architect Domènech i Montaner converted the Café Restaurant del Parque Ciutadella, his own work, in an applied arts centre where the traditional jobs were brought up to date in order to make them compatible with the most recent research and with the treatment of new materials. As Domènech declared in an article in homage to his companion Antoni M. Gallissà, "we were trying to recover arts and procedures; melted bronze and wrought iron, terracottas and golden ceramic work following the style of Valencia, metal embossments, pinced metal work, wood carving and decorative sculpture, which in those times was done badly and in a rudimentary way. Gallissà didn't stop for a moment, toing and froing from our studios to the workshops. We had reunited a group of people which was in its majority embryonic and one we tried to train in architectural work and now is the pride of the Catalan arts" (An article by Domènech i Montaner in the newspaper "La Veu de Catalunya"). Amongst many other things Domènech like Gaudí managed to get the old ceramic worker Gassany from Manises to reveal his secrets so as to adapt the ceramics to the new architectural needs. Pujol i Baucis was a great paver, tiler and mosaic arranger, as were the Oliva brothers, Mateu Cullell, Torres Muari. The tradition in wrought iron work had never been completely lost and arose with all its force in the architectural applications of the modernists: Falqués, the well-known author of the street lights in Paseo de Gràcia and in the Hall of Sant Joan worked with Manuel Ballarín; Puig i Cadafalch did so with Esteve Andorrà. We shouldn't forget Rifà, Basons or Torrebadell, nor the metalworkers Bertran i Torras, Costa i Ponces or Miret i Ascent whose works bear testimony to a creativity and professionalism quite out of the ordinary.

One of the most renowned crafts of Modernism, that of glassworks, produced crucial figures such as Amigó or Vilella. All of these craftsmen worked side by side with the architects at a time when each step of a work was as important as its creation, that is to say, the project and the plans. In fact this is arguably more important: Gaudí hardly ever worked with plans. He substituted them with sketches, elevations and models, to such an extent that the continuation of his works after his death has produced insurmountable difficulties as is the case in the temple of the Sagrada Familia.

The Catalan architects of Modernism in Barcelona

Catalan Modernism is unquestionably marked by the figure of Antoni Gaudí (Reus 1852-Barcelona 1926). There are some authors who believe that Gaudí was not a modernist given that his highly personal style can not be held within any tendency or movement. However this maybe, we cannot negate the enormous influence that this brilliant man had on Catalan art and architecture as well as on the urban landscape in the city of Barcelona. Gaudí brought valiant technical solutions to architecture and totally new ideas in the use of new materials, but in his works these daring innovations stay on a second plane. As J. C. Argan has commented, more than technique "Gaudí is violently opposed to the rationalism of the industrial civilisation; art is (for him) pure irrationalism and his technique is the technique of the irrational... (...) His architecture doesn't aim to be religious but rather sacred; it does not reveal god but rather offers the existential torment of man, he offers his city as though it were a famous painting by El Greco. Precisely for this it doesn't have deep contents, it is open immediately and totally to the perception: the form doesn't recover the structure but rather makes it stand out more; the colour doesn't recover the form but rather constitutes a whole with it. For this expressive visibility, not one of impression, Gaudí's architecture like the painting of Van Gogh and Gauguin was one of the roots of expressionism".

One of the other great figures of Catalan Modernism was Lluís Domènech i Montaner (1850-1923). He was a student of Elies Rogent, a great architectural renovator, and first director of the school of architecture founded in 1877. His main works, la Casa Vicens (1888), El Colegio de la Teresianas (1894), el Palau Güell (1889), la Casa Batlló (1907), la Casa Milà (1910), el Parque Güell (1914) and the Sagrada Familia (unfinished) are widely illustrated in this book. As early as 1878, Domènech i Montaner made reference to Modernism in his text, "in search of a national architecture", as a testimony to his precocious renovatory tendencies. Amongst his most notable works we find the publishers Montaner i Simon (1885), the publishers Casa Thomas (1898), la Casa Lleó Morera (1906), el Palau de la Música Catalana (1908) and el Hospital de la Santa Creu i de Sant Pau (1911). The collection of his work is one of the most solid and coherent in Catalan architecture. It especially stands out for the use of applied arts within a coherent whole in which the ornamentation stops being gratuitous and becomes an indispensable element: the building synthesises the result of all the arts, it is an ideal forerunner of what would later be seen in the architecture of the Bauhaus and Le Corbusier.

Josep Puig i Cadafalch (1867-1956) developed a personal vocabulary based on historical reinterpretations to which he integrated a good doses of fantasy as well as a sense of humour. Apart from studying Architecture he also researched and investigated in the areas of History and Archeology, where he made some important contributions to the History of Art in Catalonia. Furthermore he participated actively in the political life in Barcelona representing with his humanistic attitude the ideals and ethics of a nationalistic society in full resurgence. He was founder of the "Lliga Regionalista" and preseident of the "Mancomunitat de Catalunya" from 1917 to 1924. His most noteworthy houses are la Casa Ametller (1900), la Casa Macaia (1901), and the Casa Terrades or the Casa de les Punxes (19059. His most daring work is without question the Fábrica Casaramona (1911) where he employed a well balanced repertoire with great creativity.

Enric Sagnier i Villavecchia was one of the most moderate modernist architects. He remained faithful to a Neogothic style in which he introduced changes of proportions, always maintaining some schemes which give his building an air of staticness. He is the author of la Casa Pasqual i Pons (1891) and of the buildings which belong now to the Caixa de pensiones in la Via Laietana (1918), and of the Temple of the Sacred Heart in Tibidabo (1902). There were other important architects of the period such as Josep Domènech i Estapà, a cousin of Domènech i Montaner, architect of the Acadèmia de Ciències i Arts (1883); Josep Plantada i Artigas who built la Casa Queraltó (1907), Josep Vilaseca who reformed la Casa Dolors Calm (1902); Antoni M. Gallissà who directed the works in amongst other houses la Casa Llopis Bofill; August Font planned the Plaza de Torros in Les Arenes (1900); the brothers Joaquim and Bonaventura Bassegoda who designed las Casas Rocamora (1917); Joachim Codina who planned la Casa M. Malagrida (1908); Salvador Valeri, architect of the Casa Comalat (1911); Antoni Rovira who planned the house of the painter Ramon Casas (1899); Pere Falqués who designed the streetlights of Paseo de Gràcia, of the Cinc d'Oros (a square at the crossing of the Diagonal and Paseo de Gràcia) and in the Hall of Sant Joan, as well as the house of Bonaventura Ferrer (19069 or the better of Gaudí's disciples, Josep Maria Jujol, author of the Casa Planells (1924) and Francesc Berenguer.

From Modernism to "Noucentisme"

Modernism infiltrated powerfully and quickly into the city. In the same way it disappeared around the twenties and thirties, victim of the "Noucentist" criticism, a renovating movement which wanted to turn the Catalan society back to common sense and to see balance, rationality and sobriety in its art. It was not a vain vindication, given that many excesses had been committed in the name of Modernism, and obviously not all the results of the modernist adventure were equally good.

The true problem in modernist art in the years which followed was not the relative discredit in the eyes of the "Noucentists" but rather the Civil War, the post war, the consequences of the World War, the economic and political crisis and the dictatorship of General Franco. Many of those beautiful towers and galleries fell under gunfire. They destroyed sculptures, ceramics, terracottas, plasterwork. Practically all the ground floors suffered alteration as they changed owners and these renovated following the demands of fashion.

Fortunately the recent publicity campaign "Barcelona, ponte guapa", (Barcelona make yourself look beautiful), put forward by the Agència del Paisatge Urbà of the Ayuntamiento de Barcelona, has given the initiative to owners and companies, co-ordinating it with public help and funds to foment and guide the restorations and so to show us a city full of colour and beauty. To these restorations excellent interventions have been added to some of the most important modernist buildings such as the Palau de la Música or to the publishers Montaner i Simon, which is presently the headquarters of the Tàpies foundation.

ANTONIO GAUDÍ

Biographical notice

The documentary research carried out by Guix Sugrañes has led Reus to be considered as Antoni Gaudí i Cornet's birthplace, born 25 June 1852, in spite of being born in Mas del Calderer's house in the neighbourhood of Riudoms. He was baptised in Reus and his birth certificate reflects this.

Both his father and grandfather were coppersmiths and Gaudí pointed to this as part of the reason that he felt inclined towards his craft and for forms in spatial development. He lost his mother when still a child, and an older brother and sister died when he was young. Then, he assumed the responsibility of bringing Rosa Egea, her sister's daughter, up and she lived with him for quite a long time.

He studied in Reus until he entered the Barcelona school of Architecture, in 1869, from which in 1878 he received the degree in Architecture.

During his student years he planned the restoration of the Cistercian monastery in Poblet which was quite abandoned and secularized at the time. This was planned along with José Ribera y Sans and Eduardo Toda y Güell (a future diplomat who in his old age would be the restoration's sponsor).

His collaborations began shortly after with reputed architects like Francisco P. Del Villar (1876-1877, later denied in part) in the building of the niche for the Virgin of Montserrat. He worked with José Fontseré on monuments in the Ciutadella park, between 1877 and 1882. Later he worked with José Serramalera in a project for lighting the old Barcelona sea walls, along with the Paseo Nacional in the maritime neighbourhood in Barceloneta. He also planned the Benedictine convent church in Villaricos, close to Cuevas de Vera (Almería) with Juan Martorell in 1882.

Due to certain projects in his youth such as the glass display cabinet which was presented at the Universal Exhibition in Paris in 1878 he attracted the attention of Eusebio Güell, who became his main and most loyal client. After a brilliant and worldly first stage in which Gaudí participated in social and cultural activities (through the Societat Catalana d'Excursions Científiques, which looked at co-operative initiatives, and also attended rather select reunions at Güell's house), at the end of his life he lived almost as a recluse, in religious devotion. His social life reduced to the visit of a few diverse characters, attracted by the fame of his work, and who would debate his symbolic-mystic theories and his architectural and structural concepts with him and exclusively in Catalan, in his little study-room in the Sagrada Familia. Albert Schweitzer (who went to Barcelona to give concerts or take part in music festivals) tells of how he went to the Sagrada Familia to see Gaudí, and the artist, on explaining to him his mystic theories of proportions of how to submit architectural lines to the symbolic demands of expressing the idea of the Trinity, said: "This cannot be explained in French, nor German, nor English; so I'm going to explain it to you in Catalan, and you will understand what I say even though you don't know this language."

He suffered from rheumatism from childhood. During his adult life he followed a vegetarian diet prescribed by Dr. Kneipp, and he also tried homeopathic treatment and took long and regular walks. He walked from his house in the grounds of Parque Güell (from 1906 till eight months before he died), to the Sagrada Familia and to the church of San Felipe Neri, near Barcelona cathedral, every day, and would return home also on foot, so that he walked about twelve kilometres each day.

Around six o'clock in the afternoon on the 7 June 1926 he was knocked down by a tram as he was crossing a street near Plaza Cataluña, whilst following his daily walk from Sagrada Familia and San Felipe Neri. He was gravely injured. Due to his modest clothing and the fact that he was not carrying any documents which identified him, on being taken to Hospital Clinico, no one recognised him until two days later, shortly before his death. He did not regain consciousness before dying.